Understanding Dreams and (Spontaneous Images

Understanding Dreams and Other Spontaneous Images: The Invisible Storyteller applies a contemporary interdisciplinary approach to dream interpretation, bringing cognitive anthropology, folklore studies, affective neuroscience, and dynamic systems theory to bear on contemporary psychodynamic clinical practice. It provides a practical guide for working with dreams that can be used by both individuals on their own and therapists working with clients.

Erik D. Goodwyn invites us to examine key features of reported dreams, such as the qualities of the environment depicted, its familiarity or unfamiliarity, the nature of the characters encountered, and overall themes. This method facilitates an understanding of the dream in the full context of the dreamer's life, rather than interpreting individual, isolated elements. Goodwyn also introduces the mental process which orchestrates dreams, conceptualised here as the "Invisible Storyteller", and explores how understanding it can positively impact satisfaction in waking life. As a whole, the book provides a collection of tools and techniques which can be referred to time and again, as well as a wealth of examples.

Exploring dreams as a natural source of clinical insight, *The Invisible Storyteller* will appeal to Jungian psychotherapists and analytical psychologists, other professionals working with dreams with clients, and readers looking for a scientific approach to dream interpretation.

Erik D. Goodwyn is an assistant professor and director of psychotherapy training at the University of Louisville, USA. He has published on the dreams of soldiers in combat zones, on archetype theory and cognitive anthropology and folklore studies, on the psychology of rituals around the world, on combining depth psychology with symbolic anthropology, and the application of ritual theory to grief and mourning in clinical practice. His previous books include *Healing Symbols in Psychotherapy: A Ritual Approach, The Neurobiology of the Gods*, and, with Susan Greenwood, *Magical Consciousness: An Anthropological and Neurobiological Approach* (all Routledge).

Understanding Dreams and Other Spontaneous Images

The Invisible Storyteller

Erik D. Goodwyn

Routledge
Taylor & Francis Group

LONDON AND NEW YORK

First published 2018
by Routledge
2 Park Square, Milton Park, Abingdon, Oxon OX14 4RN

and by Routledge
711 Third Avenue, New York, NY 10017

Routledge is an imprint of the Taylor & Francis Group, an informa business

British Library Cataloguing in Publication Data
A catalogue record for this book is available from the British Library

Library of Congress Cataloging in Publication Data
Names: Goodwyn, Erik D., 1970- author.
Title: Understanding dreams and other spontaneous images : the invisible storyteller / Erik D. Goodwyn.
Description: New York : Routledge, 2018. | Includes bibliographical references.
Identifiers: LCCN 2018001608 (print) | LCCN 2018012064 (ebook) | ISBN 9781351252614 (Master e-book) | ISBN 9780815369349 (hardback) | ISBN 9780815369356 (pbk.)
Subjects: LCSH: Dreams. | Dream interpretation.
Classification: LCC BF1078 (ebook) | LCC BF1078 .G477 2018 (print) | DDC 154.6/3--dc23
LC record available at https://lccn.loc.gov/2018001608

ISBN: 978-0-815-36934-9 (hbk)
ISBN: 978-0-815-36935-6 (pbk)
ISBN: 978-1-351-25261-4 (ebk)

Typeset in Times New Roman
by Taylor & Francis Books

For Von
My inspiration
The light that brings me from dark seas incarnadine
And deserts of grey
To a valley of silver-green air
And mist covered groves
You make me possible
AML

In all of us, even in good men, there is a lawless wild beast nature which peers out in sleep.

Plato

Contents

Chapter 1

Foundations

> The interpretation of dreams is the royal road to a knowledge of the unconscious activities of the mind.
>
> (Freud 1900: 647)

The problem of bodies and minds

The idea that dreams are somehow meaningful and important is an extremely ancient one. What may be a surprise is the fact that dismissing dreams as meaningless is very old, too. Through the ages, the debate has continued, but ultimately the debate centers on the question of what the mind actually is. Is it a mere side-phenomenon of neural networks firing? Or does it have some fundamental reality to it that goes beyond cells and atoms?

Most simply, a dream is an experience. Everything else is interpretation. It is an experience of being in an environment, interacting with characters, with plot twists and turns, none of which is consciously created by the dreamer. Notice how that description could be used to describe the experience of waking life, also. But aren't there differences? Or should we wonder if we're all locked in the Matrix? Or being deluded by some malevolent demon? Descartes found out that pondering this question for any length of time leads one straight into what is known in philosophy as the mind-body problem. Put simply: how does the mind interact with the matter of your body (usually meaning the brain)? Is the mind created by the brain? If you think so, that is "physicalism" (or materialism). If, however, you think that the mind cannot be reduced to the workings of the brain alone, then you are a non-physicalist. There are many, many different versions of both of these, and an entire book could be written simply on this question, and many have.

But a full exploration of the mind-body problem is beyond the scope of what we're talking about. For our purposes, it is only an important issue because many of the theories that attempt to explain (or explain *away*) dreams rest on physicalist assumptions that dreams are "merely" the workings of such-and-such (usually "malfunctioning") brain mechanism and nothing more, with zero remainder. But this is simply *not* a settled matter. Thus, until that vaunted day when philosophers decide once and for all which philosophical position is true, however, we are going to have to work with what we have while trying to remain out of that quagmire. Therefore, the important things for our purposes are, what characteristics does the dream experience have? Can it teach us anything about ourselves, others, or life?

For ultimately, even if dreams are "merely" random neural firings and we are not finding but inventing meanings for them, those meanings can still cohere with our lived experience as conscious beings and enrich them. I, along with a significant number of others in the scholarly community do *not* think that dreams or the mind are reducible to whatever brain molecules bouncing around, but rather that when you have an extraordinarily complex, non-linear system such as the human brain and body, the behavior you get must be looked at holistically as well as reductively.

But enough of that. We are concerned with dreams as interesting experiences we can learn a great deal from, and we will assume that there is more to dreams, and indeed to life itself, than the mere mechanical, reflexive operations of nerve cells. Put another way, until given sufficient reason not to do so, we will assume that the whole is greater than a simple sum of the parts acting in isolation.

This may be the most important lesson about understanding dreams I can offer: that the whole – that is, the *context* – of a dream is far more meaningful and important that any of the parts, to include isolated dream images and all the way down to nerve firings. For a dream, it's *this* particular dream, dreamt on *this* particular day by *this* particular person at *this* point in her or his life that gives us the most complete understanding of the dream.

Overview of this book

In general, when reviewing dream theories and methods, it appears there is an overall need for and underutilization of dream material in various kinds of psychotherapy (Pesant and Zadra 2004). I hope to help correct that with this book. Toward that end, in this chapter we will look at a brief background on the art of dream interpretation, and in so doing also explore the subject of symbolism and why dreams can be usefully thought of as largely symbolic expressions.

Dream interpretation in the modern era begins with Freud, and afterward it has been expanded and revised a great deal by those who came after Freud. Freud's main accomplishment was in showing just how important and meaningful dreams can actually be, even if many of his more specific assertions about dreams have not held up quite as well over the years. But even in light of the shortcomings of his theory, it was a huge accomplishment, and opened the door to a great deal of fascinating work on the subject. Following Freud came many other thinkers; most notable for our purposes was his one-time student Carl Gustav Jung, who though nowhere near as systematic as Freud made a great deal of observations about dreams that have stood up remarkably *well* over time when compared to the huge amount of research into the subject of dreaming that has commenced since his time.

The present work, however, is not a review of "Classically Jungian" dream interpretation. It is rather a synthesis of many approaches to dreams – though Jung and his followers play a large part in my approach. It is a combination of classic psychoanalytic approaches to dreams (Jungian and otherwise) combined with and compared to empirical laboratory studies on dreams, as well as a healthy dose of clinical experience – my own and that of my students and colleagues working as therapists. Though I would label the present method as a "dynamic interdisciplinary" approach – following the name I call my approach to rituals in therapy as explored in *Healing Symbols in Psychotherapy* (Goodwyn 2016) – it could also fairly be labeled as "Neo-Jungian".

After taking a look at the background on psychodynamic dream interpretation, I will cover some of the common objections to the practice of it as well as the theory that dreams may be "random" and hence meaningless images. We will then look into the subject of ineffability and a general discussion of the relationship between dreams and mythology, after which I will give you what I think is the quickest and easiest way to understand a dream: I call it the "Number One Dream Hack" (meaning the key principle that can be used to understand a dream). Finally, in this chapter I will introduce what I am calling the Invisible Storyteller (IS), the hypothetical character we all have that puts together the dream story as if commenting on our current situation. To show more what I mean by this I will provide some examples from clinical practice.

In Chapter 2 I will explore the imagination and a way to look at it that will help parse out imaginary experiences that come from the conscious will vs. the rest of the psyche (including the Invisible Storyteller), along with the research that helps us understand why we should pay attention to it and what functions it may serve. Next, in Chapter 3 we will take a deeper look at how dream images, myths, and folktales are connected. Here I develop the idea of *psychological resonance* to help us figure out what to attend closely to in a dream. Resonant themes and images are "sticky" and can be found worldwide in myths and folktales. They represent powerful tools not only to understand the dream but also to engage the dreamer with her or his own "rest of the psyche".

I continue this concept in Chapter 4, where we look at the precise "nuts and bolts" of resonance as well as a number of other critical features that dreams have. These include not only resonance, but context, characters, setting, scope, storytelling features, level of conflict, overall intensity, and integrative features. We will go over Jung's thoughts on these subjects along with the more recent dream research that modifies the classical viewpoint. We will see that dreams can be measured along the various scales I introduce in this chapter and can be used as a way to understand dreams more thoroughly in a systematic way. Next, in Chapter 5, I explore the way traumatic dreams unfold in most cases, and how this helps us understand non-traumatic dreams as well, particularly with respect to the apparent "purposefulness" of the Invisible Storyteller's craft in dream-making. Contrasting this, in Chapter 6, we will look at lucid dreams (dreaming while one is aware one is dreaming), for more clues about the overall dreaming process as it relates to the dreamer's conscious will.

In Chapter 7, building on the previous chapters, we will begin to see the overall progression of dreams as aspects of the integrative process that occurs across the lifespan, and how dreams reflect this process in a way that can be illuminating. Finding an overall unity even within the fractionated multiplicity of trauma and dissociative identity disorders can show us how this process works and how dreams can be used not only for diagnostics about our life, but moving forward as powerful images that the dreamer can hold in consciousness to make progress toward one's mental health goals.

In Chapter 8, we will look at the relationship between dreams and spirituality. As throughout the ages dreams have often been ascribed a mysterious and/or divine quality, we will look at what this means given our modern understanding of neuroscience and psychiatric practice. We will explore ways that dreams can be used to develop one's spirituality if one so wishes.

Finally, in Chapter 9, we will wrap up everything covered and review the principles I have introduced here, and I will recap the methods along with some techniques you can use in therapy to take advantage of dream material and the unique strengths it has.

The talking bunny rabbit and other mysteries

In this book I will present a number of dreams for illustrative purposes so that you can get an idea of how I approach dreams. When I do this, I will present the dream in italics, then in the following paragraphs we will get into the meaning of the dream. The dreams I present in this book are gleaned from real patients in clinical practice, however, in order to preserve anonymity, I have changed certain details. This disguising of clinical material is standard practice in writing about patient care, but a curious thing happens when you do this with dreams: even changing one detail can change the overall "feel" and "texture" of a dream. That is due to the holistic quality I was referring to earlier. Since dreams are remarkably resistant to reduction to "merely this and that", it should be no surprise that changing even one detail can actually change the whole interpretation because each detail is important.

Why? Because, as I will explore in greater depth later, "meaning" itself derives from context. The same imagery dreamt by a different person in a different situation can have a different meaning because the meaning is an aspect of the whole person-image-context system. That's why "dream dictionaries" are usually a waste of time. They unwisely assume the same image has the exact same meaning regardless of context. The importance of this dream feature will become clear as we continue. Suffice it to say, therefore, that I had to constantly be aware of this issue when disguising the dreams I present in this book. I only mention it now for the sake of transparency.

That said, this is not to say that analyzing dreams in terms of various categories, parts, themes, etc., provides no information. Quite the contrary, and despite my earlier misgivings about dream dictionaries it should be said that there are universal symbols – or at least universal symbolic themes – that recur over and over in dream imagery and other spontaneous mental imagery. I just want to emphasize here that we should always try to strike a balance between what a strongly recurrent dream element *tends to mean* universally, and what a particular dream element means for the individual dreamer. Both are important aspects of dream interpretation.

Perhaps it would be easier for me to demonstrate this fact with a clinical example. Let's take a look at our first dream, from a 37-year-old female:

> *I have had this dream since I was a child. It's a recurrent dream that has haunted me for years. I'm a small child being chased by a cute bunny rabbit, but I find the bunny terrifying and run away from it. Eventually I hide under the bed. It searches around and then finds me, saying "gotcha!". I hate this dream so much I have avoided going to sleep to avoid having it.*

This dream was presented to me in case conference by one of my resident physicians in training. The resident was genuinely perplexed by the dream's meaning, which is certainly understandable. At this point I had been given no other information about the patient other than her age and gender. Upon hearing it, however, I told the resident that this patient had an extremely rigid character structure, that she was most likely severely abused or molested, that she was excessively serious and humorless most of the time, had a strong aversion to being playful and creative, and that all these things caused her a great deal of suffering. I was right on all accounts.

So how did I do that based on so little material? Well, first of all, there isn't a small amount of clinical material here. The "trick" – if you will – is that the material is in "dream language". In fact, the reason this seems like a trick at all reflects a typical approach to dreams encountered in the Western world: in other words, we tend to dismiss them as mindless, random, or zany gibberish. So using dream material to deduce clinical material seems like "magic". But it's not really a trick. It's a clinical skill you can develop, and it has even been demonstrated in empirical work (Bulkelcy and Domhoff 2010).

It starts with the fact that we are being given clinical material by way of the dream, and the details are important. For example, she has told us that it is a *recurrent* dream. Moreover, it's not just recurrent over a few months but a *lifetime.* There is also a lot of emotion in it – terror – and it is emotion that doesn't make very much sense on the surface. Why be afraid of a cute bunny rabbit? You should always take note of strange, seemingly illogical or "bizarre" aspects like this because they are not random, and they are often used to make a point. In this case the point seems to be the fact that she is running away from a harmless animal. If she was chronically running away from a demonic monster, that would have quite a different feel to it, and it would actually seem more logical! In particular, we need to look at the dreamer's behavior. She's running from something harmless, and even goes so far as to hide under a bed. This is very important for understanding patterns of behavior that are pervasive, because what we tend to do when we are awake is what we tend to do while we're dreaming. It's simple enough: we usually don't know we're dreaming, so we just carry on as we normally do. So even with just that little bit we know that running from harmless things is something she typically does, and moreover it's something that she has done *all her life.*

The part about her being abused was an educated guess. Why else would she be so afraid of cute and cuddly things? One very common reason encountered in clinical practice is that she early on learned *not* to behave that way because it would be punished. And in fact I learned afterward that this patient had suffered physical abuse from a parent, sometimes beatings so severe as to cause broken bones. Likely enough she incurred the wrath of the abuser when she did something silly or childish (as children naturally do), and came to loathe and fear such impulses because they were punished so harshly.

All that from one dream. But actually there is a lot more. And as we go I will refer back to this dream several times to illustrate different points about it that show how I was able to deduce things about the patient based on a single dream report.

General thoughts about dreams

Whenever I'm giving lectures or workshops about dreams I always encounter people who want to tell me their dreams. I have to stop them and give them fair warning: "telling me a dream might tell me more than you want me to know about you", I say. They laugh … and then they always tell it to me anyway. Upon some reflection, it seems to me that this is likely due to one of two possibilities. Either they trust me completely, which I find unlikely since they rarely know me, or, like many of us raised in largely Western "civilized" cultures, we tend to think of dreams as empty fantasy or funny, goofy brain malfunctions. Even among people who presumably take dreams more seriously – like those who attend conferences or lectures about dreams, there's still a strong sense of that legacy, and sharing dreams can feel like a parlor game.

Maybe this is because dreams often seem bizarre and funny with their unusual and sometimes grotesque/comical imagery. But often dreams seem "funny" because of our tendency to take them literally. I strongly advise against this because it will lead to all sorts of absurdities. Instead, think about what is happening in the dream and take it to a more abstract level: what is the general process that is going on? For example, one very common dream is that you are in a public place but have no clothes on; everyone has yet to notice, but you're afraid they will. Taking this literally, you might wonder whether the person has repressed exhibitionist fantasies (a Freudian approach). But this interpretation is almost never confirmed by other clinical material (the litmus test for any dream interpretation). Instead, try abstracting this event – what is "being naked" about? What meanings might it have for the dreamer? Usually it's about being "exposed". That is, feeling vulnerable, unprotected, or like everyone can see the person that you usually hide from everyone. This interpretation is typically confirmed clinically. And for good reason: worrying about what others are thinking is a part of human nature.

In any case, dreams often make plays on words like this – meaning feeling "exposed" being depicted as physical nakedness – and it's because, though we normally don't notice it, most of our thought and even language is very metaphorical in nature, and since in a dream we don't think in words but in pictures, what is really a metaphorical idea becomes a pictorial representation (I explore much of this in Goodwyn 2011). If we feel we are at "a crossroads in life" and contemplating a difficult choice, we will often dream about actually standing at a crossroad somewhere.

The art of dream interpretation: Freud, Jung, and everyone else

So from the outset the method I advocate for here has some measure of pre-dictive validity to it. This lends some credibility already. But how did this evolve in the modern era? The science and/or art of dream interpretation has a very long history (Van de Castle 1994) and has been a part of every culture known in some measure or another (Brown 1991). But for our purposes the modern art of psychodynamic dream interpretation began with Freud's now-famous *The Interpretation of Dreams*, which was first published in 1900.

In his day, Freud faced a number of theories that explained dreams as "nothing but" various mechanistic physiological reflexes, indigested food, random fluctuations in organ functioning, and so forth. But after reviewing this in his work, and comparing them to the clinical data he had accumulated during the course of developing his now well-known psychoanalytic techni-ques, he came to an altogether different conclusion regarding general dream character:

> I have been driven to realize that here once more we have one of those not infrequent cases in which an ancient and jealously held popular belief seems to be nearer the truth than the judgment of the prevalent science of today. I must affirm that dreams really have a meaning and that a scientific procedure for interpreting them is possible.
>
> (Freud 1900: 132)

Freud proposed that we differentiate what he called the "manifest" content from what he calls the "latent" content of the dream, where the manifest content is the dream imagery taken at face value, and the latent content is what Freud feels is the *actual* emotional source and various conflicts behind the dream imagery that the "dream censor" has "worked" (Freud 1900: 311–546) through various mechanisms. Thus, the dream would start with a latent wish, but then would be subjected to a variety of transformations (including condensation, displacement, symbolization, and representation) to arrive at the manifest content of the dream. Ultimately that meant that Freud saw dreams as attempts at infantile wish fulfilments (Freud 1900: 155–166), but that we did not see such wishes directly. We only saw the manifest content of the dream, which we had to work backwards from to get at the latent content.

All of this was in service of the fundamental function of dreaming, which was to protect sleep from primitive surges of affect. The transformative work of the "dream censor", which was a faculty of the human mind, served the function of allowing the subject to stay asleep when otherwise he might wake up as a result of being overwhelmed by primitive urges and drives. The primitive wishes Freud spoke of here were essentially basic primal desires, but of course he is well known for reducing many dream images down to infantile sexual drives (Freud 1900: 395–406).

In one fell swoop, then, Freud boldly put forward exactly what dreams were, what they were for, and precisely how they worked in his typically eloquent and assertive manner. But before we get into how time has treated Freud's theory, let's look at one of the first major theorists to build on, but heavily modify, his theory: Carl Jung.

After Freud: Jung and everybody else

From almost the beginning there were complaints that Freud's theory was too rigid and did not seem to entirely account for the phenomena of dreams. Jung was first among these, and though he felt Freud's theory had much to recommend it, he complained that it was in many places overly dogmatic and in general far from complete (Jung 1990: 33); instead he advocated a much more cautious approach.

But what features did Jung object to? First was the distinction between latent and manifest content. This distinction felt artificial to Jung, who believed the entire idea that the psyche would take a desire or wish and then go through such lengths to disguise it was just too hard to accept. Instead he felt that "The 'manifest' dream picture is the dream itself and contains the whole meaning of the dream" (Jung 1990: 97). Jung was therefore highly critical of the "dream censor" idea (Jung and Meyer-Grass 2008: 24–25) that was required to maintain the wish-fulfilment function intact. Thus in dispensing with the manifest-latent distinction, he also dispensed with the wish-fulfilment hypothesis, and advised clinicians to take dreams at face value (i.e., focus on manifest content) as symbolic expressions of many possible things. For Jung, dreams "do not deceive, they do not lie, they do not distort or disguise" (Jung 1953: para 189). Where Freud felt dream images were often difficult to understand because they were deliberately disguised, Jung assumed only that they were so because *we* had not yet discovered their meaning.

Jung advised above all to "stay with the original image" of the dream (Jung and Meyer-Grass 2008: 26), and then "amplify" it with various associations made at the personal, cultural, and universal level until its meaning becomes more clear. This method of amplification operates under the assumption that images are not arbitrary expressions emerging from a pure vacuum, but rather dream images emerge in a multilayered context of which the dreamer is but a small part. Much as no person utters a sentence without utilizing a language which existed long before she or he did, the dreaming mind constructs images gathered from many levels of context. Thus, for Jung, dreams were not deliberately distorted infantile urges, but meaningful utterances of the psyche that were highly valuable because they did *not* come from the conscious deliberations of the dreamer herself or himself. Rather, they had a certain intentionality to them and wisdom.

As it turns out, Jung was only the first of many to object to the above principles. Nevertheless, many continued (like Jung) Freud's original project of understanding dreams as meaningful expressions of unconscious dynamics. Jungian Analyst and physician Anthony Stevens summarizes psychoanalytic thinkers working on dream interpretation since the two giants of psychoanalysis in Freud and Jung, including Adler, Stekel, Lowy, French, Fromm, Ullman, Perls, Boss, Rycroft, and Hillman among them. Common themes forwarded by these other thinkers are that dreams are "dress rehearsals for life", thoughts that our conscious mind has neglected, symbolic expressions of emotional situations, a means to sort out important interpersonal issues, a venue to explore important fears and concerns in an *un*-censored manner, a means to strive toward self-actualization, and a symbolic means to realize life in a more vivid and connected manner (Stevens 1996: 69–82). All of these theorists appear to agree on the fundamentally symbolic nature of dream expression and its importance in possible integrative efforts, and moreover most of them focus more on manifest content as Jung did.

Stevens (1996: 19) points out that the observation that animals appear to dream (an observation that goes back as far as Aristotle and likely before) also seems to undermine the idea that dreams are disguised/censored sexual wishes. He also reviews the available evidence that has emerged since Freud to find that Freud's theories of dreams as repressed/distorted infantile wish fulfilments designed to protect the continuity of sleep have not stood up well over time – at least in the categorical form in which he presented them. Stevens (1996: 62) notes that Jung's approach to dreams appears to have corrected most of Freud's excesses and withstood the test of time and empirical research in a number of fields.

Examples from dream research support this modification of Freud's view. For example, according to dream researcher and neuroscientist J.A. Hobson, dreams do not disguise meaning: "They reveal clearly meaningful, undisguised, and often highly conflictual themes worthy of note by the dreamer (and any interpretive assistant). My position echoes Jung's notion of dreams as transparently meaningful and does away with any distinction between manifest and latent content" (Hobson 1988: 12).

Stevens reviews a large span of research supporting Jung's idea that dreams have a significant amount of innately guided structure, and he reviews a significant amount of research supporting many of Jung's more specific ideas about dreams as well (1996, *passim*), drawing from evolutionary neuroscience, ethology, attachment theory, dream research, and psychoanalytic theory, often noting with glee when more recent researchers come to conclusions Jung long ago presaged, and typically with the more recent investigators being unaware of the parallel.

Dream researcher G. W. Domhoff (2003), from whom we will hear throughout this volume, notes that the "guardian of sleep" aspect of Freud's theory has not stood up well over time either (142), though he notes that concepts of metaphor, metonymy, irony and conceptual blending "may be the germ of truth in Freud's dream-work" (168). Interestingly enough, despite the empirical support for Jung's theories on dreaming, a number of dream researchers note that Jung's theory on dreaming is deserving of more attention and has been nevertheless underappreciated (Van de Castle 1994). Psychoanalyst and dream researcher Ernest Hartmann feels that the 100+ years of research and literature on dreams since Freud have not supported the "wish fulfilment", "manifest vs. latent" content distinction, the "dream censor", and "sleep protection" theses he put forward in 1900, though many of his other ideas concerning dreams have fared much better (Hartmann 2001: 178).

Finally, one of the most troublesome criticisms of Freud is observed by Stevens, who makes the oft-repeated complaint that Freud's method of reducing dreams to infantile wishes seems on a certain level impervious to any sort of criticism – which is not a good sign if one wishes to avoid the charge of dogmatism. This criticism is summarized nicely by Jungian Analyst Yoram Kaufmann (2009: 36), who points out that any dream interpretation method is only useful if it can be validated clinically – so you can be sure you are correct and not merely placing your patient in a Procrustean bed. Kaufmann observes that in its original form, absolutely any dream could be subjected to a Freudian reduction to wish fulfilments and the various mechanisms of the dream censor. Freud offered no method of validation or self-correction to his interpretations, as Kaufmann put it: "Freud did not give us a theory, but rather a dogma" (36).

This criticism of dream interpretation theory in particular seemed to worry Jung and so he proposed a number of methods to correct it; in general he was always cautious about appearing dogmatic and presented his approach as a set of hypotheses (Jung and Meyer-Grass 2008: 2–3) that can and should be cross-referenced to other dream interpretations made, with the patient's overall response being the final litmus test. As we continue, we will point out such methods of confirming interpretation. In all, though many of Freud's ideas on dream interpretation have not aged very well, we should note that his ideas were revolutionary; his theory is the standard against which all others since him have been compared, and it is probable that only on the foundation he built was much of the subsequent understanding of dreams possible.

Dreams: random images?

But wait, some say: might this all be a wild goose chase? Might dreams be simply random images constructed in a mind that is cognitively impaired because of the sleeping state? Isn't it possible dreams don't really have any meaning or function? The most often referred to version of this old argument in the modern era might be that of Crick and Mitchison (1983) who proposed that the function of dreaming was to *forget* useless information and so dreams themselves are simply random, meaningless noise that should not be recalled or bothered with. Obviously we need to deal with these sorts of possibilities before we continue with Jung or anyone else.

As it stands, in the Western world our post-Enlightenment, Cartesian legacy has encouraged us to think of dreams as merely "mind fluff" – just random noise inside our skulls cooking up zany stuff that has no relevance to our lives. Not that everyone thinks of dreams like that, but you can't deny that it's a common approach to dreams many people have. Perhaps it makes it easier to dismiss dreams if we have such an attitude toward them.

But what is the real evidence that they are "random"? In my first book, *The Neurobiology of the Gods* (Goodwyn 2011), I work out a number of reasons why I think the "random image" theory of dreams doesn't really stand up to much scrutiny. But in fact, it doesn't hold up when studied directly either (Kramer 2007, *passim*), and furthermore the random image theory fails in everyday clinical work. Time and again, carefully looking at a patient's dreams longitudinally and putting them in the full context of a person's life yields all sorts of clinically useful information and meaning.

But there are many other reasons to reject the "random/meaningless" theory of dreaming. One is the phenomenon of recurrent dreams. Recurrent dreams are extremely common – yet if dreams are random why should this be so, outside of ridiculously unlikely coincidence? Until a random image theory can produce a viable explanation for this phenomenon, I think it's pretty safe to assume the images are not random but potentially meaningful, which tells us that exploring this possibility can be a useful clinical exercise. For one, there are measurable similarities and differences in dream content at the cross-cultural, gender, and individual levels (Domhoff and Schneider 2008), which already rules out the idea that dreams are *completely* random, though this doesn't rule out *mostly* random imagery.

But there is much more of this sort of data to count against the random imagery theory, however. Kramer and Glucksman (2006), for example, found that mood changes, behavior, and concepts of self-identity in dream reports correlated with the degree of clinical improvement achieved in therapy. A number of studies link dreaming with enhanced problem-solving capacity (Walker et al. 2002), for example, which points not so much to the imagery but to the *function* of dreaming itself. Smith (1993) reviews studies that support the idea of dreams functioning as an aid to problem solving through their images. Other studies suggest REM and/or dreaming appears to promote attachment (McNamara et al. 2001) or correlate strongly with waking attachment themes (Mikulincer et al. 2011). But showing that dreaming serves a function doesn't necessarily demonstrate that the images have any meaning; nevertheless, Kramer (2007: 12) finds that dream *content* has been found to reflect both state and trait aspects of the dreamer's psychology. Further evidence against theories of random or meaningless dreams, or against theories that consider dreams to be "deficient" or degenerative states can be found in Foulkes (1993) and throughout McManus et al. (1993), who emphasize the manner in which dreams appear to depict emotional scenarios in symbolic/metaphorical ways – exactly what Jung proposed many years earlier.

Further evidence against the view of dreams as random is provided by psychoanalyst and dream researcher Milton Kramer (2007: 129–159). In a variety of studies he reviews, dreams were found to be:

1   orderly, structured, show differences and connections between individuals
2   responsive to emotional concerns of the dreamer as well as mood-altering drugs
3   intimately connected with waking life, physical and mental health and mood.

Summarizing, Kramer (2007: 131) states: "The dream has the necessary relationships to contain psychological meaning. It is an orderly event that is structured and reflects important psychological differences, responds to immediate emotional concerns, and is significantly related to the waking preoccupations of the dreamer".

Examples like these in the literature could be multiplied, but I will stop there – suffice it to say that the idea that dream imagery is non-random and meaningful appears to have better support than the opposite hypothesis.

Is dream interpretation really valid?

So dreams aren't random; that doesn't necessarily mean they contain any sort of therapeutically useful or interesting information. Thus before we get any further into this business, we need to address the concern that dream interpretation may not actually be a valid therapeutic exercise. Essentially the argument is as follows: any interpretation method we may bring to the table is not "truly authentic" to the individual dreamer in front of us. Shouldn't we respect their autonomy to any sort of unique meaning it could be? Instead of trying to figure out what dreams mean via some method, shouldn't we just ask the patient what she or he thinks the dream image/symbol means? Isn't this superior to artificially placing meaning on the patient's dream for them? Isn't it more "authentic" to get the image meaning directly from the patient?

The response to this objection is multi-fold. First, while it may seem noble and reaching for a higher ideal of pure autonomy and limitless unique authenticity with this approach, for the most part if you ask your patient questions like "what do you think this dream means?" you will usually get shrugs and "I don't know" responses. Not that the question isn't worth asking – I'm not saying that. I'm just saying that normally patients simply have no clue what their dreams mean without some kind of method to refer to. So that doesn't give you much to work with.

Second, the underlying assumption of this approach is that dreams generally have no real meaning beyond what the patient may cook up in their head, and it privileges that meaning above all other potential interpretations. But this privilege is unjustified precisely because the *dreamer did not willfully construct the dream her/himself.* And by "dreamer" here, I mean the conscious ego of the person you are talking to. With a consciously worked out piece of art, naturally, the artist herself has first dibs on what the piece of art means. But dreams are different exactly because they simply happen to us. Something else creates them, and this something (that I name the Invisible Storyteller) is obviously outside normal conscious awareness – otherwise the dreamer would be conscious of it. Therefore, the patient's conscious personality is not a very reliable source for this information, so why should we trust it without other data to compare it to?

Third, this approach is excessively individualistic, and grossly underestimates the amount of symbolic meaning that we inherit from outside of ourselves. This is by way of our family, our ambient culture, and even our biology (the latter source I explore in depth in Goodwyn 2011). Finally, in a way asking the patient what their dreams mean is a little like asking them what their *other* symptoms mean. But if they knew that, they wouldn't be seeking professional help, would they? Helping them figure out the meaning of their dream is *our* job, after all, and not only is "well, what do *you* think it means?" essentially lazy, it is unlikely to yield much useful information beyond what they are already telling you about their experience.

Therefore, it is not at all implausible to seek out some sort of rational method with which to approach dreams to help sort out the meaning of an expression that was not consciously organized, but unconsciously organized, just as we try to sort out what all their other symptoms mean. The source of the dream was created by something *not*-ego, and it is our task to work closely with our patients to help them determine *why*, just as it is our job to help them figure out why they are depressed or anxious or what have you.

The present volume represents one of a great many approaches to dreams that consider them not as meaningless, random or deficient, but rather creative. Such approaches consider dreams to be novel and innovative utterances that dreamers benefit from recalling and incorporating into their lives – this approach is not only far older than the random or deficient-cognition approaches to dreams, but have considerable empirical support from the fields of biogenetic structuralism and cognitive neuroscience (reviewed in Purcell et al. 1993; Wilkinson 2006).

But there is more. Koukkou and Lehmann (1993), for example, argue from a neurocognitive perspective that the dream state opens up access to previously forgotten skills and memories and fosters their integration into current life. A number of studies also show a correlation between dream recall and cognitive flexibility and creativity (reviewed in Purcell et al. 1993: 245). Greenberg (1987) argues from a self-psychology perspective that dreams appear to integrate new information with prior experience in order to help adapt to current situations. Psychotherapist and researcher Ernest Hartmann, whom we will hear from throughout this volume, also shows in his work how dreams are not random but guided in particular by the emotional concerns of the dreamer (Hartmann 2001: 6–9), and even *depict* emotions in pictures. Hartmann also notes how recurrent dreams often change once their content is discussed and understood consciously by the ego (2001: 48–49).

> I believe the evidence suggests that we dream about those [emotional concerns] that have not been adequately dealt with during waking … it is the *unresolved* emotional concerns that affect our dreams. Thus, a nagging problem that has been pushed out of waking consciousness or not thought about a great deal is most likely to appear in a dream.
>
> (Hartmann 2001: 71)

Jung theorized along these lines even earlier, proposing that dreams reflected the "compensating function" of the unconscious, and Hartmann (2001: 99) seems to be in strong agreement, differing from Freud's approach in exactly the same way Jung does.

Though he is very skeptical that dreams are as meaningful and useful as many therapists (including myself) think they are, dream researcher G.W. Domhoff (2003: 163) does review evidence against the idea that dreams are completely meaningless and "random". He does, however, proclaim that the empirical literature does not support Jung's or Freud's hypotheses (Domhoff 2003: 7, 135–170); however his treatment of Jung in particular is quite superficial and comes across as a straw-man effigy lacking the nuance found in Jung's original writings on the subject – thus, considering the wealth of data that is much more supporting of Jung in particular, I would take this criticism with a grain of salt. In any case, despite this disagreement, I recommend Domhoff's work and his "neurocognitive" approach highly, as it is based on a solid edifice of very rigorous laboratory literature – Domhoff and I simply disagree on the interpretation of that data when it comes to clinical dream theory.

That said, Domhoff (2003: 18–19) reviews the literature that shows how dreams are *autonomous* and very difficult to influence with pre-sleep and during-sleep stimuli – a point Jung emphasizes frequently in his seminars and writings. Moreover, he notes that (citing Antrobus 2000: 474) when stimuli are incorporated, they are incorporated in a highly creative and ingenious manner into the ongoing narrative, suggesting a very high level of cognitive function in the dreaming mind. From the perspective I'm developing here, since this dream creating process is not the ego, these studies are essentially examining the IS itself, and its responsiveness to various stimuli and creative powers: apparently it is quite extensive.

Domhoff (2003: 33–38) further points out, as do many dream researchers, the highly symbolic manner in which dream imagery appears to be constructed, which of course has been thought about dreams for millennia, but was particularly emphasized by Jung. Domhoff's recognition of this pattern, however, cannot seem to overcome his overall skepticism that dreams "really" have such meanings. For example, he states "to the degree that dreams are like proverbs and parables, it remains necessary to study many dreams in searching for the 'generic' or underlying pattern" (Domhoff 2003: 36). I agree. But then he goes on to state:

> It may be that dreams simply provide a platform from which the client and therapist, through a process of negotiation about metaphoric meanings, can develop a new narrative about the client's life. For the foreseeable future, then, metaphoric interpretations are the fool's gold of dream theories.

It is difficult to see why he would take such an enormous leap from the possibility of a co-construction of meaning in therapeutic dream work being part of dream meaning to "fools gold", but there you have it. Apparently clinical work must appear like so much voodoo. Despite all this, he returns again to say that dreams "dramatize ongoing emotional preoccupations in many instances" (158). Isn't that precisely the point of discussing them in therapy? In all it appears Domhoff cannot decide whether or not dreams are meaningful or useful.

Nonetheless, I cannot fault Domhoff for desiring rigor and accuracy and pursuing it with such passion. And in his review he puts together an excellent summary of the Hall-Van de Castle content analysis system for dream research, to which I direct interested readers, as many of the dream research findings I review here use this time-tested method (Domhoff 2003: 67–94), and he furthermore suggests some avenues into the admittedly difficult arena of studying metaphorical thought in dreams with at least some measure of rigor (102–103). Importantly, he concludes "dream content that is not continuous with waking memories and past experiences may be indicative of figurative thought" (130). This is of course a well-known Jungian principle of dream interpretation. If it is true that, as Jung continually emphasizes, the dream "says what it means", then there is a reason why the dream is presented in such a way as to be (on the surface) *different* from what has been experienced by the dreamer – Domhoff gives the example of a series presented by a woman who dreamt frequently of riding horses and shooting guns, when during waking life she was quite afraid of both.

Then there is the basic conceptual concern about the distinction between the "original" meaning of the dream vs. the meaning that is "co-constructed" between the therapist and the patient. This distinction seems to trouble some investigators quite a bit, as we have already seen. But as I see it, the distinction between "true/original" meaning of the dream and the meaning that we create and/or discover together during the process of psychotherapy is rarely of any interest to my patients. Not only that, how do we know such a distinction is itself valid? What, after all, is the "true and original" meaning of any word, given that words are in themselves arbitrary noises? We won't find such meaning reducing our language in that manner, because *meaning* is inherently contextual. Another way to put this is that meaning "emerges" from the complex interplay of minds, cultures, environments, etc. (see Coleman 2016 for numerous examples of this principle). Whether we discover it or create it (or some combination of both) need not concern us here.

Dream researcher Milton Kramer points out that much of the final meaning attributed to a dream comes from a sociocultural meaning system of some kind, whether it be Freudian, Jungian, or what have you, just as the ancient dream interpreters had their methods (Kramer uses what he calls a neo-Freudian approach; one might call the one advocated for in this book neo-Jungian, though I hesitate to label it as anything but "psychodynamic"). Such methods he calls "dream translation" methods. I have mixed feelings about this. I agree that in order to ascribe meaning to a dream one must adopt a number of assumptions about them, just as ascribing meaning to any sentence at all requires an underlying language. It is easy to go from this observation, however, to the idea that any system at all can be used to "translate" a dream into practically anything (Kramer does not advocate this). I feel we have more of an anchor to work with here, and that is the very universality of many of the symbols we are using. Drawing on universal or near-universal symbolism provides one anchor that serves to stabilize dream interpretation. Another is the use of any assumptions that encourage the dream interpreter to "stick to the image" as Jung put it, allowing whenever possible to let the dream speak for itself as a story in pictures. As Kramer (2007: 139) puts it, quoting the

Talmud, "The interpretation doesn't create meaning, rather interpretation highlights latent elements of meaning already there", which he equates with Jung's advice: "To interpret it, we must put ourselves into the position given by the dream" (Jung, speaking in McGuire 1984: 23). In any case, I feel the present work offers a method that is grounded, precise, predictively valid, and useful, based on psychoanalytic work as well as empirical dream research.

A word about ineffability

Now that we see there is good reason to suppose that dreams are not only meaningful but can be interpreted, I want to point out that this process nevertheless has certain inherent limitations. Dream symbols, while they can be analyzed, can only be verbally explained up to a point. The reason for the limit is that they are non-verbal images and emotion-laden symbols. There is something inherent in every raw image that cannot be fully reduced to a verbal formula because imagery and pre-verbal communications are older and more basic than linguistic thought and capture the whole-greater-than-parts subjective quality of the image. Hartmann (2001: 107) argues that metaphor is "older, broader, and deeper than speech itself" and that dream images "almost always turn out to be metaphors for personal or interpersonal concerns of the dreamer."

There is truth to the story of the dancer who when asked the meaning of her routine replies: "if I could tell you that, I would not have needed to dance it." Dreams are very much like this – they contain musical, visual, and somatic communications that cannot be fully expressed in words without losing meaning. The advice Jung sometimes gives in his writing is "the dream is its own interpretation", which he attributes to the Talmud. He then augments this advice with "stick to the image", meaning that the dream image is what it is for a reason – we are advised not to be too hasty to generalize or to reduce it prematurely. We have already thought along these lines with the above "bunny rabbit" dream by considering why the dream might depict the dreamer running away from a rabbit rather than, say, a snake or a hyena (or a dragon for that matter). The idea here is to recognize that dreams are utterances that are spoken in the language of imagery and not necessarily words.

What all this means is that at the end of the day, talking about and interpreting a dream will only get us so far because we are trying to explain something that can actually only be completely expressed nonverbally. In other words, we are trying to verbalize the ineffable – which is impossible. Nevertheless, the exercise can still get us a long way, but it also explains the "pluripotence" of dream images – that is, no matter how much you talk about and verbalize a particular image, there always seems to be more you can say about it.

The disadvantage of dream utterances is that they are not semantic/conceptual thoughts with precisely defined meanings but statements of meaning uttered in the pre-verbal "language" of metaphorical *images*. I say "disadvantage" because this characteristic sometimes makes dreams difficult to understand. But in so doing dreams purchase a tremendous *advantage* in that the, in many ways richer, language of imagery and narrative is capable of representing things barely touchable with words, such as emotions, feelings, impressions, intuitions, poetic and artistic truths, the raw qualia of existence, and many more things besides.

So how do we get at them? The same way we understand meaning from any other standpoint – we examine the context. When was it dreamed, by whom, and in light of what background? Most dream interpretation methods use this principle, but it was Jung who first suggested we look far deeper for context, expanding greatly on Freud's method. Not only should we look at the dreamer's personal life situation, but we should also be mindful of cultural context, and even deeper to universal human contexts. To get at these last layers, Jung looked to cross-cultural symbolism, world mythology, and folklore. These all help to provide more contexts with which to figure out what a given dream symbol may mean.

What does mythology have to do with my patient?

Let's return to the bunny rabbit to illustrate what I mean. The idea of looking cross-culturally at what a particular image has meant to others as a way to understand what it means to my patient may at first seem odd. The Chinese and Japanese, for example, have mythological depictions of rabbits as agents of and creators of the everlasting elixir of life, thus they are symbols of life energy and other vague notions along the lines of renewal, rejuvenation, creative energy, and so forth. But, one might object, my patient isn't Japanese! So what does that have to do with her? I would answer: if the Japanese were the *only* culture to imagine rabbits as symbols of immortality and eternal cycles of creation, I would say "nothing!". But they're not – not even close. All over the world, rather, the rabbit is shown as a carrier of eternal creative forces, but moreover they are typically *hidden* carriers of this power – probably because they hide a lot and get eaten all the time by predators, and yet still they're everywhere. Also the rabbit is recurrently depicted as a go-between with respect to the worlds of matter and the worlds of spirit, and they are linked (for obvious reasons) to abundant sexual activity and playful, childlike energy – these images and connotations are *not unique* and can be found in India, ancient Greece, and Europe (ARAS 2010). It is the *lack of uniqueness* that interests us here.

But my patient doesn't know about Greek mythology or the origin of the Easter bunny or any of that stuff, counters the doubter, why would any of those connotations matter to her? Because, I argue, these connotations do not emerge randomly or arbitrarily, nor do they emerge in a vacuum from which my patient has been isolated all her life. Nor do these associations emerge for no reason. Rather, I think they are very natural associations that pop up all over the world because *Homo sapiens* tends to think the same way when given similar environments and content to think about. Everyone knows, for example, that the rabbit has a remarkable reproductive capacity, and even though it is heavily preyed upon by many animals, rabbits thrive. And honestly, how much knowledge about rabbits or mythology does one need to link bunnies symbolically to fertility, playfulness, sexuality, creativity, abundance, and childlike energy? These are associations that I think anyone would be likely to make unconsciously even without any knowledge of Greek mythology or Japanese culture, but the fact that the same associations emerge in such far-flung places solidifies the intuition that such connotations are perfectly natural and common. Thus it helps us understand what the rabbit might mean for our patient – i.e., probably the same thing. In other words, it is likely that the dream contains these connotations in our patient.

But don't take my word for it. Try it and see for yourself. In this case, using this method was precisely how I was able to deduce some of our patient's characterological problems. Notice what she is doing in this dream: she is *running from* the rabbit. So if 1) the rabbit (as depicted in her dream, i.e., harmless, cute, playful) is chasing after her, and 2) we assume the rabbit means what it typically means around the world and carries many of the same easy-to-make unconscious associations, then 3) it stands to reason that she (meaning her conscious self) normally embodies the *opposite* qualities because she has continually dreamed about "running from" them and "hiding". Therefore, it's a logical conclusion that she has a character structure that is fairly rigid, un-playful, perhaps afraid of creative, childlike, exploratory behavior. And so when I suggested that, while it may have seemed like some sort of Sherlock Holmes moment, now perhaps it is more transparent how I came to that conclusion.

But isn't it possible that rabbits mean something entirely *different* for our patient? Of course! Perhaps our patient had a very traumatic experience in which a rabbit attacked her at a young age. In which case, her associations would be more unique and idiosyncratic. In this case, rabbits would likely be strongly associated with danger, attack, surprise, and our interpretation would be *very* different! As it should be – I just spent several paragraphs talking about how meaning cannot be derived reductively but must be put in context of the entire experience. That's why you verify your intuitions about a particular image with clinical data: i.e., ask your patient – but not about overall meaning. That's what you're supposed to be doing. Rather, you ask your patient about any experiences they might have with rabbits (or whatever). Because in the absence of any sort of far-from-ordinary experience with rabbits, it's likely the "default" connotations are going to be these same ones that emerge independently and spontaneously all over the globe. And even *with* unusual connections, these default ones are still likely to be there *in addition to* the unique ones.

The Number One Dream Hack

In general, in this chapter we have been exploring the basic question: why should we assume dreams are symbolic of anything? We have reviewed some evidence addressing that question, and for more I would suggest my earlier work (Goodwyn 2011), where this question is handled at length. But perhaps I can boil it all down to a counter question: why *wouldn't* they be? The fact is, we think in metaphors and symbols all the time, and the assertion that in dreams we cease to do so for no obvious reason seems very hard to justify. From clinical material it is obvious that dreams and waking life have strong lines of continuity between them; they are not, however *literal* continuities. They are *thematic*.

Just as your mind is always churning away in the background with all sorts of unconscious processes, so is the mind while dreaming, only you the subject, while awake, live and act in the physical environment of your immediate surroundings. But while dreaming, you are in a more "internal" environment, by which I mean it is an environment produced by the imagination. As such, you cease to move and act in the physical world, and carry on in an imaginary world – but this imaginary world is not merely a phantasmagoria of random, unconnected, acid-trip-like images. No, as we saw above with the bunny rabbit dream, it is a world that reflects our waking life (you could also say that waking life reflects our dream life, but let's not go down that rabbit hole just yet). In fact, most dreams contain environments that operate pretty much the way environments do in waking life. Only rarely are the "laws of physics" violated.

In any case, we can see that the dreamer's characterological tendency to avoid creative impulses, childish silliness, and playful whimsy – that theme – is playing out in the dream, only the dream experience depicts this situation in a vivid, colorful, and imagistic language. Which leads me to perhaps the simplest way to approach dream meaning that I can offer. If you read this entire book and forget everything in it except this principle, you will still be well equipped to handle most dreams. And that principle is what I call "the number one dream hack". Here it is. At any time you are utterly perplexed by a dream, always remember you can take the content of the dream – let's call it X – and make a sentence out of it as follows:

> The Number One Dream Hack: The meaning of this dream is that you are living your life *as if* X.

It's that simple. In other words, take the content of the dream and simply plug it into that sentence: the meaning of this dream is that you are living your life *as if* you are being continually chased by a cute bunny rabbit which terrifies you.

Sums it all up nicely, doesn't it? The "trick" here (if it is indeed that), is the phrase "as if". That, I find, helps cue in all those I teach to the metaphorical nature of dreams – their "as if" quality. They are not literal memories of events. If that were the case, you would simply dream exactly what happened to you, which actually is quite rare. No, the dream is an expression of meaning – it's a story, and a strongly allegorical one, in which the dreamer is the protagonist, and the dream is the summation of one's current life experience all wrapped into dense symbolic language.

Why do we do this? I think the answer is simple: because we *can.* Notice how powerful it can be to summarize such a huge amount of information (i.e., one's recent lived experience in all its massive sensory informational material) into a compact "as if" statement. It allows us to assess what is important about what is going on right now and what isn't – isn't that the whole function of consciousness? Considering we are inundated with internal and external sensory data 24–7, the mind needs some kind of way to provide an overall gestalt that we can use to make quick, good enough decisions to go from one day to the next.

Well that's what the dream is doing. Telling a story that boils down all the extraneous minutiae into a fairly unified (even if still pretty complex) narrative that ropes together countless things into general themes and metaphorical relationships. In fact, we do this all the time, every day, all day long. When we're dreaming, we're *still* doing it. Always it grinds along in the background, this process that tries to "make sense of" what we are going through from day to day. It's saying "ok, now my current situation is *like* X".

That's why the Number One Dream Hack works. That, and it forces us not to take dreams literally, which I have found is probably the biggest barrier to understanding dreams. Recognizing, for example, that the bunny dream is not literally about bunny rabbits, but rather "bunny-like themes of life/myself" that I am metaphorically "running from" constantly because of profoundly disturbing feelings of terror they invoke. Remember, this patient suffered horrendous physical abuse … that's probably the cause of her defensive structure and tendency to run away from such feelings – they feel dangerous to her because she was likely punished severely for them. So at one time in her life, the fear she is still feeling was functional. It just isn't anymore, but it still *feels* like it is, and on a deep level.

So suggests the dream, which was confirmed by clinical material. And so we can see with this example that the dream was an expression of the person's life, covering a very large number of overarching themes and bringing them together in a dense imagistic story, an "as if" story.

The Invisible Storyteller

Which brings us to the overall theme of the book: the Invisible Storyteller. Consider, for a moment, the simple fact that when you dream you find yourself in an entirely imaginary environment, interact with all sorts of interesting characters, have conversations with them, move around, discover things, respond to things, and so forth. More often than not, these dreams are completely new experiences. They are not *remembered* experiences (except in the case of severe post-traumatic stress disorder – more on that in later chapters).

Rather, they are complex, interactive and wholly created/imaginary environments and characters, and it works better than any virtual reality machine ever invented, with full tactile, auditory, visuospatial, and even internal sensory content, all of which you experience while your body is lumped on a bed and still as a stone. It's really quite incredible when you reflect on it.

But even more profound is this simple question: who and/or what puts all of this together? After all, *you didn't*. And when you are talking to a character in a dream, you don't know what they are going to say back, do you? When you open that door in a dream, you don't know what's behind it. I often tell my students and workshop participants: if those facts about dreams – meaning they contain all of this interesting content but that *you* didn't come up with any of it – if that doesn't disturb you profoundly, you haven't thought about it long enough. Because if you didn't create all of that, who or what did?

Suddenly we realize we're not alone in our own heads ... I find that creepy. Naturally, many of us will (perhaps enthusiastically) answer the above question with "the unconscious creates it!". And given that, whatever this creative entity is, it obviously operates outside of conscious awareness, this isn't exactly wrong. But all that answer really tells us is that the dream-making process is something we aren't aware of. That's not very helpful. It tells us only *that* it is unconscious, not *what* it might be.

And whatever this thing is (if indeed it is a "thing"), one must concede that it has a creative capacity that is nothing short of astounding. Entire worlds can be created with it, creatures never seen before, languages never heard before – all sorts of outlandish stuff you have never experienced before. This entity, or process, or even unconscious personality, whatever you want to call it, is what I am labeling the Invisible Storyteller.

It's a process that I am deliberately personifying – mainly because I can't think of any reason not to – that creates dreams. Put more precisely, the Invisible Storyteller is the entity which produces imaginary experiences not consciously worked out or deliberately planned by the experiencer. This includes dreams, reverie, visions, undirected fantasy, etc.

There is an interesting line of thought that is relevant here, since I have brought up the subject of personalities. And that is the phenomenon of multiple personalities. Multiple personalities, also called Dissociative Identity Disorder (DID), occur in very rare cases of severe, often childhood trauma (Van der Hart et al. 2006). In this disorder, it appears that a person will adopt rapid, extreme changes in personality so radical that the adopted personalities have limited or no knowledge of one another. This is certainly fascinating in itself, but philosopher Stephen Braude (1995), having worked through many of these cases very carefully, makes an important observation that is relevant here, and that is, even in the severe case of multiple personalities, there is an underlying unity to all of the various personalities despite their being often so radically different.

Moreover, he makes the point that, no matter how many personalities a person winds up having, at some point *something* in their psyche must have decided that more than one personality was needed for survival. This whatever-it-is bears a striking resemblance to our Invisible Storyteller – the dream-maker. And that is because it happened outside the awareness of the person's current personality (and often most or even all of their other ones), and it is an entity with a considerable creative capacity, able to forge together entire personalities and sometimes even unique medical conditions for those personalities.

So what does that have to do with dreams? Quite a bit once you think about it – for after all, what are dream characters except alternative person-alities? They are, like the "alters" of someone with DID, personalities which have their own perspective, knowledge base, and approach to the dream environment and to the dreamer. And of course, the dreamer's own everyday personality emerged from this mysterious matrix as well, during development.

So ultimately, just based on these fairly basic reflections, we are forced to conclude that there is an unconscious process of some kind that we may be justified in calling an entity/personality (it is, after all, correlated with a human brain – if human brains are not capable of producing/correlating with personalities, what is?). Moreover, this process is capable of creating gloriously complex and extremely vivid three-dimensional environments, characters and stories that are put together outside of the awareness of the dreamer/subject. The dreamer, for her or his part, is thrown into this imaginary world night after night, and for the most part seems to behave in it just as she or he would behave in the waking environment of day to day life. And so this entity seems to have a vested interest in casting the dreamer as player in an imaginary drama. It is this entity which I label the Invisible Storyteller. And during the rest of this book, we will be finding out as much as we can about this theo-retical construct – not only defining it better, but hopefully characterizing it and understanding its behavior. And each of us appears to have one of these things associated with our minds. Or perhaps one might say it is "in" the mind or the psyche. The language quickly gets hazy here – but hopefully I have raised enough questions to guide the reader toward the intuition I'm developing. And this is that the mind has within it a powerful creative/self-organizing process that:

1   can create personalities, environments, and stories
2   puts the ego into these stories
3   constructs stories about the ego's life that follow an *as if* structure
4   is ultimately a unifying force in a person's life.

As we continue we will see that these intuitions develop naturally from dream research and clinical work – meaning not only my own clinical work, but the work of countless other therapists as gleaned from the psychoanalytic and dream research literature starting with Freud, Jung, and many others afterward.

Chapter 2

The imagination – a no nonsense look

That is exactly what dreams are – funny and serious.

(Jung speaking in McGuire 1984: 59)

The sculptor of many worlds

It should be evident that the Invisible Storyteller (hereafter the IS) is synonymous with the imagination – or at least that the IS has the imagination at its disposal to do its work, which it appears to do not only while dreaming but at other times. And this can be shown in different ways. For example, though dream research after Freud has also not supported the primary repression explanation accounting for dream recall, there is evidence that there is a cohering process that continues on hours after the dream is originally experienced and probably even longer (Kramer 2007: 45), in that the first dream reports tend to be more fragmented then later recall of the same dreams, which are expanded and better organized. There are several ways to interpret that interesting data; for our purposes it appears to support the notion that the dream making part of the psyche continually works (with or without the ego's contribution) in the background. If the dream is first experienced as a collection of fascinating puzzle pieces, then after it happens the dream-making function doesn't stop there, but keeps working to put the puzzle pieces together into "what fits best" – which may be a function of the conscious ego's active participation in this exercise, or it may simply be the IS continuing its self-organizing processing after the fact. Considering that repeated storytelling of all kinds appears to have this quality, I find it likely that both alternatives are likely to occur. Supporting this, Strauch and Meier (1996: 221–224) overall found a great deal of similarity between dreams and waking *undirected* fantasies, with waking fantasies associated with a modest increase in emotional intensity, emotional frequency and slightly more fantastical elements. Such strong overlap suggests the IS continues to work in the background even outside of dreaming contexts.

Clinically, therefore, it seems that recounting a dream to the therapist is in no way a passive exercise in "memory retrieval", but an active process of narrative formation, using raw materials not derived from the ego's directions, but from elsewhere in the mind. The process of recounting and exploring a dream with the therapist, which amounts to a selective focus and egoic attention to the dream, may actually *facilitate* the process of dream narrative developing into a more complete narrative. Thus it is evident that patients do not simply "retrieve" their dreams whole-cloth from "stored memory banks in the mind", but instead must allow some time for the initial dream experiences to naturally coalesce (with or without help from an attentive ego) into a coherent narrative. This should not disturb us because the same emotional drivers that put together the original dream will continue to operate to work it into a clearer and more concise narrative.

Since we are proposing that the IS is the creator of the dream, it is helpful to look at ways dream researchers have found that this process seems to work in more detail. One of the first principles we find is that dreams appear to take life experiences and environmental cues that the ego *missed* and incorporate them into the narrative. For example, Fiss (1993) reviews evidence from dream laboratory research that dreams pick up on many subtle environmental cues (including subliminal messages not noticed by the ego) and incorporate them into the dream material. Fascinatingly, there seems to be an inverse relationship between what the ego notices and what ends up in the dreams. That is to say: dreams in these studies reviewed by Fiss showed a high sensitivity to subliminal stimuli:

> Experimental psychology and the neurophysiology laboratories have yielded data consonant with the view that ... [dreams] are not merely passive reproductions of past events, they are *purposeful constructions* ... the dream is especially capable of bringing to our awareness facts about ourselves and the world around us that would normally remain unnoticed.
>
> (Fiss 1993: 386–7)

Fiss concludes with statements that support Jungian Analyst Yoram Kaufmann's (2009) contention that dreams do not conceal but reveal, "and they reveal extra-ordinarily well" (Fiss 1993: 397). Fiss furthermore reviews interesting evidence that because dreams are so sensitive to internal and external environment, they often contain information concerning medical diagnoses of the dreamer such as cancer, and were able to predict treatment response and outcome. Dreams moreover showed the ability to facilitate self-understanding. Fiss concludes that of all possible human experiences, dreams appear to be the most responsive of all to subliminal stimuli. Complementing Fiss's review are later results that found that suppressing a thought prior to sleep led to an increased likelihood of dreaming about it (Bryant et al. 2011), and Van de Castle's review of studies that show pre-sleep stimuli incorporate into dreams but in a creative and often symbolic manner (Van de Castle 1994: 243–245; see also

Globus 1987). Numerous studies of pre-sleep stimuli incorporation show that dreams do utilize recent events but they use them in creative ways that appear to subserve the overall themes explored by the dream rather than simply recount events (Kramer 2007, *passim*). Koulack (1993: 330) presents evidence that increased stress triggers a response that increases dream recall and encourages fitting dream content into waking thoughts, an approach that is supported by clinical experience. Alcoholics who are working on sobriety who dream about drinking maintain their sobriety longer (Kramer 2007: 104), suggesting further that dreaming is involved in problem solving activity.

Further evidence that dreaming serves a function or functions is reviewed by Kramer (2007: 165–187; see also Moffitt et al. 1993) and suggests dreaming maintains the organization and functioning of the self, improves memory and problem solving, facilitates adaptation to stress, and bolsters the integrity of the self. All of these functions can be incorporate here in our general proposal the IS is continually working toward *integration*, a subject we will explore in more depth later. Kramer concludes that dreams can accomplish their function even if they are not brought into awareness or "understood" by the ego, but that (following Jung), if such dreams – particularly important, or what I might label "resonant" dreams – are understood, then the transforming effects of the dream can be more potent (Kramer 2007: 166). Thus Kramer suggests that dreams carry the potential for ego transformation and healing if they are brought into awareness and understood by the ego, but even if they are not they can promote integration on their own. This view agrees with Jung's view that the work of individuation (the process of balancing out all the conflicting elements in the psyche) is going on all the time, regardless of whether or not we are in therapy or analyzing dreams, but that these efforts serve to accelerate or assist the natural process; Jung likens this situation to the alchemical idea that nature naturally moves all substances toward the philosopher's stone or *aqua vita*, and the alchemist merely assists and accelerates the natural process. Interestingly, Kramer's (2007: 167–187) own extensive laboratory experiments showed that dreams and dream content were reflective of the emotional concerns of the dreamer and appeared to serve a function in regulating intense affect over and above that of sleeping in itself (it goes without saying that all of this is further evidence against the "random" origin of dream content). One interesting finding was that schizophrenia correlated with larger numbers of dream characters, and moreover so did low mood, a situation which changed as the dreamer's mood improved – both of these findings we would expect if we were to view dream characters as (often) symbolic of various intrapsychic aspects in various states of dissociation and/or conflict – an idea which started with Jung.

How does this symbolic problem-solving, storytelling system develop? The most extensive laboratory study series (both longitudinal and cross-sectional) focusing in children's dreams is that of David Foulkes (1999). In these series, Foulkes found that the ability to dream developed along with the ability of a child to think symbolically and with visuo-spatial intelligence – this should be no surprise given our hypothesis that dreams are largely symbolic expressions. Children also dream about animals more than adults, which follows waking life in that children often tell stories about and think about animals more than adults do. Foulkes concludes from this interesting data that anthropomorphized animals, found so often not only in children's dreams but in their waking stories (not to mention fairy tales), are "associations [that] suggest both a means and a motive for children's self-representation in dreams via animal surrogates" (62). Foulkes worries that such dream reports (especially those from preschoolers) are suspect as "true" dream reports rather than simply stories made up on the spot by the children, but for our purposes here this distinction is irrelevant. For his part, Foulkes also comes to the conclusion that the function of dreaming is the "organization [and] integration of information … narrative is the preferred form of the serial integration of consciousness …" (149), and moreover that the various characters in dreams may be related to multiple selves attempting to organize themselves into a single identity; therefore, Foulkes's conclusions echo the psychodynamic assessment of dreams we are building here. Later work by Strauch (2005) found that when dreams were collected from children ranging from ages 9–16, though basic dream content did not change, the ability to inventively combine separate memory contents to produce meaningful narratives and scenes did improve with age.

Thus, it appears that the IS self-organizes and improves with development – this should be no surprise, of course; it has to happen at some point since zygotes don't have it. But the fact that the dream-making capacity develops *along with* visuo-spatial intelligence rather than a host of other variables helps us understand a little bit more about what the IS is really apparently for: organization and creative problem solving. The idea that dreaming is about problem solving has quite a bit of evidence behind it as well, particularly when you look at patterns across longitudinal dream series reports (Van de Castle 1994: 271). These functions of organization, problem solving, and narrative formation are something we will discuss later when we talk about *integration*.

It is not uncommon to look at longitudinal dream reports in therapy – particularly Jung-inspired versions, since therapists see their patients week after week, sometimes for years, but even researchers skeptical about psycho-analytically derived dream theories find it important. For example, dream researcher G. William Domhoff, from his perspective not as a therapist but as an experimental psychologist, notes that most clinical theorists focus on one dream at a time, with the exception of Jung (Domhoff 1993: 309). He notes, however, that focusing on a single dream outside of the larger context may be a mistake, since a great deal of information can be gleaned from long dream series. Domhoff furthermore identifies the metaphorical nature of dreams over "overly rationalistic" approaches to dream meaning (315); he quotes

Calvin Hall (Hall and Nordby 1972), co-inventor of the Hall-Van de Castle content analysis method for examining dream content in a quantitative manner, who states:

> Dreams objectify that which is subjective, they visualize that which is invisible, they transform the abstract into the concrete, and they make conscious that which is unconscious. They come from the most archaic alcoves of the mind as well as from the peripheral levels of waking consciousness. Dreams are the kaleidoscope of the mind.
>
> (cited in Domhoff 1993: 316)

The Jungian approach is in full agreement here. For our purposes in this volume, I continue to emphasize that meaning is derived from context – and a longitudinal series is part of that. More importantly, however, this evidence points to the fact that the IS has a "point of view" that is clearly different from the dreamer's. In psychodynamic theory, we might say it has a perspective that is different from the *ego* of the dreamer. That is, it's the somewhat more "objective" point of view that is interesting about this storyteller. The bunny rabbit dream is telling us something about the conscious experience of the dreamer – that she is somewhat rigid and unplayful, has a strongly fearful undercurrent that resists childlike creativity. She "runs from it" and "hides from it". But the dreamer herself would not likely be able to make this observation on her own. From her point of view, she just carries on as usual without much questioning.

The IS, however, observes the pattern from a perspective *outside* this ego. Jung noted how difficult it is to influence our own dreams, emphasizing their autonomous character (McGuire 1984: 4) – autonomous from the ego, that is. As we saw earlier, this finding has been well confirmed by laboratory study, and Kramer reviews evidence that dreams can be distinguished from confabulated dream reports that are directed by the subject (Kramer 2007, *passim*). This fact – that dreams are constructed by an autonomous unconscious process (the IS) – is why it is so powerful and useful clinically. Like the mysterious process that produces multiple personalities in the face of trauma, it decides that various fractionated personalities are needed in such an instance in order to manage horribly toxic environments and proceeds to generate them. But the personality that is presented to us in the consulting room does not typically have any awareness of this process, since this process exists *before* the conscious personality and in fact generates it. We only see one "branch" of the tree at a given time. Moreover, the IS seems to be running all the time and working towards a goal of problem solving, organizing, unifying, and integrating life experience, all outside the awareness of the ego – though therapy and other exercises can bring this process into ego awareness.

And the IS does this by creating stories with alternate personalities.

The dissociative model

But what about everyone else who doesn't have DID? The fact is that multiple personalities are instructive because they are an extreme of normal. That is, we all have multiple personalities but at a much less extreme level than those with DID. The underlying theory of the psyche that we are operating with here is the *dissociative* model of the mind. This model has a long history and many theorists have developed it since it was first proposed by 19th century philosopher and psychologist Pierre Janet. Janet had a profound influence on Jung (even more so than Freud did, see Shamdesani 2012), whose model of the mind is also dissociative, and we find the Gestalt school of trauma and recovery (Van der Hart et al. 2006) also operates with this model.

Generally speaking the dissociative model proposes that, rather than always having complete and total unity, the mind has a tendency to fractionate into various sub-personalities at any given time. This capacity has a high level of functionality in that being able to adopt various changes in overall behavioral strategy (i.e., personality) provides us with a high degree of adaptability and flexibility. But there is a cost to this capacity. And that is the tendency to fractionate *too much*, such that we can have various sub-personalities (Jung called these "complexes") operating toward different ends at the same time.

This idea is essentially a generalization of Freud's id/ego/superego idea (though it developed independently), where instead of always having only these three subpersonalities operating at varying levels of conflict with one another, you can have a variety of them operating on various levels, at any given time. The overall level of dissociation can vary depending on how much stress a person is under, for example. And the opposite of dissociation is *integration.* We will get into a lot more about integration later, but for now let's just focus on the fact that dissociation is a normal process we all experience, and at any given time you can see various degrees of it.

The point, however, is that the IS appears to be an underlying force in the process – it may be involved in the production of dissociation in response to environmental stressors/events, but it also seems to be involved in integration as well. So why would I equate the dissociation/integrative process with the IS? Because dreams have the same "objective" point of view with respect to the dreamer's point of view that the dissociative/integrative process would. Put another way, the point of view of the dream-making process and the point of view of the dreamer are not the same. Rather, the dream-making point of view appears to have a larger perspective since it is producing all sorts of personalities for the dreamer to interact with (and dream research shows dreams incorporate subliminal information), and the dreamer's own personality must come from this same creative process. This is what leads me to think that the IS is largely responsible for the management of the various personalities.

The idea that there is some aspect of the mind which manages various parts, of which the conscious ego is but one, is not a new idea. Jung proposed such a process which he labeled "the Self" (capitalized to differentiate it from the conscious self, or the ego). Without getting too deeply into Jung's description of the Self, we can summarize it as an underlying organizing center for the psyche – something that continually tries to put all the pieces together.

The point of view of the IS and the point of view of the dreamer are not the same points of view, and it seems that only the process behind both dissociation and integration would have access to such a point of view, which is why I identify it with the IS as dream-making process. So with that in mind, let's press on to see if there is more we can say about the particular manner in which the IS likes to put dreams together.

The most powerful and effectively integrating narratives will necessarily be those able to be held in ego consciousness and easily recalled (i.e., reformed), therefore we actually *want* this process to occur so that we can *use* it to do its work fostering integration. We need not trouble ourselves with a distinction between the "original and true" dream experience and the subsequently polished and better organized dream experience reported in therapy, since 1) it is the latter we will be using in therapy to gain insight and foster integration and 2) it is a process that affects *all* recall and memory anyway and so is not likely to be a confounding factor in understanding the patient but a beneficial effect of continued, close attention to the narrative.

But, one might object, doesn't this mean we are no longer obtaining a truly non-ego expression? Does this process of "secondary revision", as Freud (1900) called it, cloud our view of the IS's perspective? In most cases, no; this is because in most cases, during recall and re-telling, the ego is not actively attempting to willfully direct the imagery as in a day-fantasy, but is simply reflecting in a state of receptive attention rather than active image-formation. In cases where the ego is formulating a narrative deliberately to either deceive you or serve some other agenda, it will be obvious once you get a little practice listening to dreams. Moreover, clinically, I see this sort of behavior only rarely, and it is easy to spot since such dream reports will differ in tone and character quite a bit from dream reports gathered more honestly. Dreams *should* be surprising, unexpected and a little mysterious – these are hallmarks of a narrative *not* directed by the ego. They often have that "what the heck was that all about?" quality, at least initially. Even those better versed in dream interpretation will still have the initial head-scratching moment, at least briefly, before seeing what the IS is observing and providing the ego with an "aha!" moment. But even the most experienced dream interpreters should always respect the IS's ability to "think outside the box" and show you something you have never seen before, because just as you may learn interpretive methods in therapy, so too is the IS learning, and subsequent dreams will take everything the ego is doing into account – including therapy, which the IS often comments on, as we will discuss later.

What does dream research tell us about the link between dissociativity and the dream process? One hint that dream characters are related to dissociation is the recurrent finding that brain damage and demented states correlate with *increased* numbers of overall dream characters in several studies (Kramer 2007: 69). Furthermore, schizophrenics have more primitive (direct, emotional, and implausible) dreams, and more dreams with strangers (Kramer 2007: 100).

Harvard psychiatrist David Kahn (2013), drawing from brain-based studies of the self and dreaming argues that the self-organization properties of the brain (which allows for flexible adaptation to rapidly changing environments) are *expanded* during the process of dreaming. Supporting our IS approach to dreaming, Kahn argues that since the dream is not directed by the dreamer but is self-organizing, it provides a wider array of experiences and memories to pull together that is not obtainable while awake. As we have observed, the dream gives us a wider perspective – that of the IS.

Integration is a commonly invoked concept when studying dreams from a brain-based perspective, such as found by Hobson et al. (2000), who report various sources who confirm that dream states strongly correlate with the "integration of neocortical function with basal forebrain and hypothalamic motivational and reward mechanisms" (809).

One small study (Beauchemin and Hays 1995) of outpatients with bipolar disorder showed that shifts to mania were heralded by dreams dominated by themes of death and bodily fragmentation and injury. I have seen this pattern clinically as well in schizophrenics experiencing worsening of psychotic symptoms. This observation supports our theory that psychological fragmentation is likely to be symbolized in images – in this case as bodily dismemberment. Beauchemin and Hays (1995: 42) also review multiple studies linking dreams of death and separation as associated with poorer prognosis in cardiac patients and depressed patients showing worsening ability to recall dreams and to report fantasy. Finally, the dissociative model of the mind is carried forward by Jung as well as E. Hartmann (2001, pp. 120–129), as is the thought that dreams reflect the continued attempts to integrate after various traumas or dissociating events have occurred.

Thus, the conclusion from multiple lines of evidence is that the psyche as a whole appears to have a capacity to fractionate as a result of various environmental (and likely also genetic) insults, and that the IS appears to be involved in various self-organizing efforts to integrate it back to a state of health and balance. And furthermore, one of the ways it seems to be doing this is through the process of narrative formation and symbolism.

Symbolism

In a dream, we see the dreamer's personality interacting with other non-dreamer personalities in an imaginary environment. And the subsequent events link themselves together in a single narrative. That's why the IS is a *storyteller.* The dream is telling a story about the life of the dreamer – but remember that it's not a *literal* recalling of events. The IS uses events from daily life and images recently seen (Freud (1900) called this the "day residue"), but it rarely simply recreates events as they happened *verbatim*. Rather, dream research shows that the IS uses them in a remarkably creative manner that is not random or meaningless, but rather has *symbolic* significance.

In the previous chapter I argued that dreams and the mind may not be reducible to brain activity with "zero remainder". Nevertheless, it is not controversial that brain and mind are extremely closely connected to one another. I think they are connected in the same way that parts (neurons) and wholes (first-person experience) are connected – not as separate things, but not identical things either.

Whatever the case may be, exploring what the brain is *doing* when we dream is illuminating. The dreaming brain is very active, and actually in REM sleep the brain is more aroused (in terms of EEG activity among other things) than the waking brain is – which is why it was called "paradoxical sleep" for many years. What's different, however, is which parts are active – generally speaking, that is. In the dreaming brain, the right brain is usually more active, in particular the association cortices, the limbic system (processing emotions), and the visuo-spatial cortices, for those who know neuroanatomy. Also, the neurotransmitter tone is different; during the waking state, our brain is dominated by aminergic systems (like serotonin and norepinephrine), whereas in the dream state it is more dominated by cholinergic systems (Hobson et al. 2000). For readers unfamiliar with neurotransmitters, all this means is that while in everyday wakefulness, the brain is dominated by pathways and regions that are normally active when people report linear, differentiating and reductive types of thought processing: step-by-step thought, logical progressions, breaking subjects and events into component parts and analyzing them, and so forth. It is linguistic thinking, where concepts are well-bounded in time and space, and it is somewhat "mechanical" and closely associated with a person's conscious subjective experience – it's egocentric, in other words. Most of all this kind of thinking is literal and concrete. A cigar is a cigar, and a bunny rabbit is a bunny rabbit and nothing else.

By contrast, when cholinergic tone is dominant, thinking shifts to a nonlinear, holistic, associative, and imagistic mode. Rather than having a mechanical style, it is driven by personification and intentionality. In this state, thinking is nonlocal, boundaries are fluid and "fuzzy", and things tend to be more dissociated and detached from the ego's perspective. Most of all this kind of thinking is symbolic. A cigar might be all sorts of things. The playful side of life is *like* a bunny rabbit. (See Table 2.1.)

The summary in Table 2.1 is of course a gross simplification; most of the time we can find ourselves in either one of these kinds of thinking states at any given point. They are merely generalizations of the usual state of operations. The "dreaming brain" state, for example, can be induced by various

Table 2.1 Average growth rate in the number of company listings, 1969–2010

Waking brain	*Dreaming brain*
Linear	Nonlinear/associational
Differentiating	Contextual
Reductive	Holistic
Local	Nonlocal
Temporal	Atemporal
Serial processing	Parallel processing
Ego-directed	Detached from ego
Mechanical	Intentionality-driven
Linguistic	Imagistic

methods unrelated to sleep, including free-association, active imagination, drugs, psychosis, trance, etc., though not necessarily to the *degree* that you see in the throes of a vivid dream.

In any case, this is one of the many reasons why the Number One Dream Hack can be useful: it reminds us first and foremost not to take the dream events literally, but to ask oneself, "what does it mean to say that my life is *like* what is happening in this dream?" Since the dreaming mind is already in a highly associational, symbol-making, and holistic/contextual state, it makes sense to look at the utterances of this mind as symbolically meaningful and contextual. It seems much more plausible to look at dreams in this manner rather than to assume, without much basis, that the dreaming mind is simply "malfunctioning" and spraying us with completely random noise images that have no inherent meaning. Assuming this forces us to ask why evolution would produce a brain that engaged in such strange behavior.

But anyway. As mentioned before, the contents of a dream are images because images can express much more than words can. The old saw that a picture is worth a thousand words certainly applies here. Consider that all higher animals can communicate with one another, but only humans communicate verbally. This suggests non-verbal communication is quite a bit older than verbal communication, which of course it is. But *Homo sapiens* did not develop verbal communication to supplant non-verbal communication, rather it developed to supplement it. Generally speaking, we still communicate and think more non-verbally than verbally. And furthermore, we *think* non-verbally to a significant extent as well (Goodwyn 2011), and especially when we are trying to pull together a large amount of events and information into a relatively simple expression. This expression will be a series of symbolic images moving about in a story, but in an "as if" manner. All of the drama, experiences, pains, joys, and sorrows are *like* this dream story.

So all of these considerations lead us to the conclusion that dream images are highly condensed symbols because of the associational and holistic modality of thought that defines them. That means that whatever you are dreaming about is closely related to what is going on in your life right now, but because of the nonlocal, nontemporal nature of dream thought, it means that anything emotionally or metaphorically related to the current concerns is fair game, even if it means dreaming about things that happened 20 years ago in another country. These get pulled in because the dreaming process is about finding meaning, whereas the more linear type of thinking is more oriented toward figuring out what happened. The linear mode of thought would be more focused on the particulars of exactly how, what, and when something happened. The nonlinear, dream-mode, however, is more concerned with "what does all this mean? What is it like to live this?"

Therefore, it pays to know the full context of a patient's current situation if you want to know the full meaning of a dream. That said, since some things are universal (fear of being exposed, for example), some dreams are highly recurrent cross-culturally. Dream researchers all over the world have found some themes recur everywhere: being attacked, status striving, predatory animals, flying, falling, being pursued, sex, being socially scrutinized, swimming, watching fires, and being confined underground (Hall and Nordby 1972). To look beyond the universal symbolism of these images, however, we have to understand the dreamer's personal context.

Symbolism and "bizarreness"

One characteristic of dreams – that of so-called "bizarreness" (Cicogna et al. 2007; Doricchi et al. 2007; Limosani et al. 2011) is in the neuroscientific literature often correlated with the down-modulation of brain regions commonly associated with "executive functioning" – hence the sometimes held view that dreams are a result of some kind of "deficient" cognition. By "bizarreness" we are talking about impossible or improbable scenarios, characters and creatures that do not exist in waking life, and seemingly incongruent shifts in time, space, and environment. But I warn against labeling dreams as "bizarre"; this is because, though it has working and functional definitions in the literature, the term has a number of connotations that I think are very misleading when it comes to dream content. When a story is labeled "bizarre", it strongly suggests that it is random, wacky or nonsensical; I acknowledge that this is possible, but we must ensure that we rule out the possibility that it only *seems* bizarre because we have not fully understood its meaning, symbolism, and imagery.

Put another way, *any* story could seem bizarre except the most mundane and concrete listing of events if it is viewed in a particular way. When listening to and analyzing dreams I find more often that the "bizarre" quality of a dream usually melts away once we understand what it is finally about – that is, once we understand how the IS is *using* the particular images. This is no magic trick, either, it is a function of acknowledging that the mind is as fully capable of *symbolic* and *metaphorical* thought when constructing a dream as it is while awake. Dream research reviewed earlier strongly suggests this is so.

The key difference is, as ever, the fact that the dreamer did not construct the dream – the IS did. So we have to figure out what the symbolism is about, whereas if the dreamer cooked up a story, like "yesterday I felt a hurricane of anxiety inside me, I was feeling really low", we can just ask the dreamer if we get confused. Put this into pictures, however, and try to understand it from a literal, block-headed and concrete perspective, and you will totally miss the point: "you were low, like in a hole, and meanwhile there was a hurricane in your stomach? Wow that's bizarre!" The IS deserves more credit than that, as does metaphorical thought in general. Viewed through the same brute-literal lens, all metaphorical statements appear "bizarre", "illogical", and "cognitively impaired". It is, however, the lens (to use a metaphor) that is hampering our ability to make sense of the dream – not the dream utterance itself. And this observation applies even if dream interpretation must occur in an *ad hoc* way – meaning dreams are made sense of *as a result of our interpretive efforts* rather than the sense being "intrinsic" to the dream. But if this is so, it only shows that integration cannot proceed without (at least partial) participation by the ego. That may very well be the only way the "true" (current) meaning of the dream can be elucidated. Clinically, that's just fine – although the examples we have of lucid dreaming cast some doubt on such a *post hoc* theory; for now I shall leave it as an open question, though there is evidence that the narrative characteristic of dreams is due to intrinsic factors of the dream-making process rather than due to post-wakening factors (Cipolli et al. 1998).

In any case, so called dream "bizarreness" actually has regularities to it (see Strauch and Meier 1996: 95–104), and actually most dreams are of essentially mundane interactions in non-bizarre settings involving everyday life (122), and less than 10% of dreams were categorized as partly or purely fantastical (123), thus making blanket statements about how bizarre dreams are highly suspect. As for the observation of "cognitive deficit" theories – again, we are comparing the waking state to the dreaming state, which has different functions and may be an apples-oranges comparison. The observed down-modulation of frontal regions, for example, does not necessarily mean that the brain is "befuddled" or "in error", any more than our above anxiety-ridden example is claiming to literally be experiencing gastric weather phenomena. The dreaming state is dominated by a mode of thought that is (usually) not driven by linear, reductive and analytic mechanisms but non-linear, holistic, and symbolic mechanisms. The brain changes, therefore, may not mean what we think they mean at first glance. Moreover, empirical research casts doubt on the idea that the dreaming state is associated with radical impairments of higher order thinking in dreaming (Kahan et al. 1997).

There is a useful comparison with this state and another condition associated with down-modulated frontal cortices: Attention Deficit Disorder (ADD), where the subject finds great difficulty holding attention for long periods of time. In this case it is interesting to note that children with ADD have dreams which feature more threats, misfortunes, negative endings, and aggressions toward the dreamer. Other features like recall frequency and dream length (as well as "bizarreness"), however, *were not* different (Schredl and Sartorius 2010). This is hard to understand if dreams are naturally "deficient" cognitive states, but actually makes sense from the perspective of inner conflict representing challenges to the integrity of the ego. Having ADD is *like* being attacked all the time by an increased number of characters, and it's *like* being less able to manage one's surroundings – hence the greater number of negative endings. Thus the dream content analyses lend credibility to (one aspect of) our interpretation of the meaning of dream characters as indicative of greater fractionation and potential conflict. That is, they are symbolic of inner dynamics.

So, as we try to understand the IS, it appears we need to understand more about *specific* symbols. It is one thing to say the IS uses a symbolic language; it is quite another to elucidate what the particular symbols are actually about. Earlier, we discussed how the only way to really get at such symbols – and in fact to arrive at *meaning* in general – is to gather up as much context as possible. This consists of the patient's personal and family history, but more generally the patient's culture of origin, and finally extends to symbols that have found themselves expressed universally. In the next chapter we will explore this subject in greater depth.

Chapter 3

Dreams, myths, and everyday life

Dreams are objective facts.

(Jung speaking in McGuire 1984: 3)

So are all dreams equally important? How do we know which ones should be looked at more closely? Enter the concept of *psychological resonance* (PR). PR is a concept I have been working on for several years, and it is at core very simple and starts with one basic assumption: that some stories, images, or rituals are easier to remember than others. In other words, in general, some stories are easier to think, visualize, and retell than other stories. Consider, for instance, that there is a "Beauty and the Beast" type story in the folklore of nearly every culture studied around the world.

Folklorists classify the Beauty and the Beast story as type ATU[1] 425C, which goes: a merchant embarks on a trip intending to bring back three gifts for his daughters. The older two demand jewelry and clothing, but the youngest one asks for a rose. The merchant can't find a rose, and to make matters worse he gets lost and stays in a deserted castle where he finally finds a rose. There, an animal/beast (who is sometimes invisible) demands that the merchant return or send a substitute. The youngest daughter volunteers to take his place but refuses to marry the ugly/invisible creature, who nevertheless is kind to her. She then sees her father (often with a magic mirror) ill and she is allowed to visit him, but her envious sisters conspire to make her overstay her allotted visitation time. When she returns and finds the creature near death, she realizes she loves him and so caresses/kisses him, which breaks the spell and reveals his true self as a handsome prince/ etc. They marry.

Readers familiar with the recent Disney movies or with Mme. de Villeneuve's 18th century version of this story may mistake these sources for the story itself. But in fact, versions of the ATU 425C story have been found (Uther 2011: 252) in Finland, Sweden, Estonia, Latvia, Lithuania, Denmark, the Faeroes, England, Spain, Portugal, the Netherlands, Germany, Ladinia, Italy, Sardinia, Malta, Hungary, Czechoslovakia, Serbia, Rumania, Bulgaria, Poland, Russia, Ukraine, Turkey, Gypsy folktales, Mordvinia, Yakutsk,

Mongolia, Georgia, India, China, Japan, the Americas, the Dominican Republic, Colombia, Brazil, Egypt, Tunisia, and Morocco among others.

Consider also that myths where the entire world is flooded are also extremely widespread, found in the Ancient Near East, Celtic and Norse myth, Africa, Asia and Pacific Islander areas, as well as numerous native North, Central and South American sources (Bierlein 1994). In these cases, the myth goes: an ancient people either forsakes God or the gods or actively insults them, and so the world is flooded, but a faithful few (or one) are/is kept alive on a boat/log/rock/etc. to repopulate the world. Many think of the Biblical flood story, or look to the Babylonian precursor to it as the source of the world flood myth, but in fact this story occurs all over the world.

Here's another example, the so-called tale of the Chinese farmer: a farmer gets a horse, but it runs away and his neighbor says "that's bad news!" But the farmer says "good news, bad news, who can say?" The horse comes back bringing another horse with him. "Good news!" says the neighbor. The farmer of course replies: "good news, bad news, who can say?" When the farmer gives the horse to his son, his son is thrown and breaks his leg. "Sorry to hear that bad news," says the neighbor. The farmer: "good news, bad news, who can say?" Afterward the Emperor comes to the village to take every able-bodied young man to fight in war. Because of the broken leg, the farmer's son is spared. The farmer shrugs. In my life I've heard three different versions of this story. One is this one, reportedly from China, another from one of my residents who told a Turkish version of it, with "the king" instead of the Emperor, and a long time ago my own grandfather told me a version of this story, but set in the Wild West with a Tex-Mex flavoring to it (as he was raised on the King Ranch), with the "president's men" instead of a king or Emperor, and the farmer saying "how d'ya know it's good news/bad news?"

Diffusion or invention?

We're talking about the phenomenon of recurrent myths or recurrent motifs. It is a fact, observed by folklorists for over a century now, that all over the world, *Homo sapiens* tends to tell the same kinds of stories with the same kinds of plots and characters regardless of location or time in history. The earliest attempts to explain this phenomenon centered around two primary theories: diffusion or independent invention. According to the theory of diffusion, very early versions of these stories traveled with people telling them to all corners of the globe through various migratory patterns. Perhaps ancient Chinese storytellers migrated through Turkey on their way to the Wild West – something like that.

Independent invention, of course, proposes that no elaborate migratory schemes are necessary to concoct because people simply tend to tell the same kinds of stories independently, and storytelling itself tends to settle on similar patterns worldwide due to the fact that human minds are not that different across cultures and across the ages. Jung, with his theory of a universally inherited layer of the unconscious mind that he called the "collective unconscious", clearly leaned toward the latter sort of explanation. In other words, anyone anywhere could, on a given day, possibly produce a Beauty and the Beast, or Chinese Farmer, or world flood, just by virtue of inheriting the same common storytelling patterns and imaginative structure. Just as we all inherit the same basic human body structure and organ systems that are the same in all humans, but with local color and variations, we also inherit a mind that has a whole array of similar themes and cognitive/emotional patterns and structures in it, but again with local color and individual variations shaped by individual experience.

But one factor that is typically ignored in this analysis is the fact that even if stories "migrated" with the people telling them, in the diffusion theory there is usually no accounting for *why* a given story would have been remembered so faithfully across so many (often non-literate) retellings through so many generations rather than simply forgotten. The fact that most stories are forgotten rather than told across multiple generations is not usually accounted for in the diffusion theory – it's simply assumed that a story told will be faithfully reproduced. But we know from day to day life that this is unlikely in most cases. Stories notoriously are distorted and changed with each telling … except in certain cases. Consider, for example, that linguists and folklorists report that the folktale known as the Smith and the Devil (type ATU 330) is likely to date back to the Proto-Indo-European period, which would make this story up to 6000 years old (da Silva and Tehrani 2015). These same researchers date our old friend Beauty and the Beast to roughly the same time period. Thus, far from originating with Mme de Villeneuve, Beauty and the Beast has been around for literally thousands of years.

Most of us are familiar with the children's game where we tell someone a story and have them tell it to someone else, and so on until it gets to the last child in the room, at which point it's usually garbled beyond recognition. And that's just maybe two dozen retellings. And yet here we have stories that may be *thousands* of years old. That's not only surviving a couple dozen giggly children in an elementary school room, it's surviving hundreds of generations and even language changes, as well as migrations across thousands of miles. *That* is a sticky story. That is the definition of a story with very high PR. I hope by now it is apparent just how incredible that actually is, and how truly special these kinds of stories really are, to be able to survive such a process.

So then we are left with the fact that though stories *can* migrate, we still need a theory of *why* some stories *successfully* migrate when most disappear or become unrecognizable. As should be obvious by now, the migration and independent invention answers to the mystery of recurrent motifs are not really opposite solutions. Like so many things in life, the truth is somewhere in the middle and ten times more complicated than initial appearances. In fact, both solutions circle around the same problem: why are some stories sticky/spontaneously emergent and others are not? What is the origin for PR, which allows stories to be retold for thousands of years or to appear unlooked for in all sorts of far-flung locations around the world and across the centuries?

In some of my previous work I explore this issue in depth (Goodwyn 2013), but for our purposes here we can put it together rather simply. Some stories are "stickier" than others due to the way they appeal to a number of universal human cognitive structures and processes. So, basically anywhere, from China to New Guinea to Siberia, Ireland, or Brazil, a storyteller can cook up a story with any sort of elements in it, but only certain ones are likely to be remembered. And this is because of universal features of human cognition, emotion, and so forth, such that stories told and retold will settle into a number of typical patterns where such stories appear to have their maximal "stickiness".

Psychological resonance

So then PR is a story characteristic: it's the quality of a story, or a ritual or image, that 1) allows it to survive multiple retellings without being forgotten or ignored and 2) makes it likely to be independently invented practically anywhere. To see what stories have the most resonance, all we have to do is look at collections of world myths, folktales, legends, etc., or we can look at cross-cultural religious imagery and symbolism. These are all highly resonant by definition because they've already survived the tough filtering process of hundreds if not more retellings/recreations. The most important feature of resonant expressions, therefore, is their ability to affect the mind upon hearing them. It's perhaps not immediately obvious here, but resonant stories, etc., are *powerful*, meaning they can affect us emotionally and cognitively. That's *why* they're resonant. They enter your mind and they get stuck there, and they can change your way of thinking since they are so memorable and "easy to think". And this is true whether you hear it from somewhere else or the imagination cooks it up for you in a dream, inspiring thought, vision, or whatever.

Once we see that the debate about diffusion vs. independent invention is really about PR, we can see that highly resonant expressions will migrate, but also that any given person could produce one with a dream, or imaginative exercise, or simply clever invention, and then *that* expression can perpetuate too, and so both mechanisms likely account for the phenomenon of recurrent motifs.

So what does all this have to do with dreams? Just this: dream utterances can vary in this characteristic just like any other sort of story can. Some dreams will be highly resonant, whereas others not as much. Put another way: sometimes the IS will hit a "home run", and create a very memorable and powerful (i.e., resonant) story, and sometimes not so much. Like any other natural process, entity, etc., there's a playful trial-and-error quality to the IS. But in any case, it stands to reason that if I have a highly resonant dream on my hands, I should probably spend more time with it, pay more attention to it – and moreover by virtue of it having high PR, the patient will likely remember it, sometimes over decades. Thus it is ripe for use in therapy as material to help them integrate and heal. As we go on, we will see more examples of how to do this. Note that this is the reason for asking about our patients' earliest memories or dreams: if they occurred decades ago, they are resonant by definition in the patient's world. Otherwise they would have forgotten them as irrelevant. PR takes advantage of the fact that memory is selective; only the strongest memories survive. So if we have a memory from 30 years ago, you can bet there is a strong emotional reason *why*.

So how do we know when we're dealing with a resonant dream? Primarily two ways: one old, one a little newer. The older way was to keep a close eye and ear for themes that are found in myths and folktales. For example, in the dream of a 35-year-old woman:

> *I've been "married off" to a man in a big house on a hill in another state. I'm pretty reluctant to go, but I have to – it's weird, I feel like I have to do it to help my dad for some reason, to make him happy or something. Anyway, when I get there the house is really dark and my husband is "in the shadows" all the time. I can't see him. I'm supposed to be married to this guy but I can just hear his voice.*

This dream bears a strong resemblance to our Beauty and the Beast tale discussed above. It's actually very interesting once you start recognizing this: this person just dreamed part of a five-thousand-year old story. That will give you goosebumps if you're a romantic like I am. Instead of a castle, it's a house on a hill "in another state", and like the creature sometimes is in the folktale, the groom is invisible. Then there's the link between the daughter and her father, though it lacks a lot of the other stuff, like the jealous older sisters, the rose (a potent symbol indeed), and of course the happy ending. So it's like a folktale fragment rather than the whole folktale. But that is to be expected: we are explaining recurrent motifs as the result of a process of multiple retellings where stories are "filtered", distilled and condensed through possibly thousands of people hearing and telling the story, adding and subtracting, but with only the most resonant elements remaining, until it is finally collected by a folklorist and logged in one of the great folklore collections in use today. What any one person contributes to this process may be rather small – though not always, as I have had some patients deliver dreams with complete folktale structure (even with plot twists) whole cloth! But more commonly what we hear in the consulting room is a fragment.

But the fact that the dream matches something that has such a high level of PR as a folktale or myth, even if only partially, suggests this dream has a higher level of PR than usual. See how that works? Put another way, dreams that resemble folktales have high PR because folktales do. It's a roundabout way of getting at the PR level of a dream, but it's been the best one available for a long time. Why? Because up until recently, few people have been asking *why* folktales are so resonant and coming up with anything specific in terms of an answer. They just know that they are. And so because of that we know to pay closer attention, as high PR elements can be powerful tools in therapy, and it's just *because* of how memorable and "sticky" they are. High PR dreams are (by definition) going to be in your patients' minds anyway, so we might as well know how to recognize them for what they are and use them, an example of which I will give at the end of this chapter.

Elements of PR

There is another way to get at PR, however. One that doesn't involve learning a lot of mythology and folklore, which is fun in its own right, but honestly not everyone's cup of tea. But this second method is more recent and largely comes from my own work on applying cognitive anthropology and comparative religious study to dream contents (Goodwyn 2016). Basically, my argument is as follows: because the human mind is not infinitely variable but has a number of universal cognitive features, these features will act as constraints on the kinds of stories we like to tell and the kinds of stories we tend to remember. A vivid example I often use in my workshops and classes starts with two stories:

1   A hero enters a dark cave to rescue a princess from a dragon by cutting off its tongues or heads.
2   A hippo that is also a mosquito-man transforms into a turnip patch mist backwards every 92nd day for no reason.

Can you guess which one of these is more resonant? They both have the same number of words. And yet whenever I tell these two stories, then ask the participants 5 minutes later to recall them, only the first one comes easily. That's because I used a strongly resonant story for 1 (a fragment of ATU type 300, the Dragon Slayer), and for 2 I reversed several of the characteristics that I identify as *causing* PR. In other words, using the characteristics that I hypothesize cause high PR, I deliberately made a *low* PR story.

So what are the characteristics? I propose that there are nine, based on my readings in folklore theory, cognitive anthropology and Jungian theory among other fields of study as well as good old-fashioned clinical work (Goodwyn 2016). I invite others to add or subtract from this list, comparing the proposed features of stories that are sticky and memorable (high PR) to those that are not. The characteristics are:

1   Minimal unusualness
2   Emotionality
3   Sensual vividness

4   Indeterminacy of time and space
5   Biasing toward middle-level categories
6   Low complexity
7   Containing rhythmic or musical elements
8   Having simple plots with reversals or irony
9   Showing an apparent interconnection of events.

Let's look at these in more detail.

Minimal unusualness

By "unusual" I mean basically counter-intuitive. That is, out of the ordinary. For this characteristic, we are looking at stories in which everything happens as it usually does, *except* for one or two weird things. Like rabbits which behave and look like rabbits, but they talk and chase after you. Or your new rich husband behaves just like any rich new man would, except that he happens to be invisible. Or he is an animal. If there's no unusualness, then the story is too normal – too prosaic. The mind thinks of it as nothing of importance and it therefore isn't remembered as easily. The unusualness has to be "minimal", however, because too much unusualness just doesn't register. The hippo in story 2, for example, is just so bizarre and counter-intuitive that you can barely picture it in your mind let alone remember it. So there's a "sweet spot" in terms of unusualness that lends itself toward higher PR in a story.

Emotionality

The link between emotion and memory is well known. This is of course one of the key features of Posttraumatic Stress Disorder – the fact that extremely emotional events are *difficult* to forget even when you want to. For a story to have a high level of PR it needs to be emotional. The princess has been captured by a terrifying monster. You just got married to an invisible man. The bunny rabbit is frightening and trying to "get" you. The entire world is flooding and everyone is going to die. There's a lot riding on these events. The mind therefore zeroes in on them and they become very sticky. Fear, anger, lust, hunger, pain – injecting any of this will increase the PR of a narrative. You can include more abstract elements too, such as beauty and symmetry, or extreme ugliness – we cue in on such things automatically. The hippo story, however, is emotionally bland and neutral. What he does is "for no reason". The mind says: who cares? And so it is forgotten almost immediately.

Sensual vividness

Memory is not simply an abstract, mechanical recording of data. It's sensual. High PR expressions will be sensually vivid: bright colors as opposed to drab or bland. Sounds will be loud, thunderous, melodious, or by contrast unusually silent. They won't be mid-level static noise with no distinguishing features, however. Tactile sensations will be fascinating, textured, rich, intensely pleasurable or painful rather than "kinda, sorta, meh". Tastes will be explosions of flavor. Images will be brilliant or demonically black, and visions of perfection or absolute horror. Grey, ambiguous mush is quickly forgotten. Again, however, excessive detail and complexity will detract from PR. Environments will be vivid, but simple. Forests of crystal, cities of gold, seas of bright blue. Overly complex and detailed imagery will detract from PR.

Indeterminacy of time and space

Higher PR expressions appear to be "a long time ago in a galaxy far, far away" – meaning possibly anywhere, at any time. It's easier to dismiss things that are isolated to "this happened in Detroit on January 4, 1973 at 2:30 pm". The indeterminacy seems to evoke an oceanic sort of feeling, one where we are drifting into the realm of the universal, the godlike, the timeless, the eternal. It's just something that happens in the eternal present. I think generally the mind seeks out general principles of meaning and therefore will prioritize things that seem to apply everywhere across all times, hence prioritizing stories without a definite time or place.

Biasing toward middle-level categories

This is another characteristic that seems to be related to our general cognitive capacity for detail. Too little or too much doesn't stick. You need just the right amount. Notice, for example, that it's "a bunny rabbit". It's not too general, like "an animal", or "a mammal". That's too hard to visualize because it's not really anything – it's an abstract category, not an actual *thing.* In terms of PR, the mind appears to be unimpressed with abstractifications and ratiocinations. It likes real things. But by the same token, it's not "a rare albino Amami wild black rabbit with a slight limp and a slightly discolored left ear". That's just too much detail. We are unlikely to remember or care about all that. No, it's just a bunny rabbit. So, higher PR tends toward middle-level categories. Things like "chair" rather than "furniture" or "chaise longue", and "car", rather than "vehicle" or "convertible VW beetle".

Low complexity

This refers to the characters in the story. High PR expressions tend to have characters that have a low level of inner complexity. They show what they are about by what they do, rather than mull about with inner turmoil and conflict. The bunny rabbit wants to get the dreamer. The dragon wants to hoard the princess in its lair. The princess wants to be free. The heroes of the flood story are pious and want to survive. The Beast wants compensation for his lost rose. After that, he wants to be loved. But that's it. There's not a lot of inner complexity beyond these simple motivations because that's harder to remember and keep straight.

Containing rhythmic or musical elements

High PR expressions have a musical quality to them. Both in overall structure, such as "the first daughter did this, the second daughter did the same, but the *third* daughter did *that!*" kind of stuff, but also sometimes within the story when characters say things like "magic mirror on the wall, who is the fairest of them all?" Beats of three and four are extremely common in high PR expressions. It is easy to forget that many of our oldest stories such as *The Iliad* or *Beowulf* are actually long poems – the reason for this is that poems are easier to remember than prose, and they emerged from non-literate cultures where the storytellers essentially worked from memory. High PR expressions use this fact to enhance memorability and impact and will have rhythmic "beats" or repetitions. Low PR expressions will be monotonous and non-rhythmic, with very little or no beats or clear divisions in the story.

Having simple plots with reversals/irony

The Dragon Slayer story fragment I present above is extremely easy to follow, in part because it is so simple. The conflict is set up clearly and the players strongly drawn, then the action follows in easy to visualize, middle-level category environments. But, like the "minimal unusualness" characteristic above, if it's too simple and predictable, it's forgettable. A reversal of some kind, or irony of some kind, will make a story stickier. Anything that violates what is expected will increase PR, so long as it's *just the right amount.* Too much unexpectedness just becomes jumbled noise, like the hippo story, and so gets forgotten. So, kissing the dying Beast suddenly causes him to turn into a handsome prince. The young man who finally kisses the ugly hag in the forest causes her to turn back into a beautiful queen and he therefore becomes king of all the land. The protagonist finds his doom taking the very road he chose trying to avoid it. That kind of stuff increases PR. One common dream is reported by experienced soldiers who have seen combat (Wyatt et al. 2011): *I'm fighting an enemy and stab him, only to discover after pulling off his mask that it's really my wife and I have killed her.* That's sticky. High PR there.

Showing an apparent interconnection of events

This final characteristic shows an aspect of PR that I think may be the most important. It's that the mind is fascinated by the "big picture". When a story seems to fall into place just perfectly, as if being thought up by a higher power, we take notice and remember it. The princess is saved just in the nick of time. The three gifts given to the hero by the wise man in the woods turn out to be exactly what he needs to defeat the giant, and so win him the crown and the princess. Everything and everyone falls together like the pieces of a puzzle, as if constructed beforehand by a goddess of fate. This characteristic is why we tolerate the normally outrageous coincidences that most popular movies expect us to believe – it's because on a deep level, *we are looking for it.* High PR expressions have events, characters, and timing all work together. Though working in opposition, the dragon, hero, and princess still seem to be operating on a certain level in sync with each other, as if playing out a cosmic script. I negated this one in the hippo story with the "every 92nd day for no reason" part.

The reason I think this one is so important, however, is because – using our dissociative model – healing involves integration of various conflicting aspects of the psyche. The IS is always trying to put the pieces together, as we will explore in more detail in later chapters, and so high PR dreams will often have this element to it: that the various parts that are in conflict are secretly participating in a kind of harmony, and if we can get the dreamer to play along, often integration and healing follows.

The alchemy dream

We will conclude this chapter with an interesting example of a spontaneously resonant dream. In the latter part of his career, Jung developed an interest in alchemy – the ancient art of understanding the transmutation of minerals (see Jung 1967, 1989, 1993; and later Jungians, Edinger 1994 and Von Franz 1980). Alchemy is typically presented as a quaint and antiquated practice involving misguided proto-scientists trying to turn lead into gold – a practice that was supplanted by the light of reason and the discoveries of modern chemistry. Cue violins. But this characterization is a gross oversimplification. The practice of alchemy dates back to before the Common Era and emerged spontaneously in multiple areas – China, India, and Hellenized Egypt are among these, and the practice furthermore was usually blended with a spiritual practice of some kind (Eliade 1974; Holmyard 1990). This is where it gets interesting for our purposes.

This is because ancient alchemists to varying degrees spoke of their art as not only an art involving various minerals, but it was also an art for transforming the self through a contemplative and ritualistic program of various steps. For them, the world and the mind were not in separate Cartesian domains. Like most peoples around the world, the separation of mind and body was not rigid or absolute for the alchemists. In any case, the alchemists across the ages proposed various fascinating and highly symbolic narratives about how the cosmos and the self operated and transformed. When taken literally, of course, these narratives do not typically hold up to scientific inquiry. But taking them symbolically reveals some fascinating patterns. And in fact, most alchemists drew upon visionary experiences, imagination, dream, and so forth to propose their various theories, so looking at their theories as symbolic rather than literal is a better approach. That's where we come in (following Jung's lead, as it were).

I'm bringing this up because alchemy presents to us a unique example of PR, in that the expressions of the alchemists are highly resonant, as they repeat themselves across multiple independent paths, and survived centuries of oral and written transmission, and yet most patients you run into every day will have heard nothing about it, since in our education alchemy is mainly considered as a failed science, rather than a form of semi-religious mysticism that used minerals to symbolize its theories.

Without delving too deeply into the vast body of alchemical texts, which can be very bewildering and strange, let me summarize most of the themes found there in broad strokes, just so we can get an idea of what "alchemical" symbolism might look like (see Eliade 1974; Holmyard 1990; and Jung 1967, 1989, 1993). In many of these treatises and programs, the alchemist is shown or described engaging in the work with a "*soror mystica*" or a spiritual sister, divine guide, or muse. The alchemist then blends the minerals in an egg shaped or round vessel that is very often likened to a womb. The working of the minerals is described as involving cyclical movement, turning, and also involves adding heat. The alchemical work must also be carried out in a specifically designed place set apart from the everyday. As mentioned, the work of alchemy is just as much a spiritual/psychological exercise as it is a physical transformation of minerals, and the alchemist is supposed to be at one with the materials she or he is working with. And finally, color symbolism plays a part also, in that the primordial substance, from which the end goal of the philosopher's stone or elixir of youth is created, is usually described as black – the *prima materia* as basic substance that everything is made of. Through the alchemist's work, the *prima materia* is transformed slowly and through many steps into the end goal: the philosopher's stone, or the Elixir of Youth, or the *aqua vitae*. With it the alchemist is supposedly able to achieve immortality and turn lead into gold.

Interesting, no doubt. And resonant, as it is fairly simple, involves non-complex characters engaging in easy to visualize actions, with everything connected to an overarching goal of the highly emotional theme of achieving immortality (literal or spiritual depending on the author) via the philosopher's stone/elixir of youth/*aqua vitae*. And while some alchemists no doubt thought of this process as a literal one and were seeking wealth, most of them were relatively poor and seemed to care little for wealth, instead aiming for a more mystical transformation of the self into a "higher self" that was one with God or the Divine, however envisioned.

Of course, the number of people in most clinical populations who have even a remote interest or knowledge of this sort of stuff is pretty low. And yet, consider the following dream offered up by a 45-year-old female, dreamt on the night before psychotherapy was to begin:

> *I am going to the spa, or a gym, with my sister. We find a machine that is supposed to "make us healthy." We're not sure if we are allowed to use it, but we get on it anyway. Suddenly it encloses us in a black egg shaped apparatus and we start to tumble through it. It gets progressively hot through cycles, and my sister is panicking. Both of us tumble through in the fetal position. I reassure her that it will be ok, but I'm not sure it actually will end. Eventually it does, and it opens up. A manager is there to greet us.*

Jung felt that the first dream reported was very important:

> Initial dreams are often amazingly lucid and clear cut. But as the work of analysis progresses, the dreams tend to lose their clarity. If, by way of exception, they keep it we can be sure that the analysis has not yet touched on some important layer of the personality.
>
> (Jung 1990: 93)

Thus we are advised to pay special attention to the first dream experienced right before therapy, if we hear one.

Like the alchemist, the dreamer here is going to a "spa" – i.e., a space specifically set apart from the everyday that is dedicated to healing/health. The machine turns itself into an alchemical vessel, black (like the *prima materia*), and she herself is worked, with her sister, through the transformation, which includes turning and heat, just like the alchemists. The vessel/machine is womb-like, in that it is "egg" shaped, and she specifically uses the term "fetal position" to describe themselves. Afterward the "manager" (i.e., a "higher power") greets them – they meet with the manager at the end of the process. And of course the fact that this dream occurred right before the start of psychotherapy – a sort of psycho-spiritual exercise – is significant to our comparison.

What are we to make of this? Well, the most natural question is whether or not the patient had any familiarity with medieval European, Chinese or Islamic alchemical writings? I got the usual "um … no, I can't say that I have" response. Note also what's missing: there's no elixir, philosopher's stone, or *aqua vitae*. But the rest of it is there, which is pretty impressive since the dreamer had no conscious awareness or memory of having read any alchemical texts. But that is no mystery once we recognize that resonant expressions have the ability to pop up spontaneously in anyone. Because alchemical ideas are resonant, they have this quality.

Thus, because the alchemists described such similar processes in their writings from so many sources, it is worth considering that this dream has essentially the same meaning as the alchemists' visions regarding their work (we will talk about how to verify such a hypothesis with your patient later on). It is the concept of resonance that creates the bridge between ancient and far-flung writings and oral teachings and your patients in the consulting room. But remember that collections of resonant expressions such as myths, folktales, or numerous parallel texts from independent areas have the advantage of having been "filtered" through multiple tellings and retellings, thus allowing the most resonant elements to remain. Let's call such stories *super*-resonant. Super-resonant stories are those like Beauty and the Beast, or the Smith and the Devil – versions of which have been told for thousands of years all over the world. Like organisms undergoing Natural Selection, only the strongest stories survive the merciless process of retelling and forgetting. It is the universal cognitive and emotional constants of the human mind and environments (Goodwyn, 2011, 2016) that shape and maintain this continuous process. And, over time, stories told and retold tend to drift toward narratives of maximal resonance regardless of where they originated, whether it be in Japan or South Africa or Iceland, or your patient's dream last night.

All of this suggests that when you hear a dream report that has a number of resonant elements in it, many times the dream will look like a fragment of a super-resonant story, though as I mentioned, like the alchemy dream given above, sometimes it's already (nearly) super-resonant. Either way, though, it can be a useful exercise to consider the super-resonant narrative that the dream looks to be a fragment of as "the rest of the story". If the dreamer is crucified in a dream, for example, it's worthwhile to ask yourself, well what happens after the crucifixion? Of course the answer is the Resurrection. And when you bring that up with your patient in therapy, chances are they will respond quite strongly with that theme, given that they've already lived the first part of the story in their dream. But knowledge of resonance gives us an advantage in that the forces that shape resonant narratives operate continuously to "pull" stories toward super-resonant states. The same forces will likely operate in your patients also.

In any case, getting back to the alchemy dream, this dream provided a springboard for the discussion of psychotherapy as a kind of alchemical exercise (an idea developed at length by Jung, who thought the alchemists were better viewed as successful ancient psychologists rather than failed chemists), because I knew the rest of the story: once the process is completed, the mineral (i.e., symbolically, the ego) becomes "gold" – or it becomes equivalent to the philosopher's stone, the Elixir of Youth, or the *aqua vitae*. That is, you become integrated and whole, achieving metaphorical perfection and immortality – inner harmony, healing, and peacefulness within. That last step was not a part of this patient's dream, but it *is* where her dream seems to be "headed" (meaning pulled toward in the manner of resonant narratives), if we look at the alchemical texts that it shares so many features with.

But do we really need to be familiar with alchemy to understand this dream? I don't think so, though being familiar with any body of resonant materials makes recognizing them in dreams much easier. But you can also do it just by being able to recognize resonance by going down the list of nine features I mentioned above. Resonant dreams, I hypothesize, will have all or many of them. Non-resonant dreams (like the hippo story) will not. So let's go down the list:

1   Minimal unusualness. In this dream everything that happens is pretty much as it might happen in waking life. There's no flying dogs or talking toasters. That is, *except*, for the near-magical egg-machine that the dreamer and her sister step into, which is very much out of the ordinary. Thus, this dream is neither prosaically normal nor excessively bizarre or impossible. Modest check.

2   Emotionality. There is a great deal of fear expressed in this dream. Check.

3   Sensual vividness. The vividly pictured black egg, the fetal position of the dreamer and her sister, and the description of the spinning and heat qualify in this case. Check.

4   Indeterminacy of time and space. There is no indication of when or where any of this is happening. Just "somewhere in a spa", and we don't even know if it's night or day outside. Check.

5   Biasing toward middle-level categories. None of the images seem to dominate with their sheer level of intricacy or detail, but by the same token everything is simple and easily visualized. Check.

6   Low complexity. There are two characters apart from the dreamer, her sister and the "manager". Neither of them appear to have any great level of inner complexity. Check.

7   Containing rhythmic or musical elements. There does not appear to be much in the way of rhythmic elements apart from the turning within the black egg. We won't check this one.

8   Having simple plots with reversals or irony. The irony in this dream is that the dreamer's sister is anxious rather than the dreamer, which is different from the way in which she experiences her sister in waking life. There is also the expectation that while stuck in the egg they might "go on forever" or "die", but neither happens, which is a modest reversal of expectation. Modest check.

9   Showing an apparent interconnection of events. The manager appears just as the egg machine is finishing, which qualifies as an odd but meaningful coincidence. Modest check.

This gives us about 7 or 8 out of 9 (granted, some stronger than others) resonant features. Thus we can see that this is a highly resonant dream, and even if we knew nothing about the symbolism of alchemy, there's imagery of rebirth (the "fetal position") and the pain and fear and "heat" (i.e., intense affect) of therapy, and we are justified in linking it to therapy because of the *timing* of the dream – on the night before therapy. Furthermore, we are justified in wondering just what this patient's sister has to do with the whole process, otherwise, why would she be in there? If we operate on the assumption that these images are non-random and meaningful (the support for which we talked about in the previous two chapters), then we should be asking ourselves why the IS included her sister in this process.

A good way to think about this and get at the "why" is to ask ourselves what the dream would look like *without* the feature we are focusing on. In this case, we would ask ourselves, "why dream about her sister? Would the dream look different without her sister? How so?" In this case, the dream would be almost the same without her. The dream would still involve a sudden trans-formative process in a place of healing/health, and one that involved fear, the unknown, "heat" (i.e., intense affect), and so forth. So all that is the same, so the fact that the IS included her sister must mean that the IS "thinks" the dreamer's sister must be an important part of this process. It's *as if* her sister is going through it *with* her. The dream seems quite clear about that.

The sister character, however, is one of the things that is resonant about this dream because it matches the alchemical *soror mystica* character – the alchemist's muse or spiritual guide. There's a couple of interesting wrinkles in the patient's "version" of this process, however. First is that the sister in the dream is the one who is in need of guidance, thus in the alchemist/*soror* pair, the dreamer is in the role of *soror*, not alchemist. Interesting! Upon initial examination of this dream, I did not know what that could mean. That's ok – expect to be mystified. The IS is a very subtle artisan. Respect it. Second, this particular sister is an image of her waking-life sister and not a "sister" (we often dream of relations that we don't really have, thus they reveal their more symbolic/ metaphorical nature). So even though the IS is responsible for this character's creation, it is based heavily on the dreamer's memory of her biological sister. So this character then will be a nonverbal expression of all the emotions and history that entails. But let's also not forget that the sister is also a dream-sister, meaning she could be an image of the dreamer's own desires or feelings that are somewhat distant from the ego but "sister-like": a part of her that feels more vulnerable, in need of reassurance, in need of sisterly bonding, etc., that is – and this is critically important – separate enough from the ego to require the construction of a new character in the dream because of it. Remember the discussion of multiple personalities and the pull toward integration? Here the separation of the two characters and the facts of their behavior in the dream (one reassuring despite her own fears, the other panicking and needing reas-surance) means these two aspects of her personality are somewhat dissociated. We will have much more to say about these sisters later on.

Finally, however, we should note that this separation of sisters maintains even in the super-resonant alchemical narrative that this dream seems to be a fragment of. The alchemist is never quite *one* with the muse. Why is this? Perhaps because, in the super-resonant narrative, the meaning is that we need others to achieve the alchemical goal, even if it is an "inner guide". The ego cannot do it alone. That's a pretty profound lesson, actually. And this fact seems to suggest that a certain level of separateness is *needed.* Remember that the psyche is always undergoing fractionation and re-integration; maintaining the delicate balance between catastrophic dissociation and excessively rigid stability is the difficult end goal. The psyche seems to strive toward not a crystallized, perfectly symmetric sort of balance (that would essentially be death), but rather the kind of balance seen in an ecosystem with cycles within cycles, but stable, like a solar system. In fact, the aptness of the solar system analogy may be one of the reasons why there are so many astrological meta-phors found in mystical and religious writings, where the stable-but-moving stars and planets in their endless, complex, but non-random movements serve as an allegory for how the psyche works (when balanced), and so praying to astrological deities is also praying/communing with these same stable-but-nonlinear dynamics in one's own psyche. But more on that later.

Using resonance

So I have determined that my patient had a strongly resonant dream. Now what? What can I do with it aside from deduce certain things about my patient diagnostically (as in the bunny rabbit dream)? Well first, before you do anything else, try to get some confirmation of your interpretation with further clinical data. Given the bunny rabbit dream, for example, after hearing it and realizing that the imagery appears to be saying that my patient has a lot of difficulty with playful, creative impulses, I want to confirm that that inter-pretation is correct by following up with her. Ask some open-ended questions about hobbies, interests, playful activities, etc.

If you're way off, your patient will let you know. So what do we do in that case? File it away and leave it as an open question for the time being. Don't hang on to interpretations too tightly – this is a holistic process of meaning-finding. If your initial interpretation doesn't find any confirmation, just let it go for the time being and keep it in mind for when more information about your patient becomes available. It's all, as they say, grist for the mill. Even if this happens, remember that the dream was what prompted the follow up questions in the first place. She is the one who dreamed it, therefore it's all relevant information, and if she hadn't presented the dream you wouldn't necessarily have thought to pursue that particular line of questioning, which very well could yield a lot of helpful information even if your initial interpretation is wrong.

But let's say, as in this case, that our interpretation finds some confirmation in further clinical material. Now what? That's where the resonance can be useful. Resonant expressions by definition are easy to think and hard to forget. And given that we are using images that the patient experienced first-hand in a dream, but also emphasizing through our interpretive method that these images are not literal but *symbolic*, they can be powerful guiding metaphors in therapy. In the process of therapy with the patient who had the alchemy dream, for example, it became possible to use the imagery of her and her sister being in the black egg machine *together* to have a number of in-depth conversations about how her and her sister's upbringing (in this case, with alcoholism in the family) has influenced her and influenced her-through-her-sister, and also how her current relationship with her sister is still entangled with how she herself is doing now. The dream provided the starting point for these conversations because it showed us in no uncertain terms that they were "in it together", as siblings often are. But it also provided us with a powerfully resonant way of *depicting* how they are progressing or have progressed.

And so in subsequent sessions, you can now periodically refer to resonant imagery to put a mental picture in your patient's mind of how their life is progressing "as if" she is/was tumbling through the egg machine with her sister – but also that there is a light at the end of the tunnel (according to the IS): it will end and they will then both meet "the manager". The manager character is of course another symbol that we can keep an eye open for as the patient progresses through therapy. This can be many things, most likely being something of an "inner voice" that is in control, or the manager can even be a metaphor for the IS itself! Remember that we are working with the hypothesis that the IS aims toward psychological integration and healing, and in fact the IS creates and "manages" all the different dream environments and characters. Thus the symbols for it are likely to be of managers, "bosses", or even gods or the Godhead itself.

All that we can do without any knowledge about alchemy. But I encourage the reader to learn about super-resonant stories anyway – meaning narratives which are alchemical, spiritual, mythological, folkloric, etc. – because they represent the "end point" that fragments drift toward across countless retellings, and so they can provide something of a road map of possible ways in which a particular patient might be headed. For example, we know from our brief perusal of alchemical writings that the alchemy dream may be a fragment of the larger timeless narrative of the psycho-spiritual path to ever greater harmony and inner peacefulness, since that's what the alchemical texts are about. Since our dream here is so "alchemical", it's a good bet that our patient's IS is heading in that direction as part of a natural progression of ever more resonant inner narratives. But knowing the super-resonant material means we already know where this often goes, and so we can add questions about this process to our dialogue with our patient to see if, indeed, that is where they feel drawn. Remember, however: this method helps us merely to ask the right questions – it should never be thought of as a proscriptive exercise or a "cookbook".

In this case, we can ask her about her philosophical sense of the world, her deeper values about herself and her place in the world according to her, and what she thinks about "the bigger picture/what it all means". In so doing, we will need to be careful to avoid overly-abstract and intellectualized discussions about such things, but keeping it focused on her emotional needs with respect to fulfilment, etc. I want to know what she feels the end goal is, and what "inner peace" would look like from her perspective. Note, of course, that if she accepts the "alchemical" interpretation for her dream, what that might do: provide a sense of hope, given that she will feel like traversing a path others have gone before. It may also give her a sense of being a part of something larger than herself, given the knowledge that she is experiencing images that have strong parallels all over the world. Or if that does not appeal, she may have a stronger sense of inner coherence, as the IS comes from "within", and so gives her solid, concrete reasons to trust herself maybe just a little more than before. All these are potentially *very* healing processes that you can nurture and allow to grow in therapy in order to facilitate her getting better.

Resonance is but one part of nine principles I recommend using to help interpret a dream. We devoted an entire chapter to it mainly because it is probably the one that requires the most explanation. Luckily, the other eight are much easier to explain. In the next chapter we will look at these other principles and provide examples on how to use them in dream-work.

Note

1   ATU: Aarne-Thompson-Uther type system of folktale classification (Uther 2011).

Chapter 4

Nuts and bolts of understanding dreams – order out of chaos

Stick to the image.

(Jung speaking in Jung and Meyer-Grass 2008: 332)

So now that we have looked at some general principles on dreams, we can get into more specific characteristics and how to interpret them. In this chapter we will discuss nine characteristics of dreams to look at for clues on dream meaning. Remember, dreams are whole-cloth experiences. They are best viewed in the full context of a dreamer's life and her or his surrounding (sub-) culture. Every way we dissect a dream does a little damage to the whole-cloth nature of the dream. If we keep this in mind, however, breaking it down and examining specific qualities, images or pieces of the dream can be instructive *when we put it all back together.*

What are dreams in the clinical setting and how do we use them?

The above statement by Jung is probably one of the most often used guides to dream interpretation from a Jungian or Neo-Jungian perspective. But what does it really mean? Remember that in Chapter 1 we looked at Freud's pioneering work on psychoanalytic dream interpretation, where he made the distinction between manifest and latent content, emphasizing that the manifest content was not nearly as important because it was heavily disguised latent content that was much more important. The manifest content, according to Freud, was distorted, transmuted, disguised, and so forth by the dream censor. We saw, however, that this distinction has not aged particularly well.

And one of the first places we see strong disagreement with this principle is in Jung's work, and the disagreement has piled on since. The main point of contention is the idea that the manifest content is disguised or distorted – Jung and many others have since felt this idea was simply wrong. For example, Jung states in one of his seminars: "There is no reason to believe that the unconscious does not say what it means; in sharpest contradiction to Freud, I say that the unconscious says what it means. Nature is never diplomatic" (Jung speaking in McGuire 1984: 30).

Thus, "stick to the image" means don't stray too far from what the patient actually dreamed in your quest to discern its meaning. This he cautions against time and time again, as in:

> This is where I differ from Freud. You cannot say the symbol in a dream is merely a façade behind which you can hide and then say what the dream is. The symbol is a fact ... a symbol in a dream is meant to be what it is.
>
> (Jung speaking in McGuire 1984: 93–4).

And "one can never say of any particular dream that it has a meaning; it is always a hypothesis, one is never sure; one experiments and finds out if the dream is correctly interpreted by the effect on the patient" (Jung speaking in McGuire 1984: 20).

We saw earlier that one of the primary criticisms of Freud's method of interpreting manifest content as substituted latent content is that it is overly dogmatic and impossible to falsify. Jung was, again, one of the first of many to complain about this, but he also offered a correction to it. One of Jung's primary targets in dream image interpretation was against this idea of "substitution" – where a dream image is seen to be a substitute for someone or something else. As we saw earlier, Freud felt that a dream character could, for example, be a "stand in" for the therapist. In the alchemy dream of last chapter, for example, one might wonder whether or not the "manager" was a substitute for the therapist, or maybe a parent. But Jung would have none of this: "My method throughout has been to make no assumptions but to accept facts. In arbitrary interpretations anything can be a substitute for anything; beware of prejudices in favour of substitution" (Jung speaking in McGuire 1984: 7). And "[a] dream need not always be mysteriously related, by unconscious infections, with the parents"(Jung and Meyer-Grass 2008: 110).

Instead, Jung advocates for taking the image as is and remaining with it to understand its meaning:

> When we are interpreting ... we must be careful to be as naïve as possible, to have no prejudices in connection with the associations. Take the thing literally, concretely. How would you describe a mouse to somebody who had never seen one?
>
> (Jung speaking in McGuire 1984: 535)

Thus the dream imagery *itself* becomes a strongly anchoring factor in one's interpretation. This is what is meant by "stick to the image".

The dreamer and the Invisible Storyteller

The second principle is another one which goes a long way toward understanding dreams, and that is the assumption that the dreamer's behavior in the imaginary environment of the dream is essentially the same as what she or he will normally do while awake. This principle finds support in dream research, where dreamers behaved in dreams in a similar manner to waking life, and with similar dominating concerns (Clarke et al. 2010; DeCicco et al. 2012), but it helps us immensely once we understand the nature of the IS as a dream-constructing entity and the imagery it creates.

Jungian Analyst Yoram Kaufmann (2009), in his fascinating work *The Way of the Image*, argues that we can learn a lot about our patients by looking at how they relate to such spontaneous imagery in general: depression, for example, is often associated with a constriction of the ability to produce images; obsession, eating disorders, and fetishisms are fixations on one or one set of images; boredom is a suspension of images. Kaufmann also follows Jung by encouraging therapists not to be content to simply ask patients what they feel about their images, or ask them what they think it means – that is awfully easy, after all – but rather he encourages us to do the hard work of actually figuring out what the image means in itself. My approach is similar to Kaufmann's (and of course Jung's) in that I encourage students and residents to pursue the image as an expression of the IS with its own meaning rather than an amorphous blob of ideas that can be transformed into anything. By not "sticking to the image", it is possible to be very sloppy with dream interpretation, claiming that any dream image is a substitute for the therapist, the mother, the father, or what have you. I think it is excesses like these that encourage some to be so skeptical of dream interpretation. As Kaufmann (2009: 32) puts it: "The final arbiter of the meaning of the material is the material itself – not what it may stand for, not what it may be compensating for, but the material itself."

We must always be asking ourselves: *why* would the IS create *this* imagery just now? Recall from earlier all of the evidence from dream research that dreaming appears to have an integrating function; that it is responsive to a person's emotional life and concerns, and that it appears to depict them using symbol and narrative in highly creative ways; furthermore, note that dreaming was found to promote integration of the psyche and the dream-making IS does this with its own non-ego perspective.

Kaufmann points out that this essentially Jungian idea that the dream-making part of the psyche (the IS) has the ability to perceive the patient's clinical situation in a more impartial way and continually works to help us toward healing, integration, and perhaps even transcendence is "a staggering hypothesis", but one that he nonetheless ascribes to since he has seen it operate over decades of clinical work. I agree with his approach, however I feel it is no more staggering than any of the self-regulating and self-organizing processes that underlie human experience. I find it no more (or less) amazing than the other incredibly subtle and responsive systems of the human body such as the immune system or the cardiovascular system, and the behavior of these systems is taken advantage of in their respective fields of medicine just as we should be using the highly responsive and sophisticated mental healing system that we all have.

Thus, the remedy for dogmatic, sloppy, or gratuitous dream interpretation is what Kaufmann (2009: 31) calls "absolute faithfulness" to the dream material. By this he elaborates on Jung's advice to "stick to the image" and not stray from it with one's own or even the patient's egoic wanderings. The rationale for this approach is quite simple: it begins with the assumption that the IS says exactly what it means, as Jung might put it, and this assumption receives a great deal of support from dream research as we reviewed earlier.

It is important, however, to realize that while I may personify the IS to a degree, this personification is not exact. It doesn't behave like a human ego would. As Jung put it:

> The unconscious has no moral intention; it is just Nature, it says what is happening, as an objective event. The dream never says what ought to be or what ought not to be. We have to draw our own conclusions ... the dream is merely a statement of things which are actually going on.
>
> (Jung speaking in McGuire 1984: 110)

Jung insists on this point throughout his dream seminars, and I feel it is another anchor that protects us against sloppy or overly wild dream interpretation. Thus far, there is little evidence to suggest that dreams are necessarily "messages" to the ego. The IS does not seem to feel the ego should be "told what to do". Instead it merely reports *the story so far*. This is where we are right now, and this is what XYZ feels like to you (the ego). This principle is another reason the Dream Hack works: the dream depicts your story so far *as if* [insert dream]. As stated above, the ego then behaves in the manner it usually does. I think this is where dream interpretation and discussing dreams in therapy can help. As we go we will see these principles (and many more) in action. Dreams are thus statements of the status you are in currently, but put into pictures in a manner that Ullman (1969) refers to as "a metaphor in motion".

Storytelling

There is a theory about the function of dreams that has been around for a while: it states that dreams are about "memory consolidation" (Payne and Nadel 2004; Nielson and Levin 2007; Stickgold et al. 2001; Siegel 2001, however see Vertes and Eastman 2000) along with emotional processing (Eiser 2005).

I think this theory is generally correct, but it's easy to overlook and/or miss the potentially profound significance of memory consolidation because so often we think of memory as some kind of computer-like data retrieval. But a little reflection shows that memory does not work this way. Memory is more like a reconstructive process; we use our considerable imaginative faculties not to "retrieve" a memory, but to *re-create* it. This is much more efficient, but it means our memories are not always completely reliable and they can be influenced by current emotional and/or physiological factors.

Further links between dreaming as memory consolidation and narrative formation can be found (along with a great deal of discussion on the neurophysiology of various mental states including dreaming) in Hobson et al. (2000). However, dreams do not appear to typically incorporate just any memory items. For example, Hobson reviews the various studies that show that presleep stimuli such as films, static images, altered social environments, pre-sleep waking behavior or thought experiences, and pre-sleep daytime events all rarely find their way into dream content. It seems the IS simply has more important, larger scale issues to consider. Hobson also finds with many other dream researchers that emotion appears to be a primary organizer of dream plots rather than secondary (Hobson et al. 2000: 808–825). Studies of the precise memory sources of dream content show that exact replay of memories in dreams is rare; rather, it appears that dreams consolidate memories via binding them together into narratives via hippocampal and amygdala mediation (Nielsen and Stenstrom 2005). These investigators propose that dream narratives are driven by emotional sources and the narratives are essentially expressions of those emotional concerns in metaphorical terms – essentially the same idea we pursue here, and further empirical support for Jung's psychodynamic approach.

These findings support our contention that the IS is putting together emotionally driven, but highly symbolic stories in a meaningful and creative manner in order to better "make sense of" what has happened to us – in short as a way to "consolidate" memory. Moreover, it's not just *any* memories, but only the most "important" ones – i.e., the most emotionally relevant and (I would add) the most resonant ones. But let's think about the term "memory consolidation". If we view memory as a re-creative, imaginative process, then "memory consolidation" is *storytelling* (and re-telling, and re-re-telling, etc.). And what influences storytelling? Psychological Resonance. Remember also the Number One Dream Hack: "my life is progressing *as if* X", with X being whatever I just dreamed. So the IS is telling a story about my life, but in *as if* or symbolic terms, using the facts of psychological resonance (i.e., that they are "sticky" or *memorable*) to give an overall gestalt of my life up to now. Memory consolidation! So yes, dreams do seem to be about memory consolidation, but that phrase needs to be understood in the full light of how powerful such a process really is, and even more so in light of *exactly how the trick is done.* That is, we consolidate memory by continually telling our life story to ourselves in imagistic and symbolic terms. Why? Because images and symbols can convey a huge amount of information (much of it non-verbal, impressionistic, and emotional) in a highly *condensed* format – once we are capable of such thought, of course, which occurs in late childhood and pre-adolescence and correlating with symbolic visuo-spatial intelligence according to Foulkes's (1999) data. Doing this helps us to make sense of our world and give us a powerful heuristic tool with which to proceed.

In therapy you can detect a patient's ongoing personal narrative through the acquisition of clinical data. It's extremely important because the continually updating of personal narrative colors *everything we experience.* Such themes as "I have always been lonely", or "I'm the black sheep of the family", or "my father was never there for me" are themes you will find in the course of therapy. These are narrative elements. They are always suspect – why? Because they are often overly simple and they tend to be (in clinical populations, at least) quite negative. This is because PR works both ways – it works to preserve both uplifting stories of triumph and tragic stories of suffering and pain. Chances are good that a patient attending psychotherapy will have a number of tragic elements to their ongoing narrative. Restructuring this narrative through the process of therapy is one of the ways a person's narrative can be changed into a story that is more realistic, but also containing some measure of hope. This process involves not changing the events of your patient's life, since that is impossible, but rather the huge interpretive process of *what those events mean emotionally* to your patient. That *is* changeable.

Let's use another clinical example to illustrate what I mean: the case of Mr. A. At the beginning of therapy, Mr. A was experiencing severe Posttraumatic Stress Disorder symptoms: nightmares, anxiety attacks, irritability, and general difficulty coping. At the start of therapy, Mr. A recounted a history of severe physical abuse from his stepfather. He told the story of the worst event that he could remember:

> *I was about 11 years old. I remember hearing yelling upstairs. My stepfather was yelling and screaming again. I don't know why but I went upstairs and there he was. As soon as I showed up, he started yelling at me and screaming at me. Then he started beating me, and he hit me with a hammer, knocking me off the balcony where I landed on the floor below. I don't remember anything after that, but that's when the neighbor called the cops. That was the last beating.*

This is the version of the traumatic experience that he told at the start of therapy. Notice a few things: it's emotionally intense (and the affect displayed during the telling of this event was also intense), but it's also disjointed somewhat. Events seem to just sort of happen, and it has a somewhat surreal, nightmarish quality to it. We don't know much about *why* any of this is happening, and Mr. A even says he doesn't know why he went toward the yelling rather than go hide somewhere. It feels like pointless suffering without any explanation. It's terrifying – and this is the current "memory consolidated" story of Mr. A's life.

After a number of sessions focusing on the trauma, however, Mr. A's story changed, and the intense affect surrounding the storytelling changed also:

> *I remember he was upstairs yelling at my sister. She had broken a comb, and this set him off on another one of his rages. I ran upstairs because I was worried about my sister, and I grabbed a hammer – I thought maybe I could scare him. I was just a kid and didn't realize that wouldn't work, but you know, I had to try. When I got upstairs I told him to stop smacking her. He had her by the hair. But then he started yelling at me, calling me names. He took the hammer and popped me in the head with it, then grabbed me and threw me off the balcony. I only remember waking up later, bloody, but with the cops everywhere.*

Notice how this is essentially the same story, but the meaning of it is entirely different. The basic events are still the same – but notice how it's easier to visualize. It's still awful, but it's more resonant. And there is a lot more meaning in it, now, too. Mr. A is cast not in the light of a helpless victim of a horrible fate, but as a noble and brave soul going up against impossible odds. Like Beowulf, he faces the dragon even though he knows it will kill him. In this case defeating the dragon is not the point. The point is to face it with courage. He does so for a noble reason, also, rather than "I don't know why": to defend his sister – so he has also added the element of the self-sacrificing hero. And like Beowulf, he loses the fight – but so does the dragon.

Now it is natural at this point to ask: but did it *really* happen like that? Did he really grab a hammer and challenge his stepfather in order to protect his sister? Is this memory accurate? My answer: I don't care. I'm not a forensic investigator. I'm a psychiatrist. Pedantic concerns of perfect "accuracy" will not help our patients heal. There is a balance to strike between self-loathing and ego-inflation, where one has a healthy measure of self-worth that is neither too low nor too high. I saw that Mr. A's restructured narrative brought him greater peace, a glimmer of hope, a reason to feel proud of himself in the face of horrible things, and a way to understand those horrible things and "make sense of them" on some level. The human soul craves meaning. We are remarkably resilient in the face of awfulness, provided we can somehow make sense of what has happened. It's the patient who simply can't make any sense out of tragic events who suffers the most. We torture ourselves with the "why?" Thus, it may be a good thing that memory is so malleable: it allows us to tell our story in a different way, and one which can make terrible events bearable to some degree.

Basic principles of environments and characters

So keeping that in mind, let us return to the IS, and its continually mixing and re-mixing process of storytelling one's personal narrative. What can we say about it? We can say that dreams reflect this process of sense-making and meaning-making, and every dream is an attempt at it. That is why I hypothesize that the dream-making process is a storyteller. As mentioned, I have organized important dream characteristics into a list of nine things that are helpful to examine, in order to get a better feel for what the IS is "saying" about the dreamer and her or his current life. Some of these overlap or contribute to one another, but that is to be expected. Here they are:

1   Resonance: Developed in the previous chapter, this principle tells us just how resonant this particular dream is, and how deeply it goes into universal themes. It tells us how "big" this dream is.
2   Context: recognizing that dreams do not happen in isolation, but in the context of the dreamer's current life situation. This principle examines how the dream relates to the dreamer's current life as a whole.
3   Characters: recognizing what characters in dreams represent, either as aspect of the dreamer's own mind/life experience, or as symbols for relationships, and more importantly, why the IS uses particular people to symbolize them.
4   Setting: from abstract to familiar, the setting tells us much about the dreamer's current life situation and overall emotional quality. The details of the setting tell us more precisely *what* these things are.
5   Scope: the overall narrowness of vision vs. expansive, comprehensive view, the scope tells us a lot about the state of the dreaming ego and just how well connected s/he is with his/her life situation.
6   Storytelling: recognizing the narrative aspects of a dream adds context and meaning by putting together events in a particular order. Asking "why *this* order?" opens the door to better understanding of the dream.
7   Conflict: the overall level of conflict tells us a great deal about how the dreaming ego is relating to the rest of the mind and to the waking world. High levels of conflict, and looking at the specific imagery used in the dream often show us aspects of internal conflicts previously unnoticed.
8   Intensity: besides conflict there is overall intensity, turmoil, and general "storminess" or emotional force. This can tell us the overall level of creative/destructive energy going on at the time of the dream.
9   Integration: this final factor involves the over-arching connection between dreams that occurred over a long period of time and how the dreamer is or is not changing to meet new challenges. This principle guides us toward psychological healing, development, and expansion as we grow older.

Resonance

We've said a lot about PR already, but it's worth reiterating a few key points about it here. Remember that each dream is a product of the IS's continuous work. Not every dream is of cosmic significance, not every dream will be helpful, and not every dream will even be interpretable. Learning to tell which ones are which is the first step toward successful dream interpretation. Honestly, sometimes your patient will report a dream that is not very resonant and leaves even an experienced clinician with a head-scratching feeling of "what in the world was that supposed to be about?" I encourage you not to give up on such dreams too quickly – but neither should you dwell on them excessively. Sometimes the utterances of the IS are just too cryptic or downright weird to make easy sense of. So, spend a decent amount of time on it, but if you still can't make any sense out of it, let it go. Rest assured, clinical experience shows the IS will create another dream with the same themes later (and it will probably be better organized). You'll get another chance. In any case, PR gives us a good feel for roughly how much time to spend on a particular dream trying to make sense of it. The guideline to keep in mind: the more resonant a dream is, the more time you should give it. Some dreams come across as garbled, non-resonant noise, like the hippo-mosquito story. Don't worry about them. The IS is a tireless artist, constantly shaking things up (meaning events, images, themes, contexts), and sometimes it just doesn't fall together very nicely. That's OK. More will come, and often enough, subsequent dreams on the same theme will fit better. The IS is always perfecting its craft.

Context

Remember that dreams are rarely ever *only* about the past, even when they are rehashing events verbatim. Rather, the IS is always trying to "make sense of" the past but *in light of the present*. It's asking "what does what has happened to me mean *now* given my current situation?" In his excellent work *Dreams and Nightmares*, psychoanalyst and dream researcher Ernest Hartmann (2001), points out how traumatic dreams usually follow a typical progression from verbatim repeats of the trauma (such as a soldier being attacked in Iraq), followed by trauma happening in more recent or current environments and situations (the same soldier is now being ambushed while grocery shopping), to trauma that is "downgraded" (instead of being bombed, the dreamer is now being insulted or belittled by others), to an integrated state in which the trauma is placed in the proper context of the patient's life ("I understand that what happened to me in Iraq in part makes me who I am and I need not feel ashamed of it, nor does it have to rule my life"). As we will discuss in more detail in the next chapter, this progression occurs if all goes well. But of course sometimes it doesn't, and a patient will be dreaming of a trauma exactly as it happened 20 years ago. In this case we can deduce that the patient has not successfully integrated the trauma and is living "as if" it was still going on *right now* (notice the use of the Number One Dream Hack here). The context of "what this means now" is one of the reasons why it works. It reminds us that the IS will often use the past to give us a picture of the present.

Jung emphasized this from early on, building on Freud's emphasis on full context. And though he developed the method of comparing dream images to recurrent motifs and symbols, Jung warning against *merely* taking dream images and comparing them to recurrent symbols: "This method of treating a dream is not sufficient .... We have to ask more specific questions about the events of the previous day, and in general about the whole *individual* situation the [dreamer] is in" (Jung and Meyer-Grass 2008: 107–8).

Elsewhere he writes:

> If we want to interpret a dream correctly, we need a thorough knowledge of the conscious situation at the moment, because the dream contains its unconscious complement, that is, the material which the conscious situation has constellated in the unconscious. Without this knowledge it is impossible to interpret a dream correctly, except by a lucky fluke.
>
> (Jung 1990: 34–5).

By "complement" he means everything the conscious ego left out, repressed, or did not notice – recall the dream research reviewed earlier that shows how subliminal information has a tendency to find its way into dream content. That is the part we are interested in – the "rest of the story". That's the "royal road" to what is going on for your patient.

Characters

During development, everyone gradually forms an ego. This ego goes through multiple transformations throughout life, and the psyche is capable of producing more than one ego. This we see day to day in our ability to adopt slightly different approaches to people depending on where we are and what we're doing. On a more pathological scale, the ability to create and destroy the ego can be seen dramatically in the case of multiple personalities. In schizophrenia the ego is actually split into a primary and one or more secondary egos who feel alien to the primary ego, inserting their thoughts into it and causing hallucinations. This all traces back to the ability of the psyche to self-organize egos. In most cases, there is one dominant ego, but during the variably destabilized states such as dreaming, drug use, trance, severe mental illness, or altered states of consciousness, the ego is immersed into a matrix of other possible selves, future selves, ideal selves, hated selves, personified ideas and themes, and so forth (see McNamara 2014 for a fascinating review of these processes), and these get played out in the drama of the dream in a metaphorical fashion.

This is why many dream characters can be considered alter-egos or personified ideas/emotions – selves the current ego hasn't considered, feels alienated from, wants to be like, is disgusted by, etc. It can also be about a person in the dreamer's life and how they relate to them (metaphorically, that is). A good way to tell the difference is to ask if a particular dream character is a person that the dreamer knows or not. This approach to dream characters began with Jung (see McGuire 1984: 6–7; 29; Jung 1990) and it has found support in dream research that shows that when studying longitudinal dream series, the dreamer's interaction style with friends and relatives *that remained in the dreamer's life* closely paralleled their waking life pattern. This parallel did not hold with people who did not remain a part of the dreamer's life, however. These results again support our idea that the dreamer behaves in the dream in essentially the same manner she or he would in waking life, a fact which can be very therapeutically useful, since it can help identify unhealthy patterns of behavior, blind spots, distortions, and so on. The results also support the Jungian intuition that known characters that the dreamer nevertheless has had little recent contact with are more likely to be symbolic representations rather than mirror images of the waking life relationship (Domhoff and Schneider 2008).

Therefore, if a dream character isn't anyone they know, then the dream character is likely to be a possible self or symbol of a part of the dreamer's psyche/life (when we get to dreams and spiritual beliefs, however, this practice takes on another dimension). The task then becomes to figure out exactly what part of the psyche is being symbolized. To determine that you look at the specific imagery of the character and what they are doing. On the other hand, if it's someone the dreamer knows, then you should find out if it's someone they interact with regularly or not. If not, then we're back to considering it as a symbol, in this case a symbol of the way the dreamer was when interactions with that person were normally occurring. If it is someone they interact with regularly, then the dream character is probably about that person, but it's still primarily about the way the dreamer interacts with that person: that is, the character is a symbol of the dreamer's current interaction style with that person.

To summarize: when faced with a particular dream character, ask who is this person?

"I don't know" = symbol of the dreamer's psyche/life that is separated from the ego.

"Someone I knew 10 years ago" = symbol of how the dreamer relates to how s/he was at that time, in the settings s/he knew that person.

"Someone I interact with daily" = symbol of how the dreamer interacts with that person, from their unique perspective and in their current context, i.e., their subjective "projection" or idea of that person.

What about animals? Actually the answer here is the same, only now we are looking at "animal" aspects of the dreamer – i.e., primitive elements of their psyche, instinctive drives, etc. Which primitive part depends on the animal: wolves and lions represent different meanings than cows, kittens, or dragons, for example. This method of viewing dream animals began with Jung but has found support in the work of many dream researchers (Van de Castle 1994: 305; see also Henderson 2011), and in fact the presence of dream animals correlates with aggression and attempts to cope with challenges when dreams are analyzed with the Hall-Van de Castle content measures (Van de Castle 1994: 307).

Jung's opinion on the subject was that:

> We can say it is an instinct whenever an animal occurs in a dream, but, mind you, it is always a very particular instinct, by no means *the* instinct. A lion or a huge snake would mean something quite different.
>
> (Jung speaking in McGuire 1984: 535)

As ever, though, stick to the image. In other words, if you dream about a fairy mother, it is *not* merely a substitute for the mother: "When the unconscious says 'it's a fairy,' then please stay with it" (Jung and Meyer-Grass 2008: 195). This would be against the idea that the animal is a "substitute" for something or someone else. We saw how Jung felt about the idea of substitution as only inviting sloppy or arbitrary interpretations, since the idea essentially allows *anything* to be substituted for anything else. Take our bunny rabbit dream, for example. One commonly encountered interpretation would be to say it is a substitute for the patient's abusive mother. Still another common reflex is to assume the rabbit is a substitute for the therapist. But this style of interpretation usually falls apart if we ask "why a bunny rabbit then? Why not a hamster? Or a giraffe? Or the Snuffleupagus for that matter?" If we don't stick with the image, the possible substitutions multiply to become unmanageable. Only if there is something about the rabbit that gives us a clue to either of these connections (maybe the mother or the therapist's name is "bunny", for example, or they have a picture of a rabbit in their rooms, or *in the dream* the rabbit says "I'm your therapist", etc.), can we justify this – assuming the psyche says what it means, of course.

But this very assumption has several advantages. One is parsimony: rather than assume any dream image is *really* something else disguised or distorted, we eliminate this part and say the dream was of a rabbit for specific reasons and we simply need to figure out what they are. If the IS wanted to create a dream about the mother, then it would just use the image of the mother. Another advantage, already reviewed above, is that the assumption is supported by dream research, which time and again favors the "does not conceal but reveal" approach rather than the "disguise and substitute" approach. Finally, perhaps the best advantage is predictive validity. If I had gone with the rabbit = therapist substitution, for example, I would never have been able to predict the patient's characterological tendencies as I did. Now, of course, this could have been just a lucky coincidence; I don't think it is since I've been able to do that more than once, but I encourage the reader to try it for yourself.

Finally, getting back to dream characters, one more tendency to consider is observed by Jung: a tendency to personify one's ages in dreams (McGuire 1984: 28). That is, dreams that are about a person trying to come to grips with different life stages will depict the dreamer interacting with characters that are younger or older than herself/himself. But, as ever, before you can make this interpretation, you must be sure that the images themselves support this interpretation – these characters should be "like" the dreamer or connected to the dreamer in some way. Typical relationships would be a "step-son" or "daughter" or "uncle" (but not a waking-life uncle, a dream-uncle).

Setting

The setting of the dream can tell us something of the dreamer's state also. Here we must ask ourselves, is this a happy place? Or is it dingy, barren, dark, confining, etc. Dreamers with excessively defensive ego structure often dream of being in prisons. Depressed dreamers dream of being in barren, lifeless, and dark surroundings. Dreamers going through major transitions in life may dream of world-burning fires. So the setting gives us a clue as to what their life feels like; it tells us the "as if" quality of the feeling. Jung, for example, observed that houses generally embody the habitual or inherited attitude, the typical way of living, or the way one lives with one's family (McGuire 1984: 39).

Most dreams happen in non-specific, distorted or unfamiliar environments (Strauch and Meier 1996: 106), which highlights the fact that they are likely being used as symbols – otherwise why dream of a place you've never been in before? Interestingly, pregnant women commonly report dreams of distorted or tilted buildings (Van de Castle 1994: 391) – a clue to the symbolic nature of environments as symbolically representing the "as if you were living in X" nature of dream settings.

Scope

Scope is another clue. How limited is the vision of this dream? Is it highly limited or boundless? Is the dreamer locked up in a confined area, unable to "see" anything beyond his/her current situation? Or are they soaring across the mountaintops? (Flying dreams normally suggest themes of unlimited freedom and creativity, but also a tendency to lose touch with physical reality and stay with "head in the clouds".) Traumatic dreams that obsessively repeat the trauma suggest extremely limited scope – they are tightly bound in time if not in space, and suggest the dreamer's ego perspective is extremely limited and un-integrated, dominated by trauma, and living "as if the trauma is still happening over and over".

Storytelling

Where the analytical side of the mind links things in terms of causal chains and isolated objects interacting with one another like billiard balls, the dreaming modality tells stories. Without narrative, of course, our lives simply consist of "one damn thing after another" with no cohering theme, purpose, or meaning. As a holistic mode of thought, dreams often attempt (sometimes unsuccessfully) to tell stories about the current state of the psyche. This is another dimension to the dream that can be helpful to consider outside of character and setting. Remember, even if it's telling a story that begins when the dreamer is a child, it's still really about what's going on right now. It simply uses the story to give us context and perspective as to what the now actually *means*. In any case, the more fantastical the dream story is, the more symbolic and potentially meaningful it is; this is because the fantastical elements allow a great freedom in symbolic storytelling. Unfettered by rules of time, place, or the laws of physics, they become expressions of pure mind, concerned not with what and where, but with who and why ... sometimes.

Conflict

Another thing to think about as you contemplate a dream is to assess the level of conflict in it. Dreams of those with PTSD, borderline personality, schizophrenia, and mania are often loaded with conflict. Manic dreams, in particular, are often full of visceral, bloody conflict, complete with dismemberment and carnage running riot. Traumatic dreams that do not simply repeat the trauma are also nonetheless often fraught with conflict. It is important to remember here (especially in traumatic dreams, which usually contain conflict experienced in waking life) that a significant portion of the conflict is symbolic in nature, and descriptive of the psyche as a whole. In other words, when a dreamer's mind is in turmoil, inner conflict, or feels pulled in a hundred directions, there will be all sorts of violent conflict, storms, natural disasters, and plagues of insects in their dreams to reflect this. As your patients become more integrated, able to tolerate ambiguity, depotentiate black-and-white thinking, get back on their medications, and so forth, their dreams will correspondingly become less conflict ridden, though in many cases it does not follow a linear trajectory of gradually reduced conflict over time. Rather, what you see is fewer instances of dreams with extreme conflict. What I mean is that the dreams will still fluctuate in terms of conflict, but as a person becomes more integrated, the range of extremes will lessen.

Intensity

During development, from out of the primordial fertile chaos, the psyche self-organizes the ego, which subsequently brings order from the chaos and exerts a certain amount of top-down control over the psyche (this process, not coincidentally, is depicted symbolically in nearly all creation myths world-wide – Sproul, 1991). But the *prima materia* of the psyche is not always at a constant state of activity. There are times (drugs, mental illness, stress, trauma) when the chaos is stirred up to a high degree. The more active the psyche is, the more primitive (meaning extreme) and intense the imagery and affect will be. Dreams with mythic, godlike themes, for example, reflect a high degree of intensity in the dreamer's psyche and may reflect higher activity in the association and limbic cortices (Hobson et al. 2000). But creativity is just the flip side of chaos and destruction: in order to develop the ego, it must first be dismantled and a new one built up. Looking at the overall intensity of a dream, then, can tell us what potential for creativity/destruction the psyche is currently in. If the ego is strong, then it is time to actually embrace the chaos to a degree and look toward transformation. But if the ego is fragile, it's time to support defenses and ride the storm out!

Integration

As mentioned, the IS is continually updating the personal narrative and "consolidating memory", and it is possible and even likely that this process is working continually during wakefulness as well as sleep, but it seems especially active during dreaming sleep. In any case, the process appears to aim at integration of the various fragmented parts of the psyche. Conflict, dissociation, turmoil, etc., are of course natural processes in the mind, but so, too is integration. Sometimes it proceeds along in a predictable and healthy fashion, such as those who recover normally within a few months following a traumatic, fragmenting event. Others, however, do not recover, or recovery is significantly delayed. This delay of normal re-integration can be due to a number of factors, including genetic (such as in schizophrenia, for example), environmental (severe, chronic stress and repeat traumas), physiological (such as in severe physical illness or drug dependence), or many other things.

I often liken the integration process to the immune system. Our immune system normally works well to fight off infections, but sometimes it malfunctions or is thwarted by particularly virulent pathogens. Sometimes the immune system mistakenly attacks the organism, targeting a particular organ or organ system. Sometimes it is inherently weakened (such as in AIDS for example), and so cannot mount a sufficient defense. All of these things will hinder normal healing and eradication of the pathogen. The immune system also has an array of various defenses that are of differing levels of sophistication. Inflammation and swelling, for example, are first line and rapid defenses against suspected pathogens. They are highly non-specific responses that nevertheless work more often than not (which is why they have persisted through our evolutionary history), and so remain as defensive mechanisms. Likewise the ego has its so-called primitive defenses such as denial, dissociation and fight/flight/freeze responses. Like swelling, they are rapid, nearly automatic, and very non-specific.

But the immune system also has highly sophisticated defenses and so does the psyche. The humoral and cell-based responses are capable of pinpointing specific pathogens and creating proteins and cells that are specially designed to kill that precise pathogen and no other. The immune system can make "magic bullets", and this is the principle behind the practice of vaccination, of course. Likewise the psyche has sophisticated defenses also, which involve the so-called mature defenses, all of which involve a rather high level of integration of various emotional elements. Interestingly, the idea that dreams serve an integrative as well as diagnostic and prognostic function is not unique to Jung and can be found not only among a variety of dream theorists, but even cross-culturally among some hunter-gatherer tribes (Kracke 1993: 478). Dream researchers also support this finding: "Dreaming acts as a psychic glue to hold together the thought system and enrich it with the capacity for expansion and development ... the function of dreaming is at the same time neurobiological and symbolic" (McManus et al. 1993: 21). These authors provide additional evidence supporting the integrative function of dreaming from a neurocognitive perspective, including the assimilation of previously contradictory information and weaving it "into a greater fabric" (29). Thus we find that our psychodynamic approach has good empirical support behind it as well as clinical support from the consulting room.

In any case, the characteristic of integration in a dream is something that can usually only be seen in a dream *series*. Over time, if integration is progressing along normally, the dreams and self-stories as a whole will gradually display greater integration of elements and images. The above story of the abusing stepfather is one example. The second version, with its more coherent and resonant narrative, reflects greater integration.

Clinical examples

Ms. B, age 34, presented to therapy with symptoms of depression and reported the following recurrent dream:

> *I am by a river in a place I used to play as a kid. I remember the place used to be green and bright and a fun place to play. Now it's barren and dirty. The water is sluggish and dingy and there are old people hobbling along – it's very sad. The trees have no leaves and the grass is all brown and dying.*

Let's look this dream from the perspective of the nine characteristics presented in this chapter. With each characteristic I will add some "things to look out for" so that you can have some specific concepts in mind when you look at a dream from each of these nine perspectives. All of these, however, are really variations on the fundamental question: "why is this aspect of the dream *this* way instead of some other way? What might it mean that it is *this* instead of the 10,000 other things it *could* have been?" Asking this question helps us get at the particular meaning of the dream because it helps us stick to the images used by the IS to make the dream, rather than prematurely interpret something based on some abstract idea of what was dreamed. To understand a dream, we have to understand the dream *as it was given to us.* Jung's way of putting this was to tell his students to learn everything you can about symbolism then forget it when you ask about a patient's dream.

Resonance

Looking at the characteristics of resonance (minimal unusualness, emotionality, sensual vividness, indeterminacy of time/place, middle-level categories, low complexity, rhythmic elements, simple plots/irony, interconnectedness), this dream has a relatively modest level of resonance. There is no unusualness, except that the place appears different than it did in the patient's childhood. But no talking rabbits, flying elephants or Jedi masters. The emotionality is that of sadness and emptiness but nothing beyond that. Vividness is high, however. This is not an indeterminate time or place, though it is somewhat hazy. There is low complexity in that none of the vague, other characters have any internal complexity of their own. There is no rhythm or irony apart from (again) the changes from what they used to be. Also there isn't really enough of a plot to identify any plot twists or interconnectedness either. So, in general this dream has a moderate to low amount of resonance to it.

Things to look out for: recurrence. Why is this a recurrent dream rather than a one-off? Any time we dream something more than once it means that the IS is really trying to make sense of or understand a particular aspect of our lives or experiences. One of the key elements to dream recurrence, also, is whether or not the dreamer herself – i.e., the conscious ego rather than all the other sub-personalities, possible selves, fractionated personalities/memories, etc. – understands what the dream is about. You will find in clinical practice that when you and your patient have a clearer understanding of a recurrent dream, it will oftentimes stop recurring. This is a sure sign that you're on the right track, and it can be a very interesting experience for your patient also, since it shows in no uncertain terms that even though the dreamer did not actively construct the dream consciously, the ego's understanding and perspective can *alter* subsequent dreams. It's as if the IS is trying to figure out life, but needs the help of the ego sometimes to "get it", after which the IS moves on to other things. This can be especially eye-opening for patients who have, up until this event, assumed (more or less consciously) that dreams are really pretty random and/or just silly noise. These types of patients will initially, more often than not, report dreams to you, but often it's just more or less to humor you as their therapist, while in the back of their mind they're pretty skeptical it's going to tell either of you anything useful – this attitude I detect in a good portion of my patients, but given the typically mechanistic picture of the universe taught in many Western education systems, I can't say I blame them for it.

In any case, the effect of dream interpretation itself actually *changing* dream content can be pretty uncanny to many patients, since they are realizing that all along *something* has been dropping them into the same dream over and over again, but then once you figure it out, the dream stops recurring. It's empowering and humbling all at once. Empowering because it means we are not helpless victims to our dreams, and humbling because it means there are far more things to heaven and earth than are dreamt of in our philosophy, or put another way, because there's more going on in our minds than we are aware of, and that non-ego stuff is actually purposeful and even intelligent in its own way. The spooky feeling that accompanies this event, however, can be useful clinically, since it can open the way toward a deeper self-understanding, and a recognition that we are not simply isolated Cartesian egos floating in a sea of random noise, but people inextricably embedded in a dense world of meaning and purpose – perhaps not always easily discerned meaning and purpose but there nonetheless – and that is a powerful thought.

Of course, there need not be anything especially spooky about all this, since dreaming is a natural process like all other functions of the body and mind; the "trick" is removing the mistaken belief that it's some random mechanical process, gleefully explained away by vague references to neurotransmitters or brain networks (there is a big difference between description and explanation!). We are just far too complex creatures for that to really gain any traction.

In any case, the point is that the phenomenon of recurrent dreams, and the high resonance that accompanies that phenomenon show us that the act of dream interpretation is not a passive process. It is an active one that promotes integration because the ego, through the reflective exercise, can become more familiar with and aware of the other parts of the psyche at play. We will explore other methods for promoting integration in later sections. In this case, the recurrence of the dream suggests a slightly greater level of resonance than the initial modest amount, and so that suggests we pay closer attention to it and try to work out its meaning more thoroughly.

Context

This dream characteristic describes the connection between the dreamer's dream and her current symptoms and life situation. To understand the dream context, you often have to ask a few follow up questions. Keeping in mind that even though this riverside is supposedly a place the dreamer visited as a child, the dream is only using that imagery to tell us a story about what is going on *now*. The fact that the dreamer played by this river only serves to tell this story, i.e., that *once* it was green and verdant and full of life, but now it most notably is *not*.

Things to look out for: when elements of the dreamer's life (past or recent) are seen in a dream, it is easy to get distracted by this fact and lose sight of the particular way in which the IS is *using* the memory. In other words, it's worthwhile to ask how such dreams *differ* from the memories from which they are drawn, as they are very rarely perfect replicas of the memories. This technique is, in a way, the opposite of searching for the "day residue" mentioned by Freud (1900), where you note the elements from the person's daytime activities. Now, don't misunderstand: there is nothing wrong with noting day residue. The problem is there's clinically not a whole lot you can do with it other than identify it. Furthermore, simply pointing it out does not tell us why the IS used that bit of memory *in the particular way* that it did. That is the essence of understanding the context of the dream, because we are not just breaking down the dream into its component parts to classify them. We are looking at the dream as a coherent whole, which used the parts so identified in a particular way.

So, what I am advocating here is looking at how the IS uses memory in a specific way to weave a story. In this dream, for example, the IS used the patient's memory of a pleasant place where she played as a child. But if we stopped there and simply said "oh that's in this dream because (let's say) she was thinking about that river the day before, so that's the source of this dream" we would miss a lot of important meaning because such an analysis is extremely reductive. For instance, why *that* memory? There are likely thousands of images and sensations one experiences during a day – why is she dreaming about that one and none other? And why did she dream of that memory in that particular order, and subsequently placed in close contact with the non-memories? Surely all sorts of random stuff encountered during the day could have been tossed in there. Why was none of that included? These kinds of questions help avoid reductionistic, arbitrary, or sloppy interpretation errors. In this case we can see that the barren, muddy, dingy riverside, which is not a memory exists *in sharp contrast* to the memory, making it more meaningful *due to the juxtaposition* – the essence of context. If, for example, the memory had been of a shore that had been completely dried up before, and only now flowing with muddy water, that dream would have a different overall gestalt than this dream does, which suggests a kind of degeneration or wasting away theme, rather than the beginnings of a rejuvenation type story arc, with water (albeit muddy and slow) finally beginning to flow after a long drought.

Characters

The only characters in this dream are the "old people" that are hobbling about the riverside. They are otherwise nondescript and provide a sharp contrast with the memory the dreamer reports of the riverside as a child, where there were young people playing and frolicking. Since there is no dialogue with any of the characters in this dream, or any real interaction at all, it really leaves us with a rather lonely feeling, particularly as the dreamer is herself not old, and yet she is surrounded by old people. The overall feeling of aging and degeneration, a draining of life into stillness, slowness, and wasting away gives the scene a feeling of death.

Things to look out for: for this dream characteristic we want to take very close note of how the dreamer is relating to the other characters, asking, why is she behaving *this* way instead of the zillions of other ways she *could* relate to them? Here, she's not interacting with them at all. But what if she was? She could have been running from them, or attacking them, or talking to them, or trying to help them, or setting them on fire for that matter. But she does nothing. Why? Why is she *not* interacting with anyone? She seems repulsed by these characters, as if overwhelmed by the tragedy of their aged condition. Isn't that interesting? That gives us a clue to the dreamer's overall approach and behavioral tendencies. Remember that the dreamer will behave in a dream – being an imaginary setting constructed by the IS – as she will typically in waking life. This doesn't mean she has a phobia of elderly people, however. If that were the case, she would be more active in attempting to flee from them. Rather, she seems shocked by them, like the idea of aging is some kind of new idea rather than a natural part of the life cycle. There's also a somewhat self-absorbed quality to this dream too: why isn't she attending to the old people, or offering to help them, rather than simply recoiling from them? Thus, the things to look out for are patterns of interaction the dreamer engages in.

Another brief example may help, of a dream, reported by a 38-year-old in therapy, that has some parallels to the current dream, but shows some important and illustrative contrasts:

> *I'm in a field where I used to play as a kid, only now there are raccoons wandering around. Suddenly I'm afraid of them and decide to fly away. So I fly into a tree to get away from them.*

When asked what exactly the raccoons were doing in this instance, the dreamer replied that they seemed to be harmlessly going about their business. But look at how the dreamer responds to them: by flying away, which is "retreating into the air", which brings to mind the idea of having one's "head in the clouds". Notable, also, is the fact that flying like that is actually impossible. And yet it seems a viable option to this dreamer, who has a will such that flying becomes possible. Seeing this sort of behavior always makes me suspect that the dreamer has a vivid imagination but is sometimes a bit disconnected from physical, everyday life. So then if you were to guess from this dream that this person's general approach to things is to abstract and intellectualize away from them, retreating into the imagination even when they are harmless "animals" – which remember are typically instinctive, animal-*like* entities within the psyche or (alternatively) animal-like aspects of life experience – then you would have been correct, and further clinical data supported that. See how that works? Since dreams are often about general themes and attempts at the big picture, they often deal with overall *patterns* of behavior. And this information is often just what we are trying to figure out clinically, so it's very helpful.

Now contrast this to the bunny rabbit dream. What's similar? In both cases the dreamer is fleeing from a harmless animal. So does that mean the raccoon dreamer also struggles with creativity and play? Before we answer that question prematurely we need to be precise and look at the whole context and ask ourselves: yes those similarities hold, but what is different? In this case quite a bit. Stick close to the imagery to see what: rabbits and raccoons are not the same animals, and you always want to ask yourself, why a *raccoon* rather than, say, a rabbit, or a squirrel, or a rhinoceros, or Godzilla for that matter? Rabbits are suggestive of playful bouncing around, whereas raccoons are often culturally stereotyped as being more mischievous and clever. Their bandit-like faces get easily linked to shenanigans and tom-foolery. Also, the rabbit was actively chasing after the dreamer, wanting to engage with her, whereas in this case the raccoons are basically minding their own business. Whatever they're up to, the raccoons seem not to be all that worried about the dreamer – which suggests disconnection or even dissociation. Also the rabbit dreamer hid under a bed, whereas this dreamer *flew away into a tree.* One is physically possible and the other isn't, suggesting the raccoon dreamer is a little less realistic and perhaps more fantasy-prone, for better or worse.

Each of these details gives the overall picture a slightly different nuance, and they are important if we are to assume the dreams are not simply random noise – which they aren't. And since so often working through the imagery and taking it seriously (but not literally) yields clinical interpretations that often show predictive validity, it's a good indication that these methods are sound ones to use in therapy. I invite other clinicians to gather more data so as to fine tune these inductions about dreams. In any case, the raccoon dreamer had no problem at all with creativity and play. Instead, this dreamer too often flew into fantasy and imagination at the expense of the dreamer's own instinctive, everyday, and even slightly "mischievous" activities – i.e., physical, body presence in the here and now.

Setting

Settings are often visual depictions of overall emotional moods. A bright, sunny hillside filled with wildflowers is one thing, a graveyard full of bloody screaming zombies being eaten by roaches is another thing. Weather gets incorporated here: quick, easy, and resonant associations are almost always made between dark, overcast skies for gloomy moods, for example. And note how even our language contains these metaphors: stormy moods, "bright" moods, a "tempestuous" relationship, a "downcast" feeling, a "sparkling" or "sunny" disposition, etc., etc. Using our Number One Dream Hack: "life is progressing *as if* you are stuck by a gloomy, dying riverside with only aging people where it used to be full of life and playful vigor." That tells us most of what we need to know concerning the setting here, doesn't it?

Particularly when we compare the scene in the dream with the dreamer's reported memory of the same place, now we can see that the dream is depicting the way she *feels* in images. She feels that life has slipped away, that her childhood has been drained of life. The young people have become old. The fresh, flowing water has become stale and dirty. The previously flowering trees have become barren and dark. The bright and sunny sky has become bleak and oppressive.

Things to look out for: look at the details. They're there for a reason. In this case, why a river? To show wasting away, dessication, and death as vivid images depicting depressed feelings of lifelessness, we really didn't need the river. Is there something gained by the addition of the river in this dream, as opposed to simply a verdant field or maybe a pond or lake? Stick to the imagery: a river is a large, flowing, freshwater source. Note that cross-culturally rivers are often identified with goddesses, probably because of the connection between water and living things, and the way in which continually flowing water supports a continual flourishing of new life, new generations, etc. Rivers are sources of water for many species of animal including humans, and so a very primordial connection links rivers and "life source" ideas. These are themes that the IS often uses water images to symbolize. In many mythologies, river sources are used to represent sources of life – for example, in myths that speak of "wells of knowledge/fate/life from which all other rivers flow". Flowing rivers therefore equal flowing life "energy", or overall vigor or joy in living.

This means that the river is actually an important element to this scene because it intensifies the overall meaning of decay and death. Not only has the land become barren, but the source of life itself has become sluggish and corrupted, a breeding ground for disease and decay rather than joy. During the course of therapy, the river dreamer's dreams transformed, and we will discuss these more as we continue.

Scope

The scope of this dream appears to be rather narrow, focused primarily on the feeling of the scene itself and how it depicts overall moods that have changed across time. There is a sense that there's nothing else in the world except this place by the river, which is stifling in itself. And the fact that this dream is recurrent casts a long shadow on the entire meaning of the dream – as it always does. Recurrence suggests lack of progression, lack of change, lack of integration, as if the IS were struggling to make sense of things. The scope, being so limited, adds another piece of the puzzle to the picture the IS is painting: there is no life any more, there's only this dying river, which courses through dying trees, populated by dying people.

Things to look out for: what's missing? Where is the dreamer's family? That nothing else happens in the dream other than brooding about being in such a forlorn place suggests very limited scope, which suggests severe lack of integration. And lack of integration is lack of meaning and purpose, in the same way that the words of a sentence might be scattered by the winds and make little sense in isolation. Only when they are put into the proper order do they cohere into a whole statement of meaning. Meaning comes from the whole context.

Also, why does the dreamer linger here? Always be on the lookout for what the dreamer *might have done but doesn't do.* Asking yourself this question helps to recognize the way in which the dreamer might be locked into a habit that is keeping her in an unhealthy state. She will have the same habits in waking life. Couldn't she just walk away to greener pastures somewhere else? Notably, there is nothing in this dream that suggests she is required to stay where she is. Yet it does not occur to her to just leave this barren place and (perhaps taking one of the elderly people to help them) take a stroll over the hill where sunny fields and sparkling fountains burst forth.

Here is another example, from Mr. C, aged 45:

> *I'm in a prison cell, like the one depicted in the Count of Monte Cristo. Not much is going on. I'm just trying to figure out what I'm going to do with myself, since I have been sentenced to life in prison. After spending what seems like years in this prison, I notice something: the ceiling is missing. With some effort I climb out of it and look around. The entire prison is like this – hundreds of stone cells, with prisoners unaware that all they have to do is climb up and they can simply walk away and be free.*

If you guessed that this patient was making a lot of connections and insights in therapy you would be correct. Why? Because of the context – connecting it to waking life: this is the sort of dream one has when one is "expanding their horizons" and seeing how the only person keeping him in this prison is himself! In terms of resonance, this is what I mean by dramatic irony: the "everything is different from what you thought you knew" element of a story.

But getting back to the scope, here the scope is telling most of this story; the dramatic change in scope tells the tale. It begins with extremely limited scope and ends with a great vista across the countryside, with the prison merely one landscape feature among many. Thus, we need to have an eye here for the big picture ... the story *is* the dramatic increase in scope. Also, don't forget the reference to the famous *Count of Monte Cristo.* There is an important reason why this detail came to mind, and it isn't random. Can you guess what it is?

To answer this question, ask yourself, why did the prison remind him of *that* particular prison? Obviously it's because the IS means to give this prison the particular connotation associated with that story. Why would that be? Because it actually fits the story and adds a little more meaning – what happened to the hero in that story when he escaped his prison? He found the treasure and had all sorts of adventures. Thus there's a hint of that to be found here, too, that the prison is far from the end, though notably it's conspicuous in its absence, so it's only a *hint*. It's not an overtly expressed part of this story, but it's still there.

Storytelling

By this point the storytelling aspect of this dream should be fairly obvious. Though it's a little hokey, sometimes you can squeeze out this aspect of the dream by adding "once upon a time" to the beginning of the dream, then just going through the rest of it as dreamed. In this case: once upon a time I was playing in a verdant riverside with children playing, but now it's a barren riverside with dying people. This little maneuver brings home the importance of storytelling not to a dry recounting of events, but its importance in ascribing meaning to the current situation. If I escape a prison, it makes a big difference how I wound up there in the first place! If I was falsely imprisoned, like Dantes from the story, then escaping is a great victory (though not without its dangers). If I was put there for murder, then it's a tragedy. So the meaning of the current situation can change dramatically if we know how we got to where we are because meaning is, again, not found in the parts, but in the whole. And that means the whole not only in space, but in time.

What to look for: something called a "When-Then" moment. Since the IS tells stories in images, sometimes the meaning is contained in a "when this happens, then that happens" sequence. This method of deducing storytelling-type meaning can be attributed to Freud (1900: 349, 371) initially, which was elaborated by Jung later (McGuire 1984: 21). The riverside dream doesn't have this aspect, so let's look at a different dream to illustrate what I mean, reported by a military veteran:

> *I walk from a barren house and into a garden. Suddenly a man in a mask appears. I know this guy has killed children before and so really needs to die. I draw a knife and he draws his and we fight. We cut each other several times and are both bloody until I finally grab him and drag him into a pool where I hold him under water trying to drown him. He won't die. So I stab him in the chest, right where his lungs are. Bubbles come out but he still won't die. I stab him again on the other side. Still alive. Finally I stab him in the heart and he goes limp. Then the mask comes off and I realize he's me, but as a boy of about 10 or 11 years old. I'm in shock and quickly pull him to the pool side and try to revive him. Then I wake up in a sweat.*

This dream, if you will notice, is extremely resonant. It has the one, two, three rhythm of a folktale, and the very dramatic and shocking twist at the end. It has vivid, uncomplicated, and sharply drawn images and a clear, simple plot with a very ironic reversal. It's very emotional. I could probably write an entire book about this one dream, in fact, because there is so much in it, and even more on follow up questions. For example, when I asked the dreamer what he thought about the "garden", he said it reminded him of the Garden of Gethsemane, where Jesus was tempted by Satan right before he was crucified. That is not a random, insignificant association.

But let's look at the "when-then" of this dream. There are several, so let's list them:

1   When the dreamer enters the garden, the knife fighting starts.
2   When the dreamer drags the masked man into the pool, the ritual 1-2-3 killing begins.
3   Most of all, only when the dreamer actually kills the man does he realize he has killed himself as a child, meaning the "child killer" is, in fact, himself.

Let's look at each of these in turn. In the first when-then, the IS seems to be telling us a story about how only when entering this "garden of Gethsemane" does blood start flowing. The association of the dreamer to the sacrifice of Christ is a curious one that I think is relevant to all three of these when-thens. Why? Because the tale of Christ's death is a very resonant one (any story labeled "the greatest story ever told" is likely to be a resonant one) and the motif of death-and-resurrection can be found in widespread areas around the world in various iterations. Thus, even though this dreamer described himself as an agnostic, the very resonance of the story retains its power anyway (if the dreamer had described himself as Christian, this imagery would perhaps be even more powerful). In any case, the garden is where Jesus was tempted by evil before he was sacrificed to erase the sins of humankind. The conflict in the dream therefore seems to be a moral one by association already, between the dreamer's darker impulses and his desire to eliminate that darkness and be the "hero".

The blood spilling here, then, means that a lot of emotion and affect are "spilling out" as a result of this conflict, as blood is always linked to "life force", "life energy", "lust for life", and intense emotion (I explore this universal symbolism in Goodwyn 2011). Continuing the theme of a ritualistic sort of sacrifice finds us in the second when-then. Now the terrorist is to be "baptized" in the pool. Remember the discussion of the ways in which the IS uses water to illustrate various emotional states and changes of states? Here we have a clear pool. It's not a river or a pond, however, it's a man-made pool (stick to the images!) and therefore part of a social, organized framework rather than a wild, natural setting. Baptism is a part of countless religions worldwide, and the symbolism is very similar across the board, which suggests high levels of resonance: washing away of the old self to reveal the new self in a controlled – not wild – setting. It is a method for effecting a transformation of the participant into a new state (I discuss this element of ritual symbolism at length in *Healing Symbols in Psychotherapy*, Goodwyn 2016).

But here is the big, final when-then: once the ritualistic 1-2-3 stabbing kills the masked man, and only then, does the dreamer realize he has been fighting against a child-self that was at least *thought to be* evil. The IS is making a very clear point, however, that this person wasn't really evil. It seems to be saying *what you thought was evil turned out to be something innocent, and it was you as a child.* Powerful stuff. And the revelation happens right at the moment of death. In this case: when I kill the child-murderer, then he is revealed to be myself as a boy. When-thens are the IS's way of showing correlation and/or causation in a narrative sense. In this case, the revelation that the dreamer's enemy is himself as a boy, is *caused* by the bloody, almost ritualistic killing of that very character. It's a profound revelation to say the least.

Now let's add our "once upon a time" to get a better feel for what's going on here, told in first person, past tense (narrative style, in other words) with associations made by follow up questions added:

> *Once upon a time, I fought against a masked man who I thought was a child-killer. We cut each other in a garden that reminded me of the place Jesus was tempted by evil before he died, and also the place where he was betrayed by Judas. I dragged the man into a clear pool and stabbed him three times – first right, then left, then center, before he died in the water. I thought I had done a good thing. But then, to my horror, his mask came off, and I realized I had killed myself as a child. I tried to revive him but I failed.*

As I mentioned earlier, there's so much going on here it would take many pages to sort through it all. We haven't even gotten to the theme of "betrayal" but the garden association with Judas means that theme is in there, too. But for now we're just looking at the overall storytelling quality and what that brings to the interpretation effort. The dream here is indicative of a lot of intense and emotional reflection, and some internal revelations that are not exactly pleasant. Using the Number One Dream Hack, it's saying "my life is going on as if all this time I thought I was fighting something evil when it turned out to be my childhood I was fighting – and the fact that I killed my own childhood." That gives us the main gist of the meaning, but the details are vivid and numerous and lend themselves to further meditation.

One wonders if the masked man, even though linked to the dreamer, on some level may have *needed* to die. This question is suggested by the association with Christ, whose painful sacrifice is nonetheless *required* by the overall mythic narrative. Furthermore the association with the dreamer's own childhood is an obvious theme here, too, that demands more clinical exploration. What is it about this dreamer's childhood that "needs to die"? What happened to him that may have created this "child-killer" that is so opposed to the ego?

Finally note the incredible irony: the dreamer attacks the masked man because he is a "child killer", but in killing the child killer, he *becomes* a child killer! Note the multiple layers of irony used by the IS – he is not a child killer as in a killer of children, he is a killer who is a child. The fact that the dreamer furthermore kills *himself as a child* implicates him even more into such a vicious cycle; it's as if the IS is telling him the problem was the fighting itself. It's incredibly brilliant how it all works out in one extremely potent when-then: by hating the child killer, you kill the child killer who is a child, thereby becoming the very thing you hate ... which is you, when you were a child. Tragic, ironic, and devastating. And yet ... also somehow necessary, and furthermore it is done in a ritualistic manner, along the lines of a purification and baptism.

Rest assured, we have yet to exhaust the symbolism of this highly resonant dream.

Conflict

The child killer dream is a great example of a dream with a furious amount of conflict in it. Getting back to the riverside dream, we can see that the level of conflict is much less severe. Conflict between characters, as we saw, usually relates to various personalities, sub-personalities, selves, possible selves, personified ideas, etc., that have conflicting goals. Their conflicting goals will be spelled out in an image-told story involving those characters doing various things, with the dreamer playing the part of the ego. The dreamer and the talking bunny rabbit, for example, have a conflict, though it is not violent. It's a chase with one simply avoiding the other.

But recognizing the conflict as between the dreamer and the themes and ideas represented by the rabbit (childlike creativity and playfulness), we understand that the dreamer's behavior is indicative of her general behavioral patterns – in that case, of fear and avoidance. In the child killer dream, we had the dreamer acting out of a sense of righteous anger, though in that case it had a wild twist, primarily because the antagonist was masked, though when he first appeared he did have a knife. Tellingly, however, the dreamer made the first aggressive move.

Generally, then, internal conflict between the dreamer and various ideas, motivations, personality fragments, etc., will be depicted as various sorts of confrontations or pursuits. Lots of conflict indicates a great deal of internal turmoil. In the riverside dream, there is not much conflict so much as there is dissociation and aloneness. The elderly people are shuffling along seemingly oblivious to the dreamer and she them.

Things to look out for: ask yourself *why* is the dreamer behaving the way she or he is behaving in response to the antagonist/s? Put another way, why is the dreamer doing what she is doing rather than something else? Why, when the bunny rabbit is chasing her, does the dreamer in that case not simply stop, turn around, and say "hey, look, what do you want?" or "want to play a game?" – something totally unlike what the dreamer is doing. Why, in the child killer dream, does the dreamer immediately attack the masked "child killer"? Wouldn't he have learned a lot by even talking to him first? The character was masked – which means the dreamer attacked him without really knowing who he was. What would have been the result if the mask had come off before all the carnage? The dreamer in this case, however, could think only of attack.

When we discuss lucid dreaming – the phenomenon of dreaming while the dreamer is aware that she or he is dreaming – we will encounter some vivid examples that will tell us exactly what *does* happen when the dreamer stops and does something totally different. The IS responds dramatically – more on that later. For now, this characteristic cues us to look for the various ways in which conflicts are being carried out in a given dream, or, alternatively, the fact that conflict is low, which is also informative.

As it turns out, the riverside dream had a sequel, somewhat later in therapy:

> *I'm by that old dingy riverside again, only this time I'm in a dilapidated old shack, and the landlord is a jerk and charging me outrageous rent to live there. I'm extremely annoyed by this guy when he shows up because he won't let me get out of the lease. So I go outside and start yelling and screaming at him. I even slap him.*

There are lots of interesting variations that the IS has come up with to depict the latest "chapter" of its continual storytelling efforts. Now instead of just visiting the riverside and reminiscing, the dreamer *lives* there. This reflects that the depressed, gloomy state the riverside represents is one that the dreamer is trapped in. Note that despite the negative connotation here, it does at least represent some level of acceptance of one's current fate, whereas in the first dream there seemed to be very little acceptance of the predicament – the dreamer only recoils in horror at what she sees.

But there is a new player on the field, now: the landlord. What's his story? Well, going through our method for figuring out characters, we can guess now at why the dreamer didn't simply walk away the first time she came to the dingy riverside. That impulse or resistance to leave it is now being personified as the landlord. In other words, there's an element of her psyche that is unyielding and tyrannical, and it's holding the dreamer in this depressed place. Not only that, it is "costing her" dearly. In other words, she is being drained of her resources and her reserves – depicted in this dream as cash. Money, it turns out, works nicely as a metaphor for our overall mental energy and reserve, our ability to change things (since "money is power"), and our ability to get what we need in life (since most of us don't grow or hunt our own food). Jung hypothesized that money is often a symbol for life-energy, value or "libido" (Jung and Meyer-Grass 2008: 76). A person who grew up in a foraging society without currency would obviously not see the IS using money to represent these things. Ancient pastoral societies would often use cattle or other livestock to represent "wealth". In modern industrialized nations, we see money used in this manner as a symbol.

In any case, there's now more conflict. But even though it degenerates into a shouting and slapping match, note that it seems to be something of an improvement only insofar as there is at least some kind of interaction in the dream rather than just paralyzed horror. And this dream gives us a clue as to what might be hindering her progress – this "landlord" character, some part of her life experience which no doubt seems to be playing a part in her resistance to change and healing. An interesting exercise here would have been to ask her what this dream looked like from the landlord's point of view. We will get into this type of exercise more in later sections, but for now realize that whatever the patient did with this question would likely reflect some of the fears, etc. that kept her in this depressed state, and as such would be grist for the therapeutic mill.

Intensity

Intensity and conflict are not necessarily the same. Intensity, as I define it here, is just the overall level of "storminess" in a dream. It simply calls attention to the overall level of chaos, activity, turmoil, or what have you that a dream possesses as a whole. High intensity dreams are noisy, turbulent, full of violence and destruction, swarms of animals/insects, chaos, etc. They reflect the overall turbulence of the patient's psyche as a whole, with the ego trying its best to ride the storm out as much as possible.

This characteristic of dreams reflects a general level of emotional, creative and destructive energy that the patient lives with. I often contrast this quality with overall "ego strength". What is ego strength? It is a general term for the overall resilience of a person's ego in the face of intense emotion. A person with high ego strength will, upon learning about something shocking or dramatic, be able to stay focused and clear-thinking despite the powerful emotions that may arise. Ego strength can naturally vary but for the most part stays within a pretty well defined range. It is an irreducible combination of genetic, internal, and developmental variables. Some people simply appear to have a high level of it naturally, while others learn to increase their ego strength with various types of therapy or training, such as military, martial arts, or even competitive sports training, which is designed to "toughen" people up. Other, less intense ways of improving ego strength include mindfulness, meditation, physical exercise, healthy habits, some kinds of religious practice among other things. And of course, psychotherapy.

Those with high ego strength can withstand a great deal of stress and still function, while those with low levels of it break down and suffer functional impairments more quickly, getting overwhelmed, retreating, and trying other more primitive methods of coping such as denial, drug abuse, being inundated with symptoms, compulsions, retreating into fantasy, intense emotional outbursts, etc. Improving ego strength/resilience is one of the goals of essentially all forms of therapy. The wrinkle I am adding here is that we know the ego is only part of the picture. The rest of the psyche, including the IS, is what the ego emerged from and continues to be imbedded in, and some people simply live in a more turbulent psychological world than others. In metaphorical terms, some people may sail on a boat of toothpicks (low ego strength) but not suffer because they're floating on a serene and placid sea (low intensity), while others sail in ironclad gunboats (high ego strength) that are hammered daily by tropical storms and choppy waves (high intensity).

Intensity, then, is the overall "background turbulence" that a person lives in, and it reflects in dream content. Those who are about to flip into a manic state, for example, experience dreams that show much greater incidence of violent, bloody chaos than those who are not (Beauchemin and Hays 1995).

Things to look out for: any discrepancies between what your patient is reporting and the dream content. People can oftentimes be out of touch with their own emotions, and their level of awareness of the underlying emotional turbulence/intensity is minimal. In such cases, however, you will always be able to identify how the emotions are "leaking out the seams", so to speak. When a patient has a lot of emotional intensity, the dream content will – to the discerning clinician – reveal the nature of the emotion even when the patient may have little awareness of it, or (more commonly) have a hard time describing the emotions to you. In all cases, ask yourself, "why *this* sort of imagery instead of the many other things that it could have been?" to gain insight into the meaning of the images. Let's look at a few examples to provide some illustration, such as the following dream reported by a 39-year-old, who reported a lot of chronic daytime anxiety. This patient had a relatively high level of ego strength, in that he was able to function without falling apart in the face of what was otherwise a constant state of worry and anxiety:

> I have this recurrent dream of going outside and seeing a tornado ripping across the fields and coming for my house. I go in and frantically try to find someplace safe. Then the wind starts to destroy things and smash the windows.

Notice how the overall intensity of the dream reflects the dreamer's constant state of worry. It's *as if* he were always frantically running around trying to prevent disaster, and a tornado is always in the background causing chaos and destruction. We will see very high intensity dreams in the chapter on traumatic dreams.

And this is because intensity is affected by a number of variables. There seems to be a constitutional component to it, in that some people appear to have a lower level of intensity than others (all things being equal), but many other things can worsen it, including trauma, lack of social support, family conflicts, and physical illness. Likewise it can be alleviated by healthy habits, strong social support, and psychotropic medications – in fact one way to conceptualize the combination of medications and therapy is to think of the medications as altering a patient's baseline intensity level as we work on ego strength with therapy. In practice I don't think it is this simple, but framing it this way can sometimes help to conceptualize complicated cases and provide a clue as to which way to go when you are at an impasse clinically. The reason I don't think it's quite this simple is that high levels of intensity fractionate the psyche in general, which will include the ego – sometimes a severe enough storm can crack the seams of even an ironclad boat. Conversely high ego strength – particularly of someone who has a high degree of integration (the last characteristic we will discuss in this chapter) – can help calm the storm of intensity. Ego and non-ego can communicate, after all, and this is one of the most important goals of therapy in general: fostering a deep and emotionally meaningful level of awareness of one's fluctuating emotional intensity.

The constitutional component can be easily seen in the difference between patients with more severe mental illnesses such as schizophrenia and bipolar disorder, and patients with comparatively less severe illnesses such as depression. There is plenty of overlap here, of course, in that severe depression can come with psychotic symptoms, which are indicative of extremely high intensity and fractionation of the psyche. But in general, the neurodevelopmental abnormalities that characterize bipolar disorder, schizoaffective disorder and schizophrenia appear to correlate with greater levels of intensity and reactivity, both of which also associate with fractionation of the psyche and an assault on ego strength.

Let's look at some more examples to help sort through this. People who experience trauma will nearly always have an increase in dream intensity. Mr. D, for instance, is a patient with bipolar disorder and chronic posttraumatic stress disorder stemming from years of severe and disturbing sexual abuse from an alcoholic parent who would force him to have sex with other children while the parent watched. There was naturally a tremendous amount of shame and anxiety surrounding these events. Clinically he frequently displayed both a chronically high level of intensity combined with a fragile level of ego strength. These types of patients are obviously among the most difficult to keep functional, since this is really the worst combination. By the time he came into my care he had already been placed on disability for his debilitating symptoms. And yet, over the years he had been able to stabilize with supportive therapy and a combination of medications.

While in my care, however, Mr. D. decompensated after getting a letter indicating his disability status was "under review" and he might lose it. This even coincided with a dramatic increase in dream intensity, and he began having recurrent dreams of being bullied, attacked, beaten, and there was a recurrence of sexual abuse dreams also. His symptoms worsened dramatically as well, with worsening panic attacks, crying spells, and overall loss of functionality. None of this presented as manipulative (unfortunately we have to watch for that when dealing with potential secondary financial gain). The underlying theme was clear: his sense of security was threatened, and his emotions responded in the extreme, and with little in the way of ego strength, he unraveled rather quickly. In this case, the primary emotion behind the increased intensity appeared to be fear.

In another case, however, it was not fear but anger. Ms. E also had a long history of physical and sexual abuse that presented in a different way. In her case, her presenting complaint was only trichotillomania. Otherwise she reported feeling "fine", but the hair pulling worried her and she didn't like that she couldn't stop doing it. In trichotillomania and other forms of self-harm behavior such as cutting, I usually suspect high levels of unconscious rage in combination with a great deal of resistance to feeling angry and/or shame. This is because such behavior gives a primitive sort of outlet to the anger that otherwise has none, and it also temporarily satisfies the feeling of self-loathing that accompanies shame. I wait for clinical data to confirm my suspicion before making any interpretations, of course, but often we can identify a worsening of this behavior being associated with some sort of insult or traumatic event which aroused anger and/or shame that then is followed by the self-harm behavior. In this case, her dreams told the rest of the story, once she felt brave enough to tell them to me:

> *I keep having dreams that are extremely violent. I am taking people and strapping them to chairs and torturing them with a scalpel. I enjoy watching them bleed. I'm very sadistic in these dreams and I don't know why. In the dream the people scream in pain and I like it. These people in the dreams are always people that don't know me and I don't know them.*

In Ms. E's case, the primary emotion displayed by this dream was rage. The shame only came afterwards, when she woke up and realized how violent she had been in her dream. Intense rage is a very natural part of our fight/flight/freeze innate behavioral defenses and is very commonly aroused to a high level in cases of trauma, which we will discuss in more detail in the next chapter. For our purposes here, however, we can note the high intensity of the rage combined with not much awareness of it. But the Dream Hack tells us she is living *as if* she were carrying out all this sadistic and wrathful torment on "others" – but these others were other selves. Given this knowledge, therapy involved developing a much greater awareness of just how angry her many traumas made her, and providing her with a more integrated way of understanding and expressing that anger that did not involve shame or self-harm. It was a long and slow process.

Getting back to our initial riverside dream, note the overall low intensity of this dream. There isn't a lot of chaos or activity. It is rather an enervated atmosphere. There's very little "life energy" overall. The overall dominant emotion behind this imagery, then, is not rage or fear, both of which impress upon the ego the need for action (whether flight or fight), but rather *depression*, which reflects feelings of hopelessness and despair. The perception of help-lessness and disconnection is prominent here, with no viable options in sight. What do we do with that clinically? First identify it and help the patient see that this is the dominant feeling behind the context in which this dream occurred. Look for events that triggered the response. Help them differentiate what is and is not within their ability to change about their situation. Some-times the despair and defeatism is so paralyzing we miss opportunities that might actually change our situation. We can use the dream imagery in this case to ask "isn't it interesting that you stay by that riverside even though there's nothing to suggest you're trapped there. Why do you think that is?" A question like this can sometimes be a bit jarring, but in a good way, since it highlights how we often have blinders to our own unhealthy habits. But we can ask this because we know the dreamer's behavior in dreamland echoes their wakeful behavior.

The second riverside dream had higher levels of intensity – but isn't that an improvement? In such a lifeless place, fighting to survive is far preferable to wasting away in despair! Therefore we can see that higher intensity is not necessarily a bad thing. In fact, rare is the quality that is uniquely "good" or "bad" – it's all context dependent. Conflict, after all, is part of life, and to a certain degree it is integral and necessary for life to exist at all. So the above extremely high intensity dreams contrast nicely with the initial riverside dream, which actually has too *little* intensity. Conflict will always be present to some degree. As the saying goes, only the dead have seen the end of war. To live is to experience conflict, both on the "inside" and the "outside". Had there been any less conflict in the initial riverside dream, there would be only death, which is not what we would like for our patient.

Integration

The further progressions of the riverside dream provide good illustrations for our final dream characteristic: integration. In the first riverside dream there seemed to be very little integration. In that dream the dreamer was dis-connected from the other characters in the dream – they are merely "old people" by the shore, dried up and useless apparently. Furthermore she was disconnected from the lively part of her past on this same shore. They seemed to exist in different worlds. That said, however, integration cannot easily be judged by examining a single dream. You have to look across several dreams to assess how much integration is occurring, such as the landlord dream, and two more episodes we will explore in this section.

Integration, then, is a process defined across several dreams and across a significant period of time. It is of course the opposite process to something we have already discussed, which would be *disintegration* or fragmentation, such as in the dream about the abuse survivor and the financial crisis. Integration can be assessed via all the other characteristics by how much they have or have not changed with subsequent dreams.

Things to look out for: ask yourself, what *isn't* in this dream that could or should be? In both the initial and the landlord dreams, where, for example, is this patient's family and friends? The only things resembling either are the memories of childhood friends in the first dream, and the "landlord" (i.e., an overly rigid and taxing alter-ego or personified set of ideals the dreamer is struggling with) in the landlord episode. But actual friends and family are notable by their absence, and there is a high degree of isolation here. On the other hand, it could represent integration if previous dreams were even more fractionated, for example if the memory of childhood had been absent, or if that's *all* it was – an isolated memory of childhood relived over and over. Either one would have a significantly different overall interpretation.

Let's look at the next episode of this ongoing and continually refining story. Several months of therapy after the landlord episode, she dreamed:

> *I'm by that old dirty riverside again, only this time I'm in a house and I'm talking to a friend (not someone I know in waking life), who is about my age. It's still dingy and gloomy outside, but we're in the house and there's screens to the outside. Then talking monkeys come up to the windows. Weird! At first it was puzzling, but then I decide to let them in and we start having a conversation, about what I don't remember.*

This is a significant change from the previous dream. First, it isn't nearly as isolated as just herself and the old people or herself and the obnoxious landlord. Now she is talking to "a friend", which is one way to represent an inner dialogue with a slightly differing point of view – it's a picture of the dreamer working through similar but not identical ideas and "hashing it out" between them. It's a way to depict "self talk", since this isn't anyone known specifically but she is roughly the same age as the dreamer, which makes it likely to be a close alter ego, rather than a heavily conflicting alter ego. But what about the talking monkeys? That's certainly a minimally unusual element – note how often talking animals show up in folktales and myths. It's a resonant element and worth looking at more closely.

Let's first look at the choice of animal. It's not a rabbit, raccoon, or an alligator (or a unicorn or King Kong, etc.). The IS used a monkey for this dream and no other animal. Why? Let's consider that the monkey is an animal that shares many characteristics with humans ... it's "almost" human. So if we go with the idea that dream animals represent instinctive, animal-*like* selves, then what is most notable about this dream is that she is *talking* to them, rather than fighting with them, running from them, etc. Many times the ego is in various states of conflict with primordial emotion. Not here, though, where the emotions are "almost" human – meaning similar to the ego in rational capacity and sophistication.

In any case there's not a lot of conflict here – less than in the landlord dream, and the conflict that is there is of a more balanced variety than in the initial dream. These monkeys aren't evil flying monkeys, they're friendly talking monkeys. But again, what else can we say of the IS's choice to pick monkeys rather than some other kind of animal? Monkeys are often associated with playfulness and silly antics (as in the cliché "monkeying around"), and so are likely representing that sort of feeling, which is another contrast to the previous dream, which had an air of such solemnity and even lugubriousness. This provides us with an indirect link to the memory of the playful past riverside, only now it is occurring in the dream-present. That's more integrated with respect to time: it's not just an isolated period of time locked in the past forever.

In all there is a lot more integration in this dream than in the previous dream. There is all sorts of conversation. There's also a house, which suggests shelter and home – perhaps this reflects a certain level of acceptance of the riverside, especially considering the landlord conflict seems to be absent from this dream. Believe me, if that was still a major issue, the landlord would still be here causing problems. He is notable in his absence, which I think reflects a deeper level of self-acceptance than even the previous dream. The dreamer is getting a little more comfortable here; Jung once argued that in order to beat depression, you first have to accept it. Perhaps this dream therefore depicts progress toward that end.

Thus, as we assess a dream for its level of integration, we want to look for less isolation, more connection (both within and without, since they're likely of the same origin), less conflict, and more reference to the here and now rather than only the past or the future. Perhaps only Zen masters or other expert mystics achieve the most theoretically integrated state in which you are one with the universe, eternally present, accepting of both light and dark and possessing total inner peace. But any progress toward that ideal represents greater integration. And keep in mind that the rest of us aren't Zen masters and so dreams reflecting that level of total tranquility might actually be a bad sign, since it might be indicative of depression and despair or hopelessness rather than Nirvana.

Near the end of therapy, this dream had one more iteration:

> *I'm by that riverside again, only this time it is flooding. There are many dead bodies everywhere and the water is pouring in furiously.*

If your first impression is that big changes are happening, you would be correct. First of all is the theme of flooding. Ask yourself – how is this different from the previous dreams of the riverside? Obviously the big difference is in the behavior of the water. It's no longer stale and muddy. It's flowing – in fact, it is *over*flowing. Flooding, actually. And with dead bodies. Note that death in dreams typically signifies change rather than a final, permanent obliteration. Perhaps this is because the IS is like any natural process, in continual cycles of death and rebirth.

This dream in particular reminded me of the "world flood" myths that are found all over the globe (Bierlein 1994), that we discussed earlier. In this case we appear to have a fragment of the super-resonant myth. These myths follow the pattern: world becomes populated with people who either ignore or insult the gods, whereupon the gods or God floods the world and wipes out the old, stale, sinful, or otherwise unacceptable population, *except for a select few.* These select few survive through various methods to repopulate the world with acceptable people. Viewing this as a pictorial representation of an abstract process, we have essentially a purification and renewal, which requires clearing out the old life that had become unacceptable, to open up the way for new, fresh and acceptable life to grow.

That's what seems to be happening in this dream. The other fragmented ways of being and old attitudes, personified as characters, have apparently outlived their usefulness and need to be cleared away. Thus the flood. Recall also the highly resonant symbolism linking rivers and sources of life and mother goddesses … a flooding river suggests a surge of flowing new life and an increase in intensity that is more directly opposite the original dream.

So then, what does all this mean for our patient? It suggests that where for a long time she was living *as if* she were in a lifeless, desolate, and decaying place, now suddenly there is an upsurge of life coming from the river goddess herself that is a purging of old, decaying and withered life to make way for new life. Our dreamer is only seeing the first half of that process because she is right in it. But we know that in order to change, we have to break down the old ways of being to make way for new ways. But the breaking down can often feel like a death, flooding, burning, etc. In this case it accompanied a surge in overall intensity.

Thus, where she was previously in a very cut-off state, isolated and alone, surrounded by decay and death, we saw over time a gradual reconnection to the present, to other parts of the self in conflict, but then merely in dialogue, though at that point she was still in the dingy, depressing, and decaying riverside. Finally came a surging flood to wipe away all the old, stale, and unacceptable states of being to make way for fresh and new life. Like a purifying baptism, it cleansed away the corruption and contagion – depicted as dead bodies, but it was scary to the ego to experience this. It felt out of control. A later dream, however, shows that the feeling of being overwhelmed by this change appears to have shifted:

> *I'm taking a shower with three romantic partners I've had in the past. Not sure what's up with that, but I'm not going to complain!*

Here we see the theme of "washing" and "purifying" played out but in a very different context than before. The three partners in the shower with the dreamer were relationships that had ended on very conflicted terms. But these characters were of people that the dreamer had not had any interaction with in a long time, so we are safe in assuming these are more related to the inner relationship with who the dreamer was at the time of the relationship. Their behavior now, which is cozy to say the least, seems to indicate much greater integration than before. Integration with the past and with the idea of flowing water as well – now it is no longer a world-threatening flood with dying people, but a more pleasant shower and rejuvenation.

The common element throughout this whole series of dreams is the behavior of water: stale, stagnant and decaying, overflowing and threatening, or clean, moderated and rejuvenating. The associations made between such water imagery and ideas of purification, cleansing, as well as life-giving vigor and joy-in-living are extremely resonant. We know this because of the ubiquity of such associations that can be found not only in mythology but in rituals performed worldwide (more detail can be found in Goodwyn 2016), so it's fair to say these associations are readily available and likely to be present in our patient, especially considering how these dreams play out in conjunction with the dreamer's symptoms.

Jung observes that dreams are reactive to a person's conscious situation. When consciousness is "one sided", the dream will present the "opposite view" – however this does not mean dream contents will be the opposite of the dreamer's situation. It's more that the dream will show what the ego missed and so it will tend to be more complete. This, according to Jung will be the case particularly if the ego is "one sided", meaning plagued with various blinders. By the same token, if the ego is "near the middle", the dream will vary quite a bit, as if the psyche is content to mix things up a bit. Finally, if the ego is in an adequate and balanced place, dreams will confirm this by depicting harmonious imagery (Jung 1990: 74).

When Jung is speaking of "compensation", he is actually talking about what we term here "integration":

> We must see to it that the values of the conscious personality remain intact, for unconscious compensation is only effective when it co-operates with an integral consciousness. Assimilation is never a question of "this *or* that", but always of "this *and* that".
>
> (Jung 1990: 104)

This terminology of "compensation", however, has introduced unnecessary confusion into the dream literature, as researchers have often tried to find evidence of "compensation" by looking for dream content which represented the opposite of the conscious situation. But that's not what Jung meant by compensation. He meant integration.

Ultimately the theme we are focusing on here is the characteristic of integration, but hopefully by now it is clear that all the characteristics I have highlighted are working together at the same time in each dream. Viewing each of these will help you to make better sense of what the dreams are about and how they play into the dreamer's waking life. Patients will experience integration and fragmentation, fluctuating depending upon current situations and stressors. But overall there is a general tendency toward integration to combat the fragmenting tendencies of life experiences and conflicts, much like there is an immune system and innate healing system to bring the body back into equilibrium with itself and the environment in the face of various insults and experiential challenges. In the next chapter we will take a closer look at psychological trauma in particular and how it plays out in dream content.

Chapter 5

Traumatic dreams – fighting iron forests of dragons...

> Even when you think you are alone and can do what you please, if you deny your shadow there will be a reaction from the mind that always is, from the man a million years old within you ...
>
> (Jung speaking in McGuire 1984: 77)

As we progress I hope it has become evident that I am building an overall view and approach to dreaming with each chapter. The themes we have discussed so far, including especially resonance, integration, fragmentation, symbolism, and narrative are the main principles that help us understand dreams. In the current chapter we will look at a dream series involving trauma, in which we will get a further illustration of these principles and how to apply them.

The literature on trauma and nightmares is vast. I will highlight just a few pertinent points here. First, we should note that nightmares or trauma dreams are like any other dreams – they are responsive to our experiences (obviously) and as other dreams, they depict our current situation from the point of view of the IS. Things that trigger nightmares are (Hartmann 2001):

1   Physical illness, especially if febrile
2   Neurological diseases such as epilepsy
3   Mental illnesses, particularly early psychosis
4   Stressful life events that invoke feelings of helplessness
5   Medications such as beta blockers.

The fact that nightmare frequency correlates with general psychiatric illness, schizophrenia, suicidal ideation, dissociative disorders, PTSD, and overall emotional reactivity (reviewed in Nielson and Levin 2007) supports our general observations about nightmares here: that they reflect emotional instability and fractionation of the psyche. Note also that dreams in general appear to play a part in mood regulation (reviewed in Nielson and Levin 2007; see also Kramer 2007), as studies that track subjective dream reports with measured changes in specific brain regions typically correlated with emotional regulation show a strong relationship between dream activity as involved in affect regulation (Nielson and Levin 2007). Specifically, *contextualization* is recognized as a primary mechanism through which psychological healing (i.e. the extinction of dysfunctional levels of anxiety) occurs. Jung observed that the problem in repetitive traumatic dreams is that the event cannot be "psychified" (Jung and Meyer-Grass 2008: 21), meaning "made sense of" or put into a coherent life-narrative, an intuition which gains support from the above dream research in terms of contextualization.

Example: warrior and wounded

Our examples for this chapter come from a 39-year-old military veteran we will call Mr. E, who had been through multiple intense combat situations where his life had been endangered many times. He had personally survived multiple ambushes and bombings during his long career in the service, but had suffered with Posttraumatic Stress Disorder symptoms from the very beginning of his career, even as he had been awarded multiple medals for valor. Decorated as he was, however, he presented with severe symptoms of intermittent anxiety, depression, suicidal thoughts, flashbacks, nightmares, obsessions and compulsions, and angry outbursts, culminating in an extremely serious and well thought-out suicide plan that he was able to stop himself from carrying out before coming to seek help from psychiatry. There are a great many details in this case I will leave out and change both in order to maintain anonymity for Mr. E, but also to keep the focus on dream interpretation.

The man in wheelchair dream

Let's get into the first dream reported in therapy:

> I'm ordered by an unknown authority figure to beat up my best friend who is in a wheelchair. So I stuff him into a drainage pipe. But then I'm overcome with guilt and I pull him out of the pipe to help nurse his wounds. I feel horrible about all this.

Since this is the first dream reported, we should pay special attention to the imagery because, as we saw with the alchemy dream, the first dream often contains a great deal of the overall problems and conflicts the patient is experiencing and clinically it is often very helpful to sort through it in detail. Since it is a dream, of course, these issues are spelled out in images and stories rather than a verbal description. So what is going on here?

Since we don't have a lot of setting detail to go on (unlike, say, the riverside dreams), this dream seems to be mainly about the characters and their inter-actions. So let's focus our attention on them. There are three characters in this drama: the dreamer, the "unknown authority figure" and the "best friend" in a wheelchair. The dreamer is of course the ego, behaving as it normally does in waking life.

But who are these other two characters? Using the techniques we discussed in the last chapter, we can view these characters as largely symbolic in nature, since the authority figure is not anyone encountered in waking life at all, and the "best friend" is not actually anyone the dreamer knows from waking life either – this latter piece of information I learned from follow up questions.

Note that before we get into these characters, I want to emphasize how important follow up questions can be – there are questions about this dream, for example, that might have helped us, for example, where is all this happening? What do these characters look like? These might seem like minor details, but remember the IS does not create stories and characters randomly, but each element is put there for some reason or another, and usually it is emotionally relevant in terms of what it is attempting to express via images. The lesson to learn is that when you are listening to a dream report, ask a few follow up questions to get as much detail as your patient can recall. Now, one question that might be asked here is this: is the patient "really" recalling what was dreamed, or is she or he making it up on the spot? This question is of great importance to dream researchers, for example. But clinically for our purposes, since there is a great deal of continuity between undirected fantasy and dream content, it doesn't really matter very much. The same processes that produce the dream narrative will apply to spontaneous imagery such as reverie, active imagination, etc. – i.e., the IS. It's all grist for the mill.

So getting back to the dream – let's start with the unknown authority figure. Since we're pretty sure this character is more a symbol than a person from waking life, what might he be a symbol of? Well, obviously one possibility is that of any sort of authoritarian leanings the patient might have – we might equate this character with the superego of Freudian psychology. But we don't really have to be that specific. The image and character speaks for himself: since he is an "authority figure" then the interaction of the dreamer and this figure is a metaphor for how he relates to authority figures in general and ideas of "what I am supposed to do". This character, then, can be viewed as a personification of social pressures and rules (note that "personification" is not meant to be overly reductive – more on that in later chapters). So what else can we say about him? Stick to the image: this figure demands that the dreamer do something patently cruel: beat up a guy in a wheelchair. That doesn't speak well of our authority figure, and it puts him into conflict with the dreamer. Furthermore, he is quite vague and indistinct. This is, in itself, actually a clue to his nature as a symbolic character. It tells us that he, along with that which he represents, is a bit hazy and ill defined. So, authority, and social expectations therefore are being embodied by a vague and shadowy figure who is cruel and apparently very inflexible. But the fact that Mr. E is dreaming about this character means this set of ideas that is being personified is one which is possibly following him around and haunting him – i.e., that to a certain degree he has internalized this set of values, but it isn't very well defined, and also it's somewhat cruel and inflexible, and in conflict with the dreamer. Put another way, the conflict with the authority figure is a visual depiction of the dreamer's feeling of conflict between what he feels is right and what he feels he is "supposed" to do.

Next is the "best friend" character. Now, this character was not actually someone the dreamer knew from waking life, so obviously we are again dealing with a character who is more symbolic than one who is coming from memory. And like the "friend" dream we saw in the riverside dream sequence, the fact that the IS depicts this character as a "best friend" means this character is very "close" to the ego. In other words, he is an alter ego, and more so than the authority figure is, though he may be one too. Notably, however, the best friend is in a wheelchair. Why would the IS choose that image to depict this "other side" of the dreamer's personality? Always ask this sort of question: why a wheelchair as opposed to the hundreds of other ways that he might have been depicted?

Well, what connotations do wheelchairs stereotypically carry? Injury, weakness, vulnerability – especially in a man who is strong and fit, like Mr. E. It is notable, however, that despite this fitness, this patient suffered from chronic back pain – just to bring this a bit closer to home. Also note that in waking life this patient fluctuated a lot in terms of his anxiety, pain, and PTSD symptoms. It's *as if* he were two different people, in fact: one who was healthy, strong, and following orders, and another who was injured and vulnerable and being punished by the order-giver. Could the IS have come up with a clearer way to depict this behavior in imagery? It's difficult to see how. In any case, there are some details that we have yet to think about that are important. First is that despite the conflict between the ego and the authority figure, the dreamer at first *followed the orders.* This detail is what helps us to see that the authority figure is perhaps closer to the ego's self-identified value system than it seems at first glance. So in examining this dream, we find another principle that we can use to help us understand characters: the IS will use imagery that suggests "closeness" to symbolically depict similarity to the ego. In other words, possible selves or personifications of tightly held ideas and values will, if they are similar to that professed by the ego, be depicted as a "friend" or "relative" or something along those lines.

So how do we pull this all together to help us interpret the dream? What is the IS saying? Our method leads us to the following interpretation: Mr. E is a decorated war hero but is also suffering from severe anxiety, anger, and other posttraumatic symptoms. He seems to be caught in a dilemma concerning how he should behave toward someone who is weak and vulnerable. This person who is weak and vulnerable is, however, the patient himself, but he is disconnected from this part of himself – that he is the "best friend" is our clue here. Only if the wheelchair bound man was a *duplicate* of the dreamer, however, as we saw in the child-killer dream, would we be able to say that the dreamer had made or was making the connection between them as alter-egos. Outside of that, the alter ego quality of a character (if it is present in the form of "friend" or "relative" or "like a brother" nuances) is more or less dissociated from the ego. From the context – that is, from the manifestation of his symptoms as fluctuating from angry and irritable to anxious, isolating, depressed and suffering from back pain – we can see that he is at various times the healthy soldier or the wheelchair bound "best friend".

Moreover, he is very conflicted about all this. On one hand he seems to feel justified in beating up his vulnerable side. He feels he is "supposed" to be that way, to not accept weakness and to even punish it, even going so far as "stuffing him into a drainage pipe", which is, after all, where the garbage and waste goes. That's pretty harsh imagery when you think about it! But then, almost immediately, he feels compassion for the hurt man and pulls him out to try to help him.

This behavior suggests conflict, yes, but also a measure of hope and insight, too. Despite the conflict, the dreamer goes against "orders" and does what he feels is right – have compassion for what is essentially his own wounded side. This dream would have a different interpretation, for example, if he had just stuffed the man into the pipe and then gone about his business. That would be showing even less integration and even less insight than we have here. With this dream we have a greater hope for integration than some possible variants of it would suggest.

Prisoner and interpreter dream

Still fairly early in treatment, Mr. E reported this dream:

> I am trapped in an electrified cage with an Iraqi interpreter [Mr. E was deployed many times to Iraq and saw a lot of combat there]. The lead guy comes in with a pole with a knife on it. He tells me that if I take the knife and kill the interpreter he will let me go, and if not he will kill both of us. I told him to "go fuck yourself". So the lead guy cuts the interpreter's throat. I turn away crying because I can't watch, but I can hear the man gurgling and I can smell the blood.

This dream could have been part of a horror movie, it is so terrifying and gruesome. Generally we can see that intensity and conflict is extremely high. But let's look at it from the perspective of our nine principles (resonance, context, characters, setting, scope, storytelling, conflict, intensity, and integration). The resonance is fairly high, though there is no dramatic irony or revelations, no rhythmic elements, no minimal unusualness, and no interconnection of events. But it is extremely vivid, emotionally extreme, and the characters are simple.

The context of the dream was the early part of therapy, and so the focus was on the overall big picture, exploring his past, in particular his numerous combat experiences. So it makes sense that he would be dreaming of general patterns and overall themes. The previous dream showed one: that he has a rather intense conflict between what he perceives he is supposed to do (the authority figure) and what he feels within him is *right* to do (his emotional and compassionate reaction), and the difficulty of being caught in between these forces. Noting that one is depicted as external and one internal, already we are sensing in that first dream that the inner motivation may win the day since it is internalized. The context of this current dream was a general "sense making" process of his various war traumas – i.e., I was merely asking him questions about what he thought the impact of the traumas might be, and in these sessions he had a hard time articulating an answer to this question – this is of course very common in trauma cases.

Examining the characters in detail, we can see that the IS is giving us a clue as to why such difficulties may be. There are, again, only two characters here other than the dreamer. There is the "lead guy" and there is the interpreter. Let's look at the lead guy. It seems we have seen someone like him before in the previous dream. He is an authority figure telling him to harm someone who is innocent, only this time the IS has "upped the ante" and made this character a straightforward villain. That is an interesting change, isn't it? We're starting to see that "what you are supposed to do" is being portrayed by an outright evil actor now. This points out a very important aspect of dreams that I want to emphasize here: the characters and settings take the ego's perspective into account. This isn't a new principle; it's just highlighted very nicely here. We've seen this already. Remember in the child-killer dream, how the antagonist was masked and menacing *until* the ego killed him, and then he transformed. This reflects the ego's changing attitude toward this character and is a story of this process in vivid pictures.

When we get to lucid dreaming we will find out just how dramatically a character can change depending on the ego's perception of it. Studies involving teaching trauma survivors with recurrent nightmares how to lucid dream show that giving them the ability to confront the frequently pursuing monstrous and evil characters that chase them about in their nightmares transforms the menacing characters into benign and sometimes even humorous characters (Tholey 1988). But more on that later. Here it's just important to see how the "lead guy" being even more straightforwardly villainous may reflect a small change in the ego – one that is more suspicious of that "what you're supposed to do" feeling, one that questions it.

And this dream is the response to that – there are consequences intrapsychically for posing new questions and challenging feelings and thoughts. That is obviously the whole point of therapy – but you can see the results dramatically in dream content sometimes, and it is a powerful experience. The IS is telling us that this challenge from the ego is coinciding with an escalation in intensity. And this time instead of a guy in a wheelchair who is clearly a reflection of the dreamer himself, now we have another person who is being threatened and attacked – and notably it's by the lead guy himself and not the dreamer, though the lead guy (as before) initially tells the dreamer to kill the innocent man. It's just that this time the dreamer refuses. That is another very important contextual change across time. I hope it is clear how connecting similarly themed dreams together gives us a better view of what is happening, and that this is much more effective than viewing a single dream in isolation. This chapter in particular will hopefully show how that works.

Let's talk about the other character: the interpreter. What is he all about? Why on earth would the IS plop the dreamer into this horrible situation with an interpreter, rather than the hundreds of other characters that it could have? He's not a soldier, a gym manager, or a family member. Remember, this is a dream – he could have been put in there with Santa Claus, Tarzan the Ape man, or Pennywise the Dancing Clown, all of which would have given us *radically* different meanings. But he wasn't any of those people. Mr. E is in the cage with an Iraqi interpreter. And an Iraqi interpreter is pretty specific when you think about it. Obviously the IS produces that image to represent what it's "thinking" for a good reason. So let's work it out. First, since he is not anyone the dreamer knows, this character is likely a symbol and/or a personification of a life experience or process.

But of what? As always, the image itself provides us with the answer. What do interpreters do? Don't think literally here; think in metaphor. Interpreters *make sense of what is unknown.* They help you to understand what is being spoken of. And he's not just any interpreter – the dream is specific about that. He isn't an interpreter of French, Chinese (or Elvish or Klingon, etc.); he is an *Iraqi* interpreter. Here's where context helps. In *this* patient, an Iraqi interpreter means something different than the same character would in someone else's dream. Why? Because Mr. E has been in Iraq and had numerous traumatic combat experiences (some of which he earned medals for). In someone without that life experience, an Iraqi interpreter in their dream would likely carry quite a different connotation than in someone without that experience. Context is (nearly) everything.

But for Mr. E, an interpreter is a part of his psyche or his life that *interprets Iraq.* In other words, it's a potential self that *understands and interprets* all of the confusing, inspiring, and traumatic (among other things) experiences that happened to him there. This character can make sense of what happened to him. He is therefore obviously a very important person for our dreamer to be acquainted with. Moreover, since he is so clearly *separate* from the dreamer (i.e., he isn't a "best friend", or "twin brother", or what have you), that tells us just how separated the ego really is from that understanding. There's fragmentation here. So just in this analysis of this character, we can predict that our dreamer has a very hard time understanding what happened to him in Iraq and he needs help making sense of it. He needs *interpretation.* He needs to have meaning. All of this, of course, was also clear from his clinical presentation.

As an aside, let me point out that this craving for meaning and understanding is, I think, a human universal. As I mentioned before in discussing storytelling: we all want very much to be able to "make sense of" our lives, and we will gladly accept nearly *any* meaning if we can avoid the horrifying alternative that there is no meaning. Having no meaning is repugnant to the human soul.

Now that we have sorted out what these two characters are about, let's continue our list and check the setting and scope. Both are very limited and confined. It's a *cage*, for crying out loud. And not just any cage, it's *electrified*. The only way it could be worse would be if it was flaming barbwire! In any case, the extreme conflict between the "lead guy" and the interpreter that the dreamer is caught in the middle of doesn't happen in a cushy resort in West Palm Beach. It's a cage, like in a place where you put an animal. So obviously this setting is a reflection of feelings of intense despair and feeling trapped by this conflict. Using the Dream Hack, right now life feels *as if* he were locked in an electric cage suffering this sadistic dilemma.

If nothing else, that can help us empathize with Mr. E's emotional state – it's desperate and terrifying. The scope is similarly limited – there seems to be nothing else in the entire world but this awful cell and this awful conflict. So it's very limited and hyperfocused, with little in the way of connection between this episode and the rest of the dreamer's life. That's an important detail to keep in mind when we compare this dream to other dreams. For the purpose of understanding integration: is the scope changing at all? Are other parts of the dreamer's life being incorporated into it? Do we even see this kind of conflict again, even if significantly transformed? All questions for clinical data to provide the answers to.

Hopefully, you can see how this method is not so much a cookbook for figuring out dreams, but rather a series of questions and leads for you to follow. Coming upon the One and True interpretation for a dream is not the goal here (considering I doubt we could ever find such a thing even if we knew it existed, which is suspect). But going through this exercise often provides quick and emotionally very important themes to explore.

Back to the dream. We said earlier that the conflict between the lead guy and the interpreter is one way of expressing Mr. E's inability to make sense of his Iraq experiences and his difficulty explaining them. Why? The dream tells us: the interpreter's *throat was cut*. This, again, is an awfully specific way to kill someone. Why didn't the lead guy stab him in the heart? Or shoot him? Why go through all the trouble of putting a knife on a stick (which in some ways seems almost comically absurd)? Because "cutting his throat" has a specific meaning here: it means cutting off of communication. It means halting verbalization. His interpreter's ability to tell him what his experiences mean was cut off by "the lead guy". The IS is again explicit in naming the culprit:

that excessively rigid and clearly tyrannical sense of "what you are supposed to do". That entity is seen for what it is: extreme, excessively black and white, all-or-nothing, and drastic in its measures. There can be no compromise with the value system that this character represents. And the IS names that character as essentially responsible for the mess he is in and why he can't make sense of his trauma.

And that's why this dream is so helpful clinically: it shows what to target. Seeing it played out like that tells us that we need to target that value system that is so all-or-nothing and severe. But how? We find the answer in the behavior of the dreamer himself. First, let me make another observation here about the dreamer: his ego strength is nothing short of phenomenal. I knew this not only because of how many combats he was able to survive, and his numerous accolades for valor. I also knew this from his journals which he shared with me, in which he was able to write down his extremely intense emotional experiences without falling apart. But I really didn't need that to realize he was an iron boat in a hurricane (to use our metaphors from the last chapter). It's evident in his dream behavior. Faced with this outrageous no-win situation, he does not cave in or crumble in a heap of despair or fear. Instead he provides the lead guy with some helpful advice: "go fuck yourself". He is defiant even with no chance of escape.

On to the next characteristic – the narrative features. For this we ask ourselves: what is the narrative structure of this dream? What are the when-then moments? We've identified that the IS does not shy away from making observations about the ego's decisions. The most important when-then that emerges here is this: when he tells the lead guy to fuck off, the lead guy kills the interpreter. This is an observation about the consequences of the ego's response: strong though it may be, it doesn't help! We must ask: what else might the ego have done here and might that have made a difference? Note that I'm not interested in finding the answer to this question (because some-times there are no easy ones to be found). I am interested in fostering the reflection that arises in asking the dreamer this question. I might ask: isn't it interesting that you chose *that* response to the lead guy's choice? Doesn't that, on a certain level, imply that you are *accepting* that choice as a valid one? Remember the child-killer dream: in that dream the dreamer didn't even ask the masked man any questions. He just attacked ... and look what that led to – for better or worse. We have a similar situation here. Rather than trying to reason with the lead guy, or trying to persuade him to set them free, or even trying to taunt him into coming into the cage, the dreamer merely accepts the choice as the only option and tells him to sod off. Which leads to the inter-preter being silenced in a gruesome, bloody way. So when we really look at the overall structure of this dream, we see something interesting: that the dreamer's defiant attitude and unwillingness to even try to talk with the lead guy is part of the problem. The conflict is so intense here because both sides are extreme and unwilling to even *try* to negotiate. Now, it is certainly possible that no compromise could ever be reached. But the point is that neither he nor the child-killer dreamer even tried. They immediately took their place in the conflict and started defiantly attacking. All that did was escalate the conflict. Since what we are doing here is trying to foster integration, we must take note of such seemingly irreconcilable conflicts where they are depicted.

The "ceremony at noon" dream

Roughly halfway through his treatment, Mr. E reported the following dream:

> *I'm in intense urban combat in the states, trying to find a bomb. I was in nonstop combat, using all kinds of weapons, and I was also shot and stabbed. Then we had to stop because of a ceremony at noon. I went to the dorm to get my dress blue uniform, and a bunch of people were there I knew throughout my life, but they were sleeping and hungover. I came in bloody and dirty and wounded. I got the idea I was not liked. I asked about my uniform and everyone pointed to the corner where it hung, dirty and wrinkled and I was devastated. Next thing I know I'm back fighting and my boss is telling me I am "doing a good job". Finally I find the bomb, but I can't disarm it. I'm alone and it explodes.*

Notice that we are no longer in Iraq. We are "in the states". According to the Dream Hack, life feels *as if* he were back home and still fighting a war and trying to find a bomb, *as if* my military identity is soiled and damaged, and *as if* even finding the bomb won't stop it from exploding. Resonance here is moderate, having many (but not all) of the criteria, including vividness, intense emotionality, clear, simply drawn figures, an eerie connection between events at the noon ceremony and the unity in the sleepy, hungover people, and then the dark ending. Reason enough to stick with this dream a while.

What about the context of the dream? At this stage in therapy we were still sorting through the events of his past and attempting to identify the long-term effects. We were continually trying to identify any conflicting values or ideals he had (such as the ones so clearly illustrated by the previous dreams). Outside of therapy, Mr. E was starting the process for separation from the military since we were nearing the end of his military career (he was receiving an honorable discharge). Thus, it is worth comparing this dream to those therapy and non-therapy life experiences.

We have several characters here, but most of them are vaguely characterized and are pretty clearly symbolic. The "people from my past" don't behave in a manner that identifies them with those actual people (whom he had no recent contact with), so we are safe in assuming these characters represent not the people so much as those parts of his life when he was interacting with them. Thus, a room full of "people from my past" is a visual way of depicting a collection of memories that he is trying to reconcile with his current situation.

Before we get further into that, however, it's worth noticing that he is reliving urban combat, but the very interesting detail is that he is *not* in Iraq. He is "in the states". Thus he is back home, so obviously this is not reliving a memory. The IS is using imagery that is related to his Iraq combat memories, but jumbling it up in his current life back here in the U.S. This juxtaposition is an important indicator of integration, which we will get to in a moment after we consider the other interpretive principles, but it also shows a certain level of incompleteness of this integration, since it is a *jarring* juxtaposition. He isn't stuck in the past, but instead the past is invading the present – neither of these is preferable in the long term.

Further notes on the setting and scope: both are expansive, but not limitless. Larger scope suggests the IS is weaving a larger tapestry, considering multiple elements from the dreamer's life and attempting to put it into a single narrative. Of course, the IS is always doing this, but sometimes it works with smaller materials to look at something more closely, while other times it is trying to "memory consolidate" a much larger swathe of experience in order to pull everything together as best as possible. Dream scope is how to tell when it is doing which. In short, the scope of this dream is quite large, but not as large as it could be, such as when we have those rare dreams that attempt to encompass the entire universe and all the realms of the gods and mortals alike, putting them into a truly mythic narrative. Such dreams are quite rare indeed, but always worth examining very closely.

A few more observations about the setting here. Unlike the previous dreams we have actually two main scenes rather than one: we have the sprawling urban combat scene, and we have "the dorm" area. The episode in the dorm, in fact, punctuates the dreamer's continual battle in the urban combat area. So what's going on here? What is the significance of the dorm? Why did the IS choose a dorm for a middle scene instead of a bar, or a football stadium, or the Himalayas (or Xanadu, or planet Mars, etc.)? A dorm is a place of camaraderie and of rest, but it is certainly also a social atmosphere as well, and it is very interesting that the IS chose to jam these two seemingly unrelated scenes together like this. Of course the point is that they are *not* unrelated at all.

In terms of narrative, the juxtaposition suggests meaning by the context the story gains as a whole. Let's look a bit closer at what happens in the dorm. Since we have decided that the various characters of the dorm represent the dreamer's life in pictures of important people from the past, we need to ask the question: why are they all sleeping and hungover? That's a curious element to put in there, isn't it? And it isn't just "some of them"; they're *all* that way. What does "sleeping and hungover" suggest in a more metaphorical sense? If you're lost here you can Dream Hack it: "it's *as if* I'm in a room full of memories, but those memories are barely conscious or they're sluggishly active". So this is the IS's way of observing that these life experiences aren't particularly vigorous or even conscious to the ego. Furthermore, we need to understand the dreamer's feeling of "not being liked". This seems to suggest a kind of fractionation, a disconnect between the ego and, in fact, the rest of his past. In Dream Hack terms: it's as if his past doesn't like who he is now, which may be a reflection of the ego's perception that he is a "bad person" – like he imagines they would think ill of him now "if they knew". This sort of feeling of shame often accompanies trauma and the images of the dorm episode appear to reflect that.

Further confirmation of this interpretation is found in the rest of the dorm episode: they all point to the uniform hanging on the wall (in unison – an eerie detail that suggests interconnection here) and he is devastated to find it is dirty and wrinkled. Now, ask yourself, what is the uniform probably symbolizing here? Anyone who has military experience can tell you: it's a symbol of your military persona, your military bearing, your standing within the military, etc. It is an outward, material sign of your participation and belonging to a specialized cultural group. There is a lot of cultural status that accompanies that, and it also isn't just a sign of belonging, it's a sign of *what you have done to earn* that status, as are each of the medals you have on the uniform. And as such, it is an extremely important symbol. The military takes great pains to *make* this the case in each soldier. Through the process of training, you are taught to take care of your uniform because it is a reflection of your military status. It's furthermore a large part of your identity, particularly for a man who joined as a 19-year-old still developing his identity, although identity development never actually ends. The IS continually asks the ego: who are you? And the stories it creates from past experiences and pure imagination are continued attempts to answer it. In the current dream, the uniform is a concrete, tangible expression of that identity. There are a lot of regulations regarding exactly how the uniform is to be worn, and of course all the medals received (tangible symbols of your military deeds in themselves) are to be placed on it in a precisely predetermined way.

There is a function to all that nitpicking: it helps preserve the symbolism; consider how angry many veterans get when they find someone walking around in a military uniform who either never served or did serve but is wearing it "incorrectly". Why get so angry? Because the uniform is a symbol of deep emotional issues: group belonging, but also pride in membership in that group, and also there is the sense that you only get to wear it if you *earn* it. Not just any bozo can put one on; the anger arises because if that kind of behavior were unchallenged, it would quickly diminish the meaning of the symbolism. Everyone would catch on that the uniform only meant the wearer just wore it for the heck of it. If just anyone can put it on and wear it any old way, the symbolism falls apart. So the "rules" that are put in place, which act in exactly the same manner as taboos practiced by countless cultures world-wide (lots of examples in Goodwyn 2016) serve to solidify and maintain the symbolism of the uniform to a high degree of meaning. So then, given all that, what is the significance of Mr. E seeing his uniform *dirty and wrinkled* when there is a ceremony to be performed? It's a sign that the ego experiences an intense amount of shame and self-doubt, *as if* his uniform were corrupted and soiled. The ego perceives his military identity to be blemished and of low worth.

And when this happens, then he is plunged back into combat, told he is doing a "good job", finds the bomb, but can't disarm it so he dies. Note that there is a common lay belief that we never die in our dreams – this is false. Death of the dreamer can and does occur in dreams. Anyway, what is all that about? Since we're on the storytelling principle, having considered resonance, context, characters, setting and scope, we can look for "when-thens". I see two big ones: first is "when I feel ashamed of my uniform, then I go back to endless fighting and looking for a bomb, and I'm told this is good by 'the boss'". Second is "when I finally find the bomb I can't disarm it so then it blows up".

What observation is the IS making with this story? Let's look at the two when-thens, each in turn, remembering that when-thens are symbolic ways to represent linkage, correlation or even causation, only not in a literal sense but in an allegorical sense. The first one links the sense of shame and dis-appointment with going back to the continuous urban battle "in the states". It ties together through juxtaposition the sense of shame and the "as if I'm still fighting even though I'm home". There's no resolution to the dorm scene. He is just going back to the old habits. Also, note that the uniform is tattered and wrinkled through no fault of the dreamer's. Believe me, if the dreamer had *caused* this situation, the IS would not shy away from depicting it. But it didn't depict that. It shows things as they are, at least from the "perspective" that the IS has – a non-ego perspective. While the dreamer is likely to feel he *should* be ashamed, since the IS did not fault the dreamer in the narrative, the IS does not apparently think this is a valid point of view. This is interesting, to say the least, and a very important distinction.

In any case, another interesting detail is that the "past life" characters are sleepy or hungover. One wonders what they might say if they were "more awake" – i.e., more clearly conscious. We will see the answer to that question in a later dream. In any case, the narrative seems to tie together his distorted perception of wrongdoing with his going back to the search for the bomb. Always ask yourself, why does the dreamer do what s/he does in the dream instead of something else? In this dream, he merely reacts emotionally – he's "devastated". What else might he have done that he doesn't think to do? Why doesn't he fix his uniform, for example? Why not ask who messed it up? Why not just buy another one? All of these actions would have changed the overall dream interpretation a lot. The fact that all he does is respond with intense emotion to the perception of his loss of military identity and pride means he accepts this judgment to a significant degree and then "finds himself" back in the endless urban battle.

The when-then strongly suggests that going back to the battle is therefore a kind of retreat. But since he didn't actively turn around and run back outside, but instead simply "found himself" back in it suggests it isn't a conscious decision on the part of the ego. He's not aware that this retreat is happening, he's simply swept up by it.

What about the detail of the "ceremony at noon"? This is actually two details. The first is that he is "supposed to attend a ceremony". What kind of ceremony, we may wonder? Without anything else to go on, we can surmise that the ceremony has something to do with his transition back to civilian life. The opening scene, after all, shows that they are blended together – this is not a situation that we want to be in! Clinical experience shows that combat veterans with trauma symptoms are often in exactly this state depicted in the dream. They're home, but the battle rages on in their head. They have not successfully re-entered the civilian world. The IS seems to think a ceremony is called for, or would normally happen (but didn't in this case).

Ceremonies are rituals. And in fact, many societies around the world, ancient and modern, have rituals that punctuate this part of a warrior/soldier's life. We, however, do not have much of a ritual surrounding this practice in our own culture (Goodwyn 2016). Since the purpose of transition rituals like this is to help facilitate a mental change in the participant from soldier to civilian, we might speculate that a lack of such a ritual may, in some cases, coincide with a lack of adjustment. Whether or not this is true for all soldiers returning from war may be debatable, but it seems that in *this* case, the IS is thinking the dreamer seems to be missing out on such a ritual. And this is evident from the when-then in the dream: *when* the dreamer is called "at noon" to end the fighting and participate in a ceremony, and he doesn't go through with it, *then* he just goes right on back to the fighting.

Note the particular way the IS sets this up: the endless urban chaos is *suddenly stopped* because of this pending ceremony. That is no small statement! It gives us strong reason to suspect the IS thinks this ceremony – whatever it is – has the potential to end the conflict and make it and the bomb irrelevant. The IS is mum on the details of the ceremony, which may mean the details aren't as important as the *general idea* of a ceremony of some kind.

This brings us to the final when-then we will look at: *when* I find the bomb alone and I can't disarm it, *then* it explodes. So what is the IS expressing here? The first question to ask, as always, is why are these images put this way and not some other way? The biggest thing I notice here is that *the dreamer is alone* when he finds the bomb. Why isn't someone helping him? Might that be the main reason he can't disarm it? Notably, the dreamer doesn't go looking for any help, either. And observations about the dreamer's behavior are a tool that you can use in therapy when discussing the dream – something along the lines of "isn't it interesting that you chose to try to disarm the bomb by yourself". Often that gets a response like "hmmm … yeah, why didn't I get help?" In other words, exploring dream content in this manner with your patients can foster reflectiveness.

In any case, let's consider the principle of integration. This dream appears to be about integration perhaps more than the others we have considered so far. I say this because the IS appears to be giving us an update on how the process is going, and the verdict is that the dreamer is struggling mightily to integrate not only the various aspects of himself, but also struggling to re-integrate into civilian life. The IS is stating in pictorial form that he is behaving as if still in combat even though he is back home. And furthermore, there is "a bomb". We haven't considered this image thus far, so now let's take a closer look. In order to figure out what the IS is using image X to represent, sometimes you can ask yourself questions about what X is/does/means in a more general sense. Here, for example, we can ask ourselves "what do bombs do?" The answer is, of course, that they "blow things up". Put another way, they *fractionate* things. Bombs cause *dis*-integration. Bombs also cause chaos and disorder. They destroy what took years to build. They dismantle and tear apart things. Make more sense now? The bomb is representing the threat of severe fractionation and breakdown.

What better way to represent the theme of possible overwhelming breakdown and descending into chaos than a bomb? So in his struggle to make his way in "the states" (i.e., in civilian life back home), he is not only behaving and feeling *as if* he were still in a war zone, but also there is a huge pressure to avert the pending possible disaster of total breakdown of the ego and psyche fragmentation. And one of the usual cultural ways to fix this situation is to have "a ceremony at noon" – noon being a natural punctuation mark to accentuate the "transition" nature of such a ritual "from morning to afternoon" (note also that rituals often align with celestial/solar/lunar cycles in order to align the participants together with them, to make them through ritual performance to be a *part of* the cosmic order). In any case, *not* participating in the ritual meant the urban conflict and the threat of annihilation are not averted, he is plunged right back in it, and in fact even when he finds the bomb he cannot disarm it – making the entire search for the bomb a wild goose chase.

Thus the IS appears to be saying that the dreamer has not integrated within or without, in part because he is blocked by shame (very common in trauma cases of all kinds, clinically), which isolates him and keeps him fighting and frantically searching. The final when-then intimates that all that searching, especially *alone* accomplishes nothing but the destruction of the ego. Not a very pleasant message, but the IS does not appear to exist to comfort or criticize the ego so much as to observe and present the current "big picture" to consciousness in as comprehensive a manner as possible, and from a different perspective from the ego's. One final note – we have another recurrent character: the "boss". Notice, again, that this authority figure is as unhelpful as ever, though in this case the authority figure is not ordering him to hurt anyone or kill an interpreter, instead the boss is simply encouraging him to keep doing what he is doing, which is going in circles.

Ghosts and gargoyles

Several months later Mr. E reported the following dream:

> *I and some others were fighting monsters and gargoyles. Everyone else was using guns but I was using a sword. Then an old friend who was a fellow soldier in Iraq appears and we talk. He told me he had died and I realized I was talking to his ghost.*

This dream presents quite a change in tone from the last dream. In terms of resonance, it has minimal unusualness in the gargoyles and monsters, some emotionality but not quite as much as before, and it seems vivid enough. The characters are of moderate complexity, but there isn't a very clear plot; however there is an interesting surprise at the end in the revelation of the soldier being a ghost. So, there is a moderate level of resonance here. The context of this dream was further along in therapy, when the patient was getting closer to separation from the military *and* we were discussing the sources (meaning the environmental triggers) related to his symptoms, pinning them down to various events in Iraq and before.

In terms of characters, we have only the dreamer, his "friend" and (apart from the monsters) a bunch of non-descript "other soldiers". These others are fairly straightforward: they represent "the group" in a very general sense, and it remains general because the IS doesn't bother with making anything specific about these characters. I think the IS uses just what it needs to represent something in its continual storytelling efforts, and so if certain details are omitted, it is usually because they aren't needed – which is all the more reason to take notice when details *are* present.

But these soldiers being so vague tells us plenty, actually. It tells us plenty in providing a context and contrast to the dreamer, showing us how he relates to his peers when they're fighting "monsters and gargoyles". Which leads us to the next characters to be discussed: the fantastical enemies. Monsters suggest a disconnect with the combat experiences he described earlier. After all, the dreamer never fought any monsters, he fought enemy soldiers. Thus we appear to be in a more idealized setting; this interpretation is supported by the fact that the dream isn't set anywhere in particular. It has the detached feel of a video game, rather than a grueling combat experience.

Then there is the interesting detail that everyone else is fighting with guns but he is fighting with a sword. That is a curious detail, isn't it? Why would the IS depict that? First, it shows an important difference between the dreamer and the perceived group – insisting on fighting with a sword suggests even further idealization. And what about *swords* in particular would tempt the IS to use it as a symbol? Why not a hatchet, or a chainsaw (or a light saber or a flamethrower, etc.)? Unlike many weapons, the sword is far and away the most romantic of weapons, used by heroes of old, knights, and kings.

So what is going on here? Dream Hack it: the IS is saying "it's as if you're still fighting, but not enemy soldiers in theater; instead it's like you are in a fantasy world with mythical creatures, and you are alone in your use of a sword". Looking at it this way brings out the inflated quality of this dream: the ego seems out of proportion – larger than life. That this is a fantasy ideal is hinted at by the monsters and the use of the sword as if he were a "great warrior of old", even as his buddies resort to more mundane and practical weapons.

It might be easy to be critical of this idealization and fantasy element, but that would be overhasty. Who knows how many times he drew from the idea of the mythic warrior-hero in order to get him through what otherwise might have been many terrifying situations. Remember: this patient's ego strength is very high – might this be one of the reasons for that? Fantasy and idealization can be functional just as often as it can be impairing, and an inability to draw upon the inspiration, focus, emotional strength and resilience that resonant or super-resonant stories provide can be as impairing as withdrawing too often and too deeply into such fantasies.

Drawing inspiration from idealized characters like gods and heroes can be rejuvenating and incredibly empowering, but runs the risk of ego inflation – in which case the ego begins to feel it is *identical* with the archetypal character rather than merely drawing inspiration from it. Jung felt that the identification of the ego with various godlike figures was typically due to a discontinuity of consciousness – i.e., fractionation (Jung and Meyer-Grass 2008: 97). You might see this sort of inflation in a dream where the dreamer is Superman or Batman, for example, or a powerful wizard, king, the President, a celebrity, a saint, or religious figure such as God, Jesus, Mary, etc. Such identifications with idealized characters can be seen in waking life in the grandiose delusions of patients with psychotic illnesses such as schizophrenia or bipolar disorder. In these cases, the psyche is fractionated and the ego is so fragile as to be "taken over" by godlike idealized characters.

Luckily for us, the IS will observe when this is happening and comment on it in the process of dream-making. If the ego is identifying with such a character, the ego will be imbued with super-powers, be it a celebrity or religious super-being, etc. If the ego is merely inspired by such a being, they will be separate in the dream. The dreamer will *meet* Alexander the Great rather than *be* him. Note that if you *do* happen to be Alexander the Great, then it would not be inflated to dream it! It is the *contrast* between who you are and who you are dreaming yourself to be which tells the tale. In the current dream, for example, it is the dreamer that is fighting monsters with a sword, not unlike Sir Lancelot, say. But ask yourself *how much* inflation is going on here? I would say that while it does suggest inflation, it is only a modest level of it. After all, he is a sword wielding warrior, but he is *not* Luke Skywalker or King Arthur or Beowulf. Here the dreamer is merely a heroic fighter, he's not the Greatest Warrior of the Age.

But even in the case of the dreamer fighting dragons, hurling lightning bolts, or waging battle with entire armies, we want to ask ourselves: what might such a grand level of inflation be in response to? Remember the dream about the ceremony at noon. Dipping into the fantastical can be a balm against soul-crushing shame and doubts of self-worth (when this normal healing tendency is taken to a chronic, pervasive, and pathological extreme is when we see Narcissistic Personality Disorder). And I think the degree to which a particular person may do this is a simple reflection of how fantasy-prone they are. Patients who are very fantasy prone will often retreat into fantasy (mainly because it is easy for them) when they need to in order to counter feelings of inferiority or worthlessness, or sometimes simply to stave off boredom (which in itself can be an indicator of minimal engagement with one's own life).

In general, however, health is indicated by balance. We don't want to be plunged into the abyss of worthlessness, nor do we want to be manic with grandiosity and unable to function, nor do we want to ping-pong between these two extremes, which (of these three) I see most often in therapy. Fluctuations like this will always occur, but so long as the extremes between which the ego bounces are modest, that is often the best we can hope for. Jung emphasizes the important distinction between differentiating the ego from inflated fantasies while at the same time not cutting off the inspiring images from the ego at the same time (Jung and Meyer-Grass 2008: 184). Only the Zen masters and Stoic Sages among us will always see ourselves exactly as we are, fully accepting of our place in the world, neither dwelling on our shortcomings nor wishing for things beyond our actual reach. The rest of us mere mortals will be riding waves of this sort of activity, and this will reflect in our dream content, as the IS sees not only the world, but the ego's reaction to it, and it then will put what it "sees" into a narrative in pictures and feelings to describe the scene. And on the following day, if it "sees" the same thing, the ego will have a recurrent dream.

So let's get to the final character in the dream: the "friend". This character is, again, not someone Mr. E had any recent contact with, and so is likely being used by the IS to represent more who he was when that person was a part of his life than really telling us much about the actual person. This person is also a "fellow soldier in Iraq", which is another clue that he is a reflection of the dreamer – an alter ego. But the twist comes next: he's talking to a ghost. Interesting! So then why a ghost? That's a pretty important detail and seems critical to the whole interpretation of what is going on here. What is the reason for depicting this man as a ghost? Let's stick to the image: a ghost is a person who is *dead*. So, whatever we might want to say about the dreamer's Iraq self, the IS went through the trouble of making sure we knew this alter ego is permanently gone and no more. Of course, this is a dream, so it's still possible to speak with the dead, and so talking to him is possible. But the fact that he is dead is important because it means the IS thinks his current ego is quite a bit different from who he used to be, and yet he is still "in contact with" this older self and is engaging in important dialogue with him (i.e., *as if* talking to a ghost).

Let's Dream Hack it: when you talk to your Iraq alter ego, you realize that guy is dead and gone. Put another way, who you were in Iraq isn't really you so much as an "old friend". An old friend who is dead and gone. But even though he is not alive anymore you can still dialogue with him and learn from him.

The IS seems to be making a point about the past-ness of Iraq here, which is a clear progression from the previous dream which had him fighting in the present, "in the states", in the here and now. Instead now he is having a dialogue, and the past is being placed in its proper context, where it belongs – in the past.

Setting and scope are rather vaguely defined here in terms of location, but expanded in terms of *time*. This is an important detail to note: scope can refer to space or time (or both). Since he is, at the time of this dream, mentally progressing *as if* he were engaging in dialogue with the "ghosts of the past", that suggests a clear delineation of the past *as* past, rather than *living in* the past, as he was in the previous dream. Again, the contrast between what is dreamed and where he is now gives us important information about how his current life *feels*. If you feel *as if* you are still fighting the battles of the past, then you will dream about being in the past, or the past will be present in a vivid way in the dream. If, however, you are achieving a higher level of integration, then the past will not be overwhelming you and will be put into its proper place and context.

The storytelling principle also gives us another clue as to the meaning of his fighting monsters in a modestly inflated manner. The when-then states: when you fight in that way, then you begin to engage in a dialogue with your past, but unlike before, the past *stays* in the past. This detail indicates that perhaps the inflation is functional and healthy rather than excessive and unhealthy. As for the friend, he's a ghost – alive (because you can talk to him), but dead (because he is no longer present). So that suggests the inflated manner of looking at his combat experiences is actually more healthy than not. And judging by the extreme guilt, shame, and horror he experienced in the various traumas (witnessing dismemberments, decapitations, and worse), this is a significant observation by the IS here.

Remember the two stories given to us about the patient who, as a child, was hit by a hammer by his step father? The second story had more heroic and story-like elements to it. There was a feel of noble sacrifice and heroism in the second story that coincided with a great reduction in symptoms. A similar process appears to be happening here, and shows the importance of frame in self-narrative, and of the positive effects of a modest amount of inflation.

Conflict and intensity are moderate, though certainly have been much higher in other dreams from Mr. E, and this suggests a reduction of inner turmoil. The enemies are generic "foes" of a fantastical nature – in effect they are place holders for "the enemy". It even feels *fun* to a degree, rather than horrifying. Since it isn't anyone specific (like many of the endless minions in action movies), there's not a lot of anger, hatred, or anything really to draw a lot of attention to these creatures, which serves to focus attention on the dreamer and the meaning of his own actions. The conflict, therefore, is more one of maintaining ego integrity against "the forces of chaos and evil" and other such vague threats from "outside", rather than from conflicting desires or self-hatred.

Thus, this dream appears quite a bit more integrated than several of the others discussed up to this point. Not only is the past put in its proper place, but there is more harmony (even if in a brother-in-arms against a common, abstract enemy type), and there is dialogue with alter-ego type characters rather than bloody conflict, such as with the "lead guy" in the interpreter dream.

The drunk man dream

Nearing the end of treatment, Mr. E reported the following dream:

> *A drunk guy tried punching me so I moved and he missed and fell, hitting the table and cutting his neck open on it. I started first aid and felt bad for him. Not once was I mad at him for trying to hit me. Then I woke up.*

For this dream, we note that there is only a modest amount of resonance apart from the slight twist of the dreamer not being angry with the "drunk guy" for trying to hit him. And we only know this is a twist based on previous, highly conflicted dreams full of fighting and combat. As resonance is on the lower end, we should not expect a lot of deeply non-verbal and abstract symbolism, but something simpler and more straightforward. The emotion in this dream is present, but somewhat tempered rather than dramatic. By this point you may have already discerned what this dream appears to be about. Nevertheless, the dream does have resonant elements, including clear plot, and simplicity of characters. This moderate level of resonance compares interestingly with the gargoyle dream in that the resonance it has is for different reasons – i.e., different qualities of resonance are represented here, more related to ease and directness of storytelling rather than vivid, wild imagery.

The context of the dream was that Mr. E was nearing the end of therapy. So whatever else we may glean from this dream, that it is happening at the end of therapy is not a coincidence. Rather, the way the IS is crafting this dream likely has that meaning included in it, and the IS is likely offering commentary on that process as well. In Dream Hack terms: "nearing the end of therapy and everything discussed up to that point is *like* learning to take care of a man who is experiencing drunken rage and not hating him for it. It's also like recognizing that man is actually harmless and has *cut his neck.*"

That last part is interesting, isn't it – the cutting of the neck. Remember the interpreter in the prison dream from much earlier in therapy? In that dream, the "lead guy" cut the neck of the interpreter, and the dreamer was powerless to help the interpreter. Here, reflecting a greater sense of command of his surroundings, the dreamer is able to attend to the injured man and administer first aid. Also, contrast this dream with the early dream where Mr. E is ordered to hurt a wheelchair bound man and "stuff him in the drain", after which he feels terrible and tries to help him. This dream seems to be playing around with many of the same themes, but these themes have evolved since then, reflecting the changes the ego underwent in therapy.

What about the characters? There are only two: the dreamer and the drunk guy. No "authority figure" – significantly. Like before, since the drunk character is nobody the dreamer knows, and therefore a personality created by the IS, we can view him as an alter ego or at least a personification of an idea or theme. In this case, it is an angry man, so possibly reflective of Mr. E's anger. As before, the anger is a separate personality so we can see the modest dissociation of it here, but I think more important is the ego's response to it, and the IS's insistence that this anger is harmless because it is "drunk" – i.e., it is dimly aware and minimally conscious or reflective. A considerable change from the wrathful and unstoppable enemies of the previous dreams (and in fact, many dreams that stem from trauma).

The dream therefore strongly suggests that Mr. E is getting a firm handle on the angry and raging feelings that everyday experience was previously provoking in him and causing such suffering. This interpretation was strongly supported by clinical material, as he displayed a marked reduction in symptoms of anger and irritability. How did this happen? By the hard work of therapy that involved seeing his anger not as an unstoppable enemy, but rather as a less dominating force, this force being an understandable consequence of trauma that is nevertheless frequently inappropriately applied because it is primitive. In the IS's depiction, it is "drunk", or minimally aware of the surroundings, and so somewhat forgivable. And whereas previously such outbursts were followed quickly by a deep sense of shame, now we see that it is merely regrettable but not catastrophic, and we can go to work, like the dreamer does, in healing this side of his life experience. Healing the neck, then, means the same thing as before, only whereas the IS showed that the interpreter was muted by the "lead guy" (i.e., a personification of his perception of rigid and unforgiving expectations), here we see that the angry man injured not the ego but *himself*, and the ego takes up the task in healing him so he can speak again, allowing him to verbalize the anger rather than need to lash out physically. It's amazing how often the Kindergarten advice given to children to "use your words!" rather than act out emotions applies to psychotherapy in adults. We are, after all, merely older children.

As for the setting, we have no information whatsoever, which means it was forgotten (which is not a neutral observation), or it is simply sweepingly generic and applicable anywhere. The scope is intimate – only the dreamer and the drunk man – but the generic setting applies it to anyplace, which actually suggests a large scope. Further details would help us to pin this down better, if we had them.

Storytelling factors include a very important when-then: when the drunk man lashes out and hurts himself, the dreamer sets to healing the man. This is the most important insight offered here by this dream, I think, because the dreamer could of course have done ten thousand other things besides this. But instead of beating the man to a pulp, or calling the police, or running away, all of which would have given us a dramatically different sort of interpretation, he offers aid. Our goal for therapy being integration means this is a positive sign that the patient is responding to therapy. If he hadn't been, the IS would have said so, and bluntly. But it didn't – so this bit of clinical data helps us to get a more objective view of our patient's condition since he did not create the dream narrative himself.

The conflict and intensity both are fairly muted in this dream. There is no real threat to the dreamer posed by the drunk man, and overall the scene appears stable. It's not all happening during a thunderstorm, for example, or an earthquake, both of which would signify much higher levels of intensity. Taken as a whole, this dream, especially when compared to earlier dreams which deal with similar themes, appears to show a much greater level of integration. The ego is flexible, aware, and not overwhelmed. He is neither an inflated super-being nor a downtrodden insect being crushed by the fickle hand of Fate. He is in control of his surroundings and at an appropriate level, and compassion even for those lashing out at him is present.

The Basic Training dream

The final dream we will discuss from Mr. E was reported in the last few sessions of therapy:

> I'm at basic training and one of my previous female fellow troops was there and we started dating. I never really thought of her like that, actually, she was more like a sister to me. But in the dream she is the adopted daughter of my commander. He didn't want her to date me, and said that if I continued he would kick me out of the military, which is pretty funny.

The commentary included in this dream report is every bit as important as the dream content itself. It's all part of a whole that aids in interpretation. As before, the resonance is fairly muted. It's still pretty clear, straightforward, and there is emotion present, but there are no giants, talking monkeys, gargoyles, or indestructible bad guys. This suggests there is not a current need for massive, mythic narratives to make sense of life, rather the IS appears to be polishing and fine-tuning. But there is still some dramatic conflict – more of the soap-opera type rather than the epic warrior type – and that tells us things are likely going fairly well, focusing on things higher up on the hierarchy of need than raw life-death survival.

Yet there are still some very profound elements here. Dream Hack it: "it's *as if* I'm in Basic Training". The context is that he is separating from therapy and from the military as a whole. Is it not striking that a patient separating from the military would dream of being in "Basic Training"? After all, Basic Training is what you learn at the beginning, so obviously the meaning is related the patient's transitioning from military life to civilian life, as the last time he was a civilian he was a teenager. He is at a new beginning, and so needs a new "Basic Training". Joining the military is a big transition, which is part of the purpose of Basic Training, and now the IS is using that imagery to depict another big transition with another Basic Training. He was re-evaluating everything he had learned and absorbed in the military.

Which leads us to the characters – other than the faceless "other recruits" there are only two besides the dreamer: the commander and his adoptive daughter. The daughter, let's call her F, is described as "like a sister to me", and yet he is dating her. This is perhaps the most resonant image in the dream of all, as it is merely one step away from dating an *actual* sister, which would reflect the mythic motif of the brother-sister union. The IS has downgraded that super-resonant motif: not a divine marriage between brother and sister deities but a dating of someone who is "like a sister". I think the reason for depicting brother-sister unions in mythology is that the imagery reflects a union of the masculine and feminine aspects of a person/the universe. The IS is merely personifying the (stereotypically) feminine aspects of the dreamer as a woman and showing how these characteristics, as perceived by the dreamer, interact with the ego.

In other dreams (not analyzed here), these aspects of the dreamer were depicted either as pretty but helpless damsels in distress or as critical "bosses" – this is the first time in the series where the dreamer is in a fairly non-conflicted or non-idealized relationship with a woman. That is naturally quite significant. So, like the "damsels in distress" characters that Mr. E often dreamt about earlier in therapy, the characters would often be beautiful and young – indicators of high value, but to a man of equal youth and vigor – the contrast between prospective mate character and dreamer makes a difference. An ego that is less mature (irrespective of age) will likely, then, depict a symbol of less mature value and attraction as a youthful beauty.

Classically (for Jung) this character can be labeled as an "anima" character. Without getting too deep into the technical details of this concept (some of which are still debated in Jungian circles), we can conceptualize this as the seemingly "feminine" characteristics that the dreamer has, personified into a female dream character. In a female dreamer, the "masculine" characteristics would be personified also and labeled an "animus" figure. Jung used these Latin terms for "soul" to emphasize that such characters can be very profoundly impactful on the subject because they contain the extremely powerful emotion of attachment, sexual intimacy, and/or various forms of serious commitment. And though the division between "masculine" and "feminine" ways of being was more rigid in Jung's day, the tendency to make this distinction is so strong and universal that this conceptualization of dream characters is still relevant today, so long as it is not taken too far.

So another way to look at the "damsel in distress" (or its corresponding young male in distress) character is to view it as a way to depict just how polarized these ideals are in our dreamer. A dreamer may, for example, strongly identify with masculine ideals. Now, granted, "masculine ideals" are not set in stone and written into the stars. There are many variations across the globe, but certain themes recur very frequently, and this may have significant biological contributors (Goodwyn 2011). Some highly recurrent virtues labeled as "masculine" are strength, courage, resilience, and achievement, for example, whereas virtues labeled as "feminine" might be empathy, nurturing, healing, etc. I am not attempting to critique these value systems here – that work I leave to gender theorists and sociologists. I am merely pointing out that pervasive gender norms will find their way into your patients' dreams and it's important to know how to recognize them. The IS is resourceful and will use whatever raw materials it has to craft the dreamworld.

Taking our strongly masculine-identified dreamer, then, it will be common for him to have hero-rescues-damsel themes running through his dreams, because his feminine qualities are distant from him, perhaps repressed or cut off/dissociated for various reasons (such as being immersed in a dangerous environment where stereotypically feminine virtues such as nurturing and expression of sincere feeling are devalued). Though I hasten to add, damsels that the dreamer does *not* bother to rescue is certainly possible, and potentially quite concerning. More often than not, though, a dreamer attempting to rescue the damsel is engaged in the work of trying to get in touch with the feminine qualities he has distanced himself from, and the more mythical and fantastical the setting is, the likely more idealized and deep the split is. Remember the Dragon Slayer story (ATU type 300)? Understanding the basic theme at work here helps us understand why that folktale is super-resonant. It's a universal concern, and the story depicts the symbols in vivid detail. What about the female trying to connect with her idealized and mysterious masculine side? That, I think, is the primary theme behind another super-resonant tale: the Beauty and the Beast story (ATU type 425C).

In the current case study, Mr. E had the damsel-in-distress sort of dreams often early in treatment, where he was trying to rescue a damsel from an invincible enemy (another recurrent character we found was representative of his trauma and war-triggered angry side). In his waking life he played this very same drama out in his relationships – unsurprisingly these were disappointing to him. Nevertheless, trying to "rescue" his nurturing side from his angry and wrathful side is a worthy goal, and the IS depicted this situation whenever it was occupying his life. She is, after all, worth saving. But again, she is a highly idealized character in this case. She is young and helpless, vulnerable, and her worthiness is depicted in a simple visual and primitive manner via her great beauty and high social station, just as the Prince in the Beauty and the Beast story is shown to be valuable by his beauty and high social station in the end. But we should note that she is also quite passive and devoid of real humanity.

The problem, then, is not that he is trying to rescue her, but that this idealized and nearly super-resonant setup is far too high in the clouds. It's important but not grounded in physical, tangible life. All relationships likely contain this archetypal seed that triggers the emotional bonds, but they must play out in the messy and complicated world of physical, mortal life. And only a (more) mature ego will understand that on any level. Rescuing damsels, then, represents an early phase of the manifestation of this universal and timeless reconciliation of masculine and feminine that occurs both "within" an individual, and between she and he in physical life (even in the case of LGBT individuals this drama plays out, but the details of the imagery usually adapt to the individual's sexual preferences). Its players are vivid and fascinating, but mere sketches of real human beings. They contain the essence of reality, but lack all the messy – but tangible and gloriously visceral – details. Ultimately, these stories stick with us and recurrently emerge in the imaginations of millions because they behave as if they want to live and be played out in the day-to-day all-too-mortal lives of human beings.

But the IS must work with the materials it has. And so if the ego is less sophisticated and mature, it must craft its versions of these universal dramas in more idealized and (in some cases) almost cartoonish simplicity. As the ego develops and becomes more mature and balanced, however, the IS will be able to represent an anima or animus character with a more mature and grounded beauty; a beauty that shines amid flaws, scars, etc., and in fact made radiant and gorgeous not *in spite of* these things, but *because of them*.

In any case, this character is not a flawlessly-beautiful-but-helpless damsel in distress – which suggests all the above considerations – nor is it a harsh and critical "boss" woman, which might suggest low self-worth and shame, but a person who is on his level in terms of maturity. Furthermore, that she is more than merely the personification of a theme or idea but actually something of an *alter ego* is suggested by the "like a sister" qualification. She is like a Ms. E, as it were – the patient but from a female point of view. In super-resonant mythologies, the archetypal theme of a perfect balance between masculine and feminine strengths working in concert is depicted many ways; some are quite abstract, such as the Chinese Yin-Yang symbol, but others less so, as god and goddess marry and give birth to a line of kings, etc. Interestingly enough, it seems that the closer to everyday human life the story in which this motif is inserted becomes, the more tragic the outcome. Gods and goddesses such as Zeus and Hera, Freyr and Freya, Isis and Osiris, and so forth can marry and have children without any negative consequences. But in folktales involving humans inadvertently coupling with siblings, the union typically results in tragedy (ATU type 938). Perhaps the lesson learned from world mythology and folklore is: we are not gods, and we can't get away with their kind of shenanigans. More seriously, the drama played out by gods is of a thematic and abstract order, representing powerful and more universal themes of union and balance, depicted (accurately and vividly) by the actions of the lofty gods. Having the same drama played out by human beings, however, loses some of the abstract nature of the imagery and must be adapted before being played out in the world of less-than-perfectly-ideal physical life.

In any case, notice that F is the "commander's adoptive daughter". This is a curious detail that demands a closer look, and it was this detail in particular that made me think this dream was about the patient's relationship to the military in general. Why? Because his date is linked with the commander in this manner. And in fact, the commander does not want this dating to happen.

Haven't we seen variants of this commander character before? The "authority figure" who ordered him to beat up the man in a wheelchair, the "lead guy" who cut the throat of the interpreter, the "commander" who told him he was doing a "good job" running around the city looking for a bomb he was ill equipped to disarm, etc. Here he is again, making our dreamer's life difficult. And the dilemma posed to him is: you cannot stay in the military and date her. You must choose one or the other. Put in other words, if you plan to get in touch with your feminine side, you have to give up the military (as you perceive it, it must be added). Furthermore, he is faced with this while in "Basic Training" – what is the significance of that? Well, if we view each part, meaning the Basic Training and the dating, in isolation, it doesn't seem very significant. But we *cannot* interpret dream images in isolation. Context matters! We must look at the whole cloth as well as the individual strands, and in this case, that the date-or-military dilemma is posed *in the context of* Basic Training strongly suggests a Dream Hack of the order: "transitioning out of the military and out of therapy is *like* dating someone who was like a sister to you and the adopted daughter of the commander, and it's *as if* you can't date her and stay in the military." I think this particular dream probably reflects the way in which the ego is already questioning things he learned from the very start.

The somewhat inflexible way in which this dilemma is posed is of course a reflection of the ego's inflexibility with respect to these two ways of being (meaning "dating" or "military"). It was very hard for Mr. E to be a mighty warrior, nearly invulnerable, bound to extremely high standards of honor, *and* at the same time be a man "in touch with his feminine aspects". Understandable! And the IS depicts it just as it is without comment, as it always does. The fact that he is separating anyway winds up being a relief – a way out of the dilemma that doesn't involve sacrificing either, both of which have value.

Thus, coinciding with an overall improvement in symptoms and making the necessary adjustments that go along with transitioning out of military life, Mr. E's dream content reflected these changes and even showed a few additional nuances, such as the link between the patient's relationships with the opposite sex and also any "feminine" qualities he saw in himself, as he found new ways to look at his military career in whole. As mentioned, it seemed at this stage that the ego perceived the two to be irreconcilable. Despite this, however, Mr. E did not appear all that distressed, as evidenced by his "which is pretty funny" comment at the end of the dream report. Since he was separating anyway, who cares?

In terms of integration, the IS seems to be reporting a lot of improvement. The conflict between ego and "authority figure" is much less severe (but still present), the intensity is fairly low, and the challenges between ego and feminine character are improving also, with neither an inflated "knight in shining armor" fantasy nor shame-filled recipient of harsh criticism (or being blown up) involved. There is still also conflict between the theme of meaningful emotional connection and the theme of belonging in the military and this dream sets up the conflict as essentially irreconcilable (and again, the ego does not challenge it in the dream, which suggests a certain acceptance/ internalization of this dichotomy). But the dilemma is robbed of any sort of catastrophic consequences since Mr. E is separating anyway – therefore it is simply made irrelevant. In a different context, such as if the dreamer were *not* separating, we can see that the entire timbre of the dream would be quite different! But that's why we have to consider the full context of the dream when interpreting it. You can't break up a dream into parts, analyze them, and then stop. You have to keep going and put them back together to see how it all fits into a larger meaning.

Finally, I will wrap up this series with a quick observation about the IS's choice to have F be the *adopted* daughter of the commander. Why adopted? Why did the IS go through the trouble of adding this seemingly odd detail? It could just have easily been that F was the biological daughter of the commander. Perhaps this nuance was added to suggest that while the daughter and commander are necessarily linked (and hence the dichotomy between relationships and military belonging), the bond is not quite as permanent and binding as if she were his biological daughter. I think it means the ego may not *entirely* buy into the dichotomy; Dream Hacking it: "it's as if you're dating the commander's adopted daughter" is just a little less intense than "it's as if you're dating the commander's *daughter*". It's a subtle point, but it's there nonetheless.

The trauma progression

By now you have likely noticed a gradual change over the course of these dreams from Mr. E, beginning with bloody conflict and impossible situations, gradually calming down to less conflict and more upbeat images. Full disclosure, however: the above dream progression represents an overall trend in a case with a lot of fluctuations. What changed was the imagery and the intensity and conflict, but it was gradual and only visible in the long view. To use a metaphor to illustrate what I mean, if you tracked the fluctuations of dream intensity and conflict over time it would look like a wave, with high peaks and troughs (with the peaks very high intensity and the troughs death and despair imagery), but over time the *amplitude* of the wave settled. The extremes became less extreme over time, except at points where Mr. E had life setbacks or acute stressors, which would *increase* the amplitude again, only to – in time – have them calm back down. This pattern I have observed across many different clinical cases to the point of thinking it is likely a general pattern of dream content.

And there is support for this perspective coming from other dream researchers and theorists. Ernest Hartmann, for example, in his book *Dreams and Nightmares* (Hartmann 2001), using a variety of post-trauma dream reports and studies, shows how trauma dreams follow a typical progression, starting from (nearly) exact repeats of the trauma to slowly incorporating other elements of life outside of the trauma, followed by an overall tempering of the violence and chaos, going from being outright attacked to merely feeling vulnerable without being attacked, and gradually back to everyday dreams which I would label moderate to low resonance which deal with smaller day-to-day concerns rather than whole-lifetime or even cosmic scope levels of thematic content.

This is the case of *normal* trauma dream progression, and clinically it correlates with symptom reduction. That is, extreme symptoms correlate with being very early in this progression, whereas more muted or minimal symptoms correlate with being late in this progression. I want to emphasize, however, that this progression is not a rigid and inexorable or mechanical process. Allow me to illustrate. Let's propose that the above progression can be described as a "Trauma Dream Progression Track" happening in a given order, using labels A, B, C, D, and E.

The Trauma Dream Progression Track:

A: near exact repeats of trauma
B: similar trauma with other elements thrown in
C: peril downgraded from bodily attack to verbal attack
D: peril downgraded to feeling vulnerable without attack
E: return to daily concerns with a few bounded references to trauma.

In the ideal case, following a trauma, the patient's dreams will start at A, then over the next few weeks or months travel in order to B, then C, then D, and then E, such that we can describe the overall process as ABCDE. This ideal progression represents the normal mental healing and integration following a given trauma. It is ideal because it assumes one simple trauma, followed by no subsequent traumas in an otherwise neutral environment. But life is hardly ever so considerate, and so this progression is not common in clinical populations (in the general population, however, it is likely to be much more common). Instead we can see patients stuck at A for years – even decades. This obviously tells us a great deal of clinical information, in this case that the patient has been unable to experience the normal healing process that occurs following a trauma. In Dream Hack terms, it's *as if* they are reliving the trauma day after day.

We can also see patterns like ABCDA, where the patient was getting better but then was hit by a new trauma, sending her or him back to A to begin again. Another pattern might be ABC, where the patient stays at C for a prolonged period, because of course any of these stages can be prolonged. Or we might see ABCBCDCBC ... etc., where a patient struggles over the course of years and sometimes decades, but is hindered over and over in the process, causing backtracking, followed by the hard work of healing, followed by yet more setbacks, and so on.

Obviously people vary greatly in this overall scheme. Some heal quickly, others more slowly, and the contributors are both biological, environmental, and in large part an irreducible combination of both in various mixtures. Those with disorders such as schizophrenia or bipolar disorder are naturally slower healers. Those with strong, supportive social networks and good health habits tend to heal more quickly. Those with multiple traumas will find it harder to heal, just as someone suffering 30% burns will struggle more than someone suffering 10% burns (all else being equal, of course). Other factors that can hinder healing include drug abuse, rigid and maladaptive character-ological structures, various chronic illnesses both mental and physical, repeat traumas, chronic stress (financial, relational, family, etc.), poor health habits (i.e., the usual suspects of poor diet and no exercise), social isolation (a *huge* factor), and so forth.

But at all times, the IS tells us where the patient is *today*, even if the patient, for whatever reason, cannot. That is, when the dream occurs, the IS is telling us how they are doing as a whole at that time. This is why looking at a long view in terms of dream series content can help us determine more objectively how our patient is faring.

Chapter 6

Lucid dreams – and soaring to Asgard

> We are quite probably dreaming all the time, but consciousness makes so much noise that we no longer hear the dream when awake.
>
> (Jung and Meyer-Grass 2008: 3)

A lucid dream is a dream in which you are aware that you are dreaming. It is therefore a special case which is different from the usual dreams we are discussing in this book, and while I discuss other special cases (such as the dream-within-a-dream) in later sections, I felt the lucid dream had enough on its own to merit its own chapter. The subject of lucid dreaming outside of a clinical context is a vast and fascinating subject. But here my primary aim is to narrow our focus on lucid dreaming to its relevance in clinical work, and to integrate the phenomenon into my overall theory of dreams as products of the IS as well as provide some suggestions for what to do with them. Therefore in this chapter I will not present a comprehensive literature review of the lucid dream as space does not permit, and that has been done well in a variety of other sources anyway such as in the work of lucid dream pioneers Stephen Laberge and Howard Rheingold (1990), just to name one. Though the subject of the lucid dream stretches back millennia, Laberge was perhaps the first to work with lucid dreamers and carefully document their experiences using sleep laboratory techniques, bringing "scientific legitimacy" to something mystics have known for ages. Their work is therefore very interesting on its own regardless of clinical concerns.

But the fact that we can lucid dream at all raises some interesting questions about the theory of the IS I am working on here. Remember that in general, a key feature of this book's approach to dreams is the recognition that dream content is not created by the ego, and so provides us with clinical data that is valuable for that reason. It is created by something else that is non-ego, whether that be some kind of process or (I think more likely) a kind of over-arching "deeper self" or non-conscious personality from which all the other personalities, including the ego, originate. This process or sub-personality (or super-personality, if you prefer) I am labeling the IS. It appears to "decide" when and how to respond to trauma and other environmental stresses, what sort of ego to create, along with alter egos to compare, contrast and debate with in dreams, and its "thoughts" – if indeed they can be called that – are metaphorical picture-thoughts which have a perspective that is wider than the ego. I'm using quotes here because I am hesitant to personify the IS too much, since it may be some sort of natural non-directed process, but that said, if we deny the IS any sort of intentionality or goal-directedness, it becomes a puzzle as to how the various personalities generated by it could emerge from something which has none. As mentioned in Chapter 1, if we pursue this line of questioning very much we wind up with philosophical and metaphysical (rather than clinical) questions. In any case, while I certainly have my ideas about how to answer these questions, I will leave them to future work and do my best to remain metaphysically neutral. For now.

Anyway, we can see that lucid dreaming is unusual in the sense that the dreamer actually has quite a bit more control over the imagery and narrative of the dream than the usual case of non-lucid dreaming. If we think in terms of a spectrum of willful directedness with respect to imagery, we have normal dreaming on one end, pure daydreaming fantasy (where everything that is imagined is dictated by the ego) on the other end, and lucid dreaming apparently somewhere in the middle. The unique thing about the lucid dream, then, is that the dream content is under the *partial* control of the ego, rather than completely in the hands of the IS as in a normal dream. At the same time, however, it is not *entirely* under the ego control as it is in a daytime fantasy. It seems therefore to be a kind of hybrid state, which it shares with other over-lapping but non-identical hybrid states such as trance, active imagination, reverie, and so forth.

So what can we learn from this phenomenon? If your patient reports one, are there any special considerations? Given that we are conceptualizing a lucid dream as a dream which is more ego-controlled than IS controlled, obviously that means the answer would be "yes". What follows, then, will be a discussion of the implications of lucid dreams on our theory, as well as things you can do with patients who have lucid dreams.

Dream imagery as symbols of the dreamer's perspective

Earlier we discussed how the appearance of a dream character will reflect the way in which the dreamer perceives or feels about the thing being represented or personified. A primitive emotion will appear often as an animal. Playful feelings can be represented as bunny rabbits, whereas feelings or thoughts the ego is trying to avoid can be represented as shadowy, malicious characters chasing the dreamer, or they can be monsters, demons, "terrorists", or what have you.

This principle is actually empirically demonstrated quite strikingly in lucid dream reports. In some of the earlier studies of lucid dreams (Tholey 1988), subjects who experienced recurrent nightmares found that when they were taught lucid dream techniques and courageously faced the characters that were terrorizing them in their dreams, the dream characters often changed and became less threatening. Later research supported the technique of using lucid dreams to treat nightmares and PTSD (Soffer-Dudek et al. 2011; Zadra and Pihl 1997). Purcell et al. (1993: 238) even found that lucid dreaming had positive effects on those studied in both cognitive and motivational spheres.

Laberge and Rheingold (1990: 189) add, however, that attempting to make the characters disappear rather than interact with them can have the opposite effect! This behavior strongly suggests that the way such dream characters behave is tightly correlated with the ego's attempts at dealing with them, which is exactly what we would expect if we were to think of them as personifications of life issues/problems/alter egos/etc.

Thus, with this study we have direct support for the idea that a change in ego attitude *causes* dramatic changes in dream content. Other, more indirect support comes from clinical practice, where I and other therapists have found that interpreting and understanding a dream or recurrent dream image in therapy can cause a shift in dream content, as is discussed throughout this volume. Note that this also confirms our intuition that dream characters can often be conceptualized as alter egos, and that conflict with them coincides with internal conflict, whereas reconciliation with them in therapy, which consists of dialogue with the therapist and exploration of various previously unconscious motivations or desires, will usually result in a change in behavior between the dreamer and such alter egos.

Lucid dreams and the IS theory

So what else can we learn? There are a number of opportunities that lucid dreaming can offer, as well as a few pitfalls. Let's look at the opportunities first. First, notice how up to this point all of the dream work done in therapy has been required to be done in hindsight; that is, the patient has the dream, may or may not record it, and then if she or he remembers it, the patient brings it into therapy to discuss it with you. Any insight offered or gained is in retrospect. Lucid dreaming, however, allows one to work with dream material and characters *in situ* and *in medias res*. Recognizing that you are dreaming, for example, and utilizing the techniques we have discussed so far, we can apply the insights learned in therapy directly to the dream itself. In the dream series of Mr. E, there were a large number of dreams reported where he faced invulnerable enemies. Time and again, especially early in therapy, he faced such characters, and therapy involved pointing out to him that he always chose fighting no matter what, which resulted in the enemy simply getting back up for more mayhem. Using the techniques developed here, we came to the conclusion that such enemy characters were personifications of his trauma-induced rage that spun out of control, and behaved in Dream Hack terms "as if attacking me and I can't defeat him." As therapy progressed, his rage diminished, and such conflicts lessened also, culminating in the "drunk attacker" dream, where he was able to manage a reconciliation by offering the man aid, despite being swung at.

The lesson learned through therapy was that the dreamer cannot defeat trauma-induced rage by *attacking* it. How do we know that? Because the IS showed us exactly what happens, since the dreamer continued to utilize this method to attempt to deal with this character early on. And every time he did so, the "terrorist" (as it usually was) simply got back up. The when-then told us: when I use my favorite coping mechanism (fighting) to try to deal with this character, it doesn't work. The IS also gave us further clues in this case by equipping the dreamer with inferior weapons such as knives, sticks, or rocks, "as if I am ill equipped to handle this character", which of course he was.

In the case of normal dreaming, we can approach this recurrent theme by offering up observations to the patient along the lines of "it seems that no matter what is going on, your go-to strategy is always to fight and attack and never anything else ... isn't that interesting?" This alone may stimulate enough thinking to cause a change in attitude that might show up in altered dream content. In Mr. E's case it did. But in the case of lucid dreaming, the next time he encountered this character, and remembered that attacking him never worked, he could have tried something else entirely. Given that we strongly suspected this character is a split-off aspect of the dreamer, fighting it would only perpetuate the split rather than alleviate the suffering. Clinical data supported this conclusion. Furthermore, since integration is our goal, the dreamer can try something integrative, such as talking to the character, trying to understand his point of view, or even inviting him to the pub to discuss it over a pint (this last suggestion is very likely to be effective in the case of the author of this book). Much like the Tholey study, then, we can expect that such efforts are likely to change the dream character much more effectively than continued endless fighting.

Is there a difference between this technique and the more cerebral, language-based and abstract method offered by therapy? Is the lucid dreaming method likely to be as effective as the therapy method? I think it may be even *more* effective, since in therapy you are merely talking about changing attitudes, whereas in the dream you are *acting out* such reconciliatory efforts in the dream environment, and so engaging not only your mental but (dream) body intentionality toward the goal of integration. For reasons I explore in much greater depth in my previous book *Healing Symbols in Psychotherapy* (Goodwyn 2016), I suspect this is likely to be even more effective, as it engages multiple levels of being and not only the cerebral.

But encouraging integration by diffusion of conflict is not the only exercise one can do in a lucid dream with dream characters. Recognizing characters as anima/animus figures or alter egos can be approached in a lucid dream and questioned directly, for example, as in the following dream report of a 36-year-old male in the early part of a Jungian therapy:

I'm wandering around a large city that looks old and European, like Rome, maybe, with the old world buildings and cobbled streets, small shops and open-air markets. There's a lot of activity going on. I find a fruit market where a lady about my age is there before a big clock tower. She has dark hair and a Mediterranean appearance, and says a polite greeting. Then I look up to the clock and notice I have a hard time reading the numbers on it. Just then I realize I am dreaming. I take a moment to marvel at just how real and vivid everything is, taking time to run my hand along a stone wall of a building, amazed at how solid and strong it feels. Then I look at the lady and realize she is a dream character, and decide to see what she has to say to me. It is a powerful thing to look directly into the eyes of someone whom you know is a dream person. I respectfully greet her and ask if I can do anything for her. She says she is here to teach me an ancient language. I thank her but the dream fades before I can find out more from her.

There's quite a bit going on here, as hopefully by now the reader can identify. Briefly, the "old world" city (since the dreamer is American with European ancestry) denotes a certain "delving into the past" that is commonly seen in dreams reported in therapy – especially early on when many of the sessions are focused on getting a full "history" for the patient. The clock tower, also, seems to be there to emphasize this same idea. The intensity is elevated (lots of bustling people milling about), but it isn't violent or scary like a hurricane or war zone would be. The psyche is simply very "activated", possibly indicating that therapy is successfully "stirring things up" in this patient. Going through therapy (and whatever else is going on in the patient's life) is *as if* he were in a bustling old city full of activity.

The image of a "fruit market" is interesting, suggesting that the lady is someone who can supply "fruit". This dream, in fact, provides us with an example of another interesting thing the IS does, which is make visual puns with common parts of speech. Someone who feels she is involved in making an important decision, for example, will find herself literally "at a crossroads in life". Someone with whom you can have "fruitful" discussions may literally have fruit to offer. Note, however, that this lady has a fruit *for sale* – not for giveaway. There is a cost to reap the benefits from dream characters; it's unclear what this cost might be, but money typically is used to represent the concepts of value, effort, or even prestige, particularly those of us raised in the post-industrialized complex civilizations of Western first world nations.

In any case, the dreamer uses the fact that he can't read the clock tower as an indicator that he is dreaming. The inability to read easily is, in fact, one of the so-called "dream signs" identified by Laberge and Rheingold (1990) – that is, a sign that one is dreaming. Other dream signs include: malfunctioning technology, inconsistencies in environment, and being able to use superhuman powers (there are others discussed at length in the lucid dream literature). This dreamer was familiar with the idea of lucid dreaming and had done it before, and so was able to recognize when he was dreaming (this time). He also was familiar with a few Jungian concepts, such as the anima concept, and so thought this character might be an anima figure, whom he should get to know better.

Was he right about this in-dream interpretation? I think it is likely – first, she has an aura of the past all about her, in her "Mediterranean" appearance and the fact that the city is "like Rome maybe". The connotation of Rome is of the foundations of the Western world. Thus she and the city bear a strong amount of symbolism that seems to suggest the strong weight of the past (both in people and in events). It makes a very good symbol for the unconscious grounding from which the ego has emerged; the IS's domain, in fact. And so as Jung classically described it, the anima character is one who in fact represents the unconscious as a whole and gives it voice (and in a woman, the animus performs this function). Does the fruit seller fit this bill? Well, given that she is appearing to the dreamer in order to teach him "an ancient language", I would say yes. Sadly, the dreamer did not get to converse with her any more. But if he had another lucid dream later, he could *look for her*, and perhaps find her to continue the conversation. That's one possible use of lucid dreaming in therapy. Once we have a framework for understanding just what these dream characters are about, then we can formulate a plan for how the ego can interact with them in a manner which fosters *integration*, the ultimate goal of therapy. The dreamer's intuition to treat this character with respect and ask to help *her* was a good sign that the ego is interested in integration. After all, the dreamer could have done many other things, such as run away from her, cuss her out, attack her, or hit on her, all of which would not necessarily have moved him toward greater integration between the ego and the rest of the psyche.

Another thing the dreamer does is pause and simply marvel at the dream itself and how *real* it all feels. I recommend any lucid dreamer do this at least once. It is an unforgettable experience to reach out and touch someone or something, and have every detail vividly realized in all the senses, even tactile and kinesthetic, and *know* that it is a dream. Note that I emphatically refuse to say "know that it is *just* a dream". I know better than to be so dismissive and reductive about dreams. Particularly after you have done this in a lucid dream, you come to realize just how incredible the mind, and the IS really is – capable of conjuring up incredibly "realistic" (if that is even the right word) worlds, and whole hosts of characters to inhabit them, each with their own appearance, idiosyncrasies, habits, voice, etc. The effect of simply pausing and reflecting seriously on this fact can be eye-opening for your patients, hopefully drawing them away from the all-too-often encountered attitude, inherited from our post-Enlightenment, Cartesian legacy, that the world is simply an empty, mechanical, and clockwork universe, and our imaginations mere pale imitations of this universe. If anything will convert you to a more Romantic view of the world, it is gazing face-to-face with the creative genius of the IS.

And in fact, we should not miss the detail that the dreamer here had the association that the city he was in was "maybe Rome", perhaps another "Romantic" play on words?

Grief work can also be done with lucid dreaming. As mentioned in some of my earlier writing on grief (Goodwyn 2015), the pathway to integrated vs. complicated grief often involves coming into a new relationship with the deceased (regardless of whether or not the patient believes in any sort of survival of consciousness after death) that is not as conflicted. Lucid dreaming is an avenue, then, available to the dreamer to encounter a dream character version of the deceased, through which the dreamer can have conversations about whatever might be troubling them.

It is well known in grief that many times working through such conversations can be therapeutic. In a lucid dream, they can be carried out "in person" with the deceased. This technique is not one that has been subject to rigorous study that I am aware of, but has been encountered clinically. In Chapter 8 we will discuss some of the psycho-spiritual issues this practice could raise and my suggestions for how to use them effectively and promote healing and integration. For now, however, it is important to point out that this particular technique – seeking out deceased loved ones in order to converse with them and help the grieving process – requires an experienced lucid dreamer. Not only does the dreamer need to be aware of how to induce lucid dreams, but in-dream they need to be able to seek out the loved one (often achieved through "willing" it to occur) but to be able to stay in-dream while the conversation is happening, both of which require practice. If your patient happens to be able to learn these things, however, you have this tool available.

Another tool that can be used to foster integration is to have the dreamer leave the dream ego and "enter" the bodies of other dream characters during lucidity to foster greater levels of empathy and interpersonal understanding (Tholey 1988). This is the lucid-dreaming version of an exercise I have patients go through frequently which we will discuss later, that of recounting the dream to me from the point of view of one of the other characters. Tholey simply had lucid dreamers do this *in the dream*.

The limits of lucid dreaming

For all the potential that lucid dreaming has to promote integration, it also has some pitfalls. I will highlight two main groups of pitfalls. The first group of these stem from essentially the same feature that lucid dreams have, and that is their susceptibility to the desires and whims of the ego. As we have been discussing throughout this volume, the main benefits of learning and working with dreams is that their source is *not* the ego. Because of this fact, we can see in vivid terms what other creative processes are going on in the patient's mental life and what those processes "think" about the patient's current situation. If I'm right in thinking of the IS as a kind of "deeper self" than the ego with a wider perspective, then dreams are an excellent way of understanding what this process is doing, and it's precisely because dreams are not constructed by the ego, as are (for the most part) daydream-type fantasies.

But lucid dreaming is not quite as "pure" as normal dreams are in this sense; though they contain the vividness and realistic quality of normal dreams lucid dreams are a hybrid state in which the ego can actually change and direct how the dream goes. Lucid dreamers report being able to do all sorts of wild things in dreams including fly to chosen locations, meet chosen people, or give themselves supernatural abilities. Sometimes lucid dreamers do these sorts of things for the sheer thrill of it – it's like being in the world's most sophisticated Virtual Reality simulator.

And so the pitfalls here are the same as you might find in any fantasy-prone individual. Dominating the scene and action of a dream in this way is obviously a good way to mask the craftsmanship of the IS, which becomes relegated to a sort of reactive element of the mind, creating characters and scenes under the direction of the ego's will (this in itself is very interesting, but perhaps less relevant to therapy). Therefore it is hard to get at the IS's insights in the case of an overly willful and dominating ego that may be engaging in such practice to counter feelings of inferiority by being powerful in the dreamscape, which means the imagery is being driven to a much larger degree by ego fantasies rather than the observations of the IS. Therefore the pitfall we are identifying here is that a skillful lucid dreamer can, in fact, use her or his skill as a kind of escapism from the IS, hijacking whatever dream she was having and forcing it through ego desire into a different kind of narrative, making the raw imagery of the dream less useful – at least in terms of how "objective" or non-ego it is.

Of course this in itself is certainly clinically relevant, and like all things it is grist for the mill of therapy, but the focus changes: in such a case we will want to inquire into such underlying feelings, with an aim toward what underlying feelings might motivate the dreamer to manipulate her or his own dreams in such a brute-force manner, rather than letting go of the imagery and allowing it to self-organize in a more organic manner. Doing so lets the IS speak more clearly, and as such, if the dreamer is able to do this while remaining lucid, it means the patient can engage in a more meaningful conversation with the rest of the psyche and so have a better chance to promote integration.

Interestingly enough, even in this case, the Dream Hack still works fabulously: "right now life is moving *as if* whatever problems you are having you just avoid, making your life into what the ego would rather it be via sheer force of will." Since putting it this way highlights the escapism and ego defensive functions being engaged by this process, it tells us clinically what we need to know.

The second limitation placed on lucid dreaming, however, does not come from the ego, it comes from the IS. In a number of cases reported by dream research, lucid dreaming often does not typically involve total and complete control over one's dream (Laberge and DeGracia 2000), and in a few cases I have observed clinically also, it seems the IS will actually not *allow* the dreamer to do this indefinitely. For example:

> *I am in a well-groomed park at night and within a short time I realize I am dreaming. As I have done several times before, I decide to leave the current environment in order to find a particular person I want to dream about. But a voice speaks from the night sky: "Stop! You are not allowed to do that." It is the voice of the Moon Goddess herself. Shaken, I apologize and stay where I am.*

The dream developed from there into a different story, and the dreamer lost lucidity and was swept into the narrative. But the first part of this dream is what is so relevant to the subject of lucid dreaming. These sort of reports make me suspect that the IS is "watching" even when the dreamer is using lucid dreaming techniques, and resorts to brute force techniques itself if need be. Curious indeed! In therapy this dream was used to suggest the dreamer take a break from lucid dreaming techniques, except to observe and dialogue in a more passive manner, and important insights were gained from that.

Overall, lucid dreaming presents some unique possibilities, and nothing about the phenomenon seems to go against our general interpretive principles thus far. If anything, lucid dreamers provide an opportunity to integrate in more direct psychological ways than what we do in therapy, assuming we can avoid the pitfalls associated with lucid dreaming.

Chapter 7

From suffering to integration – the storyteller's map

> The disaster of the whole world stems from the fact that people think that others have the same psychology they do.
>
> (Jung speaking in Jung and Meyer-Grass 2008: 69)

The concept of integration and meaning

One way to frame the overall process of what the IS does is as a continual process of asking the ego "who are you?". The way it attempts to answer this question is by telling stories: lots of them and continuously. With each story, I believe the IS attempts to tie together the pieces of a person's life, trying to work it into a coherent narrative. And so it provides the materials to *answer* the question just as it poses it; but in order to really get a handle on this question of "who am I?" we need to have a rough idea of what the answer is supposed to look like.

A little reflection shows that it can be surprisingly difficult to answer this question just posed out of the blue. Consider that normally when someone asks "who are you?", you might answer with where you come from, or what your job title is, or even what your hobbies are. But do these seemingly incidental things truly constitute "who you are"? It doesn't seem so. But perhaps the method we are using to answer this question is flawed. We cannot, for example, look at slices of a person's life and examine each of them individually, looking for evidence of whether any of them qualify as "truly essential" or "truly part of who we are", any more than we can look at an isolated electron and try to determine what sort of object it was a part of before we started looking at it. An electron can be a part of a rock, or a piece of cheese, or the Queen of England. No amount of looking at such an electron in isolation will tell us anything about that. We have to look at the whole thing before we can get an idea of "who/what it is".

The same thing applies here, I think: it is the entirety of a person's life experiences, origin, instincts, loves, desires, social network, family, personality quirks, etc., that provide the answer to "who are you?". Who I am is my story, and my story is who I am. The whole is greater than the sum of the parts in isolation. We are given identity by our context within a greater bio-psycho-social-spiritual net. And so I think the IS seems to want to pull everything in a person's life together and try to make some kind of whole out of it, and it does this tirelessly and continuously. The IS is never content to simply list the events of one's life in a meaningless jumble of "one damn thing after another". The IS wants to understand what it all *means*. Of all the examples we have studied so far, this should be evident, but it is difficult to demonstrate without looking at dreams reported over long periods of time by the same dreamer, particularly if they are in therapy, since the goal of therapy is to enable progress and change toward healing. In any case, the trauma series of dreams presented previously show this very quality, culminating (when last we left Mr. E, anyway), with the "Basic Training" dream. Is that the end of the story? Well, of course not! That story only ends at death (as far as we know).

Anyway, all that said, what do we really want when we are asking for the meaning of a dream? As dream researcher Milton Kramer (2007: 143) once put it: "what does meaning mean?" This is actually a very deep question that has been fielded by more than a few philosophers over the ages – I make no pretense to attempt to summarize all that has been thought on this subject. Rather, here I must humbly present merely a working theory of meaning to help us clinically, and I will leave more thorough treatments on the subject of meaning to the experts.

So, for what it is worth, and for our purposes regarding dream interpretation, I think the best way to answer this question is to equate meaning with context. That is to say: the meaning of a dream is the entire gestalt looked at as a whole, just as the answer to "who am I?" is the big picture and full context of how we relate to everything else. To reduce identity and meaning to a handful of isolated facts is to commit the same error as looking at an isolated electron and trying to figure out where it came from. Thus, to reiterate, the meaning of a dream will emerge out of the whole-cloth picture of all the parts of which it is composed, all working together as a coherent unit. That is, the meaning is the collection of relationships between all the parts, players, and scenes, across all the time considered, up to now (which means it is subject to change).

I think this works as a theory of dream meaning for two reasons. First, notice how this places a *contingent* meaning on the dream. The dream has the particular meaning it has based on everything I know about when it occurred and as much as I can about how all of its contents relate to everything else in the dreamer's life – today. Tomorrow, however, a new element may be dreamt or lived that can change what came before it; this is because we are equating dream meaning with context, and context changes over time as life continues and new things are experienced, layered upon the old ones. So this definition of dream meaning, therefore, is malleable, just as is our own understanding of who we are, as obviously they are related.

I think that we risk a potential pitfall when we define meaning as if it were a singular, final, immovable entity that exists to be discovered for all eternity. To ask, "what is the true meaning of this dream?" is to risk this hazard, because it tempts us into thinking we may be able to "translate" or "decode" the dream once and for all. Note that I especially dislike the term "decode" because it implies dreams are in a "code" to begin with. They aren't. The IS says exactly what it means. It just does not use a language to say it. Or, more accurately, the "language" it uses is pre-verbal and image-driven rather than verbal. But I do not think these utterances can have a "final" interpretation or meaning necessarily. I don't think dreams (or languages, for that matter) work like that. The same electron could be removed from one object and placed in another and its behavior will change considerably, and hence "what it is" cannot be separated from "what it is a part of" without doing considerable damage to the original thing we are trying to determine. A pizza and an elephant are both made of electrons, protons, and neutrons – but what a thing is constituted by is *not* the same thing as what it *is*. All the more so for human lives. Each dream has a context – it is dreamt by a person at a particular time in a particular situation, dreamt upon a history of everything that came before. Tomorrow, however, something new may be thought or experienced that therefore *becomes* a part of the context of yesterday's dream, *as we recall it now.*

The related second point is that equating meaning with context helps to explain *how* the meaning of an entire story can suddenly change with the addition of a single element. Remember that dramatic irony or plot twists constitute one of the characteristics of psychological resonance in a story. Story tellers use this fact all the time in constructing their stories, but the reason it works is because the *meaning* of a story – i.e., its current context as a whole with all of its parts working together – can change with the addition of one element. To use a famous example from movie history (and at the risk of spoiling a plot point), up until the finale of *The Empire Strikes Back*, everyone thought that Darth Vader and Luke Skywalker's father were two different characters, and the meaning of the story (up to that point), involved a young man's quest to emulate his lost father whom he idolized his entire life, and in opposition he faced the evil man in a mask before him who stood in his way, trying to stop him from achieving that noble goal. They battle for several scenes, until Vader, crippling Luke, tells him to surrender, saying "Obi Wan [Luke's mentor] never told you what happened to your father." Luke responds with "He told me enough. He told me you killed him." Then, with a single line uttered by the villain, the entire meaning up to that point transformed from the ground up: "No. *I* am your father."

A similar, huge plot twist can be seen in our "child killer" dream from earlier. How is this possible unless meaning is a function of, or at least heavily overlapping conceptually with, context? Like all of us, Luke partially constructed his own identity out of who his father was – *that* context. And so it goes, a vast network of connections and interlacing events, people, and places, all combining to give a complex, yet unified whole – but which can change with the addition of a new element that is sufficiently impactful to send reverberations through the entire network.

The child-killer dream was another example of the IS engaging in a powerful meaning-making construction. One that pulled together the dreamer's childhood, his longstanding inner conflict, and his spirituality even, into a single utterance of meaning that could itself be changed yet again by subsequent events. And this is because *context* does not simply mean the connection of everything involved to everything else, it also means connections *across time.*

So, the IS, then, is always working and crafting together stories in an attempt to elucidate meaning by identifying relationships and depicting them visually, weaving together elements from lived experience, from the imagination, from other people, from the surrounding culture, from the past, from speculation of the future, and trying to put it all together, with new experiences folding into the mixture every day as more life happens. And given enough time and lack of interruption, it is likely that this self-organizing process could bring things together in a powerful, resonant narrative for anyone at any point in their life, as it seems the process is continual. The IS, then, provides a centripetal force to the psyche as a whole, trying to pull together the ego into a harmonious integration with all the other alter-egos, possible selves, personified ideas, etc., into a working unit. Note that integration means all the parts are working together – not that they are identical.

But opposing this nascent centripetal force are centrifugal ones: trauma, illness (acute and chronic), and grief, for example. And one of the most powerful anti-integration forces operating in the psyche comes, ironically, from the ego. It should be evident at this point how this can happen; in many of our examples we have seen how an over-defensive ego, overly rigid ego, or at the other extreme overly lax ego (in terms of boundaries) can hinder the integrative process. An ego which ping-pongs between crushing shame and inflated fantasy can hinder progress. An insufficiently reflective ego can hinder the process. And the dreams reported will show these behaviors and their consequences night after night.

Using dream symbols in therapy

But dreams are useful not just for diagnostic purposes. They can foster insight simply through discussing the imagery and brainstorming about what they may mean – note that even engaging in this enterprise will surreptitiously enroll your patient into treating dreams as potentially highly meaningful events to be taken seriously. Of course not all patients will respond to this approach, and that's fine. The issues will arise anyway; it may just be more difficult without the direct observations of the IS to help you as therapist.

But not only can dreams be used to foster insight – and they are very good for this – they can be used therapeutically in a more active manner. For example, you can point out themes to the patient that you notice from the above analysis. Themes of chaos and turmoil, intensity, inner conflict, setting, scope, characters, and context can all be wrapped up in an empathic "as if" statement: "this dream seems to tell us that you're living your life as if you're in a warzone". "This dream is saying that it's like you've imprisoned yourself somehow." "Maybe you're dreaming about fighting with an old friend from high school because you feel at war with who you used to be." "This dream says you often punish parts of yourself because you feel you have to." Most patients can relate to such statements on some level or another – they do not have to be super-sophisticated or grasp every nuance of symbolism to get what you're saying.

The dream content can also be used in other creative ways. In the case, for example, of a benevolent dream character (such as commonly seen in trauma cases where a loving grandparent, a goddess, an angel, or "spirit" of some kind offers aid to the ego) that represents a healing, integrating impulse within the psyche can be communicated with in the patient's imagination to varying degrees: "What would your grandfather say about that, I wonder?", I might ask Mr. E, whose deceased grandfather showed up in several of his dreams offering advice and/or comfort. In the case of a recurrent dream angel, for example, you might offer something like "The angel seems to want you to let go of your anger toward your sister, what do you think?" – assuming that is how the angel is behaving in the dream of course. You can "get away with" statements like this because the dream content comes directly from the dreamer. It's not you that is saying it, it's the contents of their own mind! The question of how seriously your patient takes this sort of thing flows normally into their own world view and religious beliefs (the subject of the next chapter). If they believe in angels or spirits, then they may take such a dream character very seriously – this can be quite beneficial for dismantling unhealthy defenses in a non-invasive manner.

I've found that people with sincere religious beliefs are very open to this sort of intervention and respond well to it. Even highly skeptical patients can learn to take dreams seriously, provided you give a solid (at least reasonable sounding) scientific and/or clinical basis to do so. Most patients, however, do not need a philosophical defense and will be satisfied with a few reassuring statements. Either way, engaging in this sort of imaginary exchange is a way of getting disconnected parts of the psyche to "talk to" one another, and so promote integration.

Integration is, after all, the goal we are after. And this appears to be the goal toward which the IS continues to strive through its storytelling efforts. This is accomplished by taking the previously cut off or dissociated elements of the patient's psychic life and creating meaning by proposing *relationships* between those elements and the ego, pulling them together in a single coherent narrative that "makes sense" of their life, even when many of those elements are painful, traumatic, disturbing, or repulsive. The second dream of the violent step-father, for example, is far more integrated: even the disturbing and repulsive elements have their place in the overall story of the ego heroically standing up for his sister against an insurmountable enemy, where getting hurt – though very painful – wound up attracting the attention of the authorities and helped bring an end to the suffering.

Mr. E's profound inner conflicts and hyper-polarized conflicts slowly balanced out over time as his feelings of anger and terror (both brought about by the trauma) de-escalated as the ego found ways to understand them and *contextualize* them (Hartmann 2001). It is the contextualization – the establishing the firm and clearly defined *relationships* between previously cut-off and isolated and intense memories and affects – that makes meaning and creates "perspective".

Some tools to use for fostering integration

As should be increasingly evident by now, the act of merely discussing a dream with you can actually help foster integration because, as we learned from evidence reviewed earlier, the storymaking process does not stop after we have the dream. Dream researchers have noted that with subsequent retellings, the dream becomes more coherent and organized. Thus, it is likely that the mere attention of the ego helps to "water the garden" that is the IS, allowing the narrative to develop and grow into a more complete memory-consolidating, psyche-integrating tale (whatever level of integration we may be at presently).

Jung observed this ongoing process that dream researchers refer to also, and talked about the integrative process that occurs outside of awareness as going on continually, but requiring consciousness to progress forward (McGuire 1984: 224–5). He compares the dreams of the chronically mentally ill, which often had hopeful and colorful symbols of hope, which would encourage you if you heard them in your clinic, but that since they are so ill, you cannot get them to engage with this process – their ego is too fragile and they will not listen. Afterward you may find such a patient having destructive and chaotic dreams, only to have them renew again later. "It is just a process of nature, with no intervention on the part of consciousness. So I conclude that for such a process as the building up of the individual, consciousness is indispensable" (McGuire 1984: 225). As we saw from the dream research, however, even when not especially participated in by the ego, dreaming seems to serve several problem-solving and mood-regulating functions – which means Jung may have overstated a little here. Recall also, however, that on top of this essentially autonomous process, it was also found that engaging with them more fully led to clinical improvement. Thus, the IS's work is always going on (Jung called this process "individuation" – Jung 1954), but actively reflecting on dreams and working on making sense out of them improves its efficiency, much as giving antibiotics to someone helps the immune system destroy a pathogen.

You will also find that images brought up in dreams can be referred to in therapy time and again as vivid symbols of chronic issues that need to be attended to. The following recurrent dream illustrates this principle, from a 54-year-old male:

> *I'm in an unfamiliar forest, and I'm not exactly sure which way to go, but I'm not walking along the worn paths because I know they won't lead me to where I want to go. Instead, I'm hacking my way through dense under-brush and looking for a new trail to get on.*

By now the reader should know, without anything else to go on than this, that the dream could mean quite a few things – it depends on the context. The emotional valence of the dream is one of exploration and not fear, conflict, or danger, so we're not especially expecting a lot of internal conflict. But the patient's current life situation tells us a lot: he is a recovering alcoholic, and he has successfully been maintaining sobriety for several months and further-more presents in therapy as engaged and actively working on continuing it.

At this point we have all we need to understand the dream – in this case it's quite straightforwardly intelligible using our Dream Hack: your current life experience feels *as if* you're blazing a new trail for yourself in a challenging, but not terrifying "forest". A few comments are in order: in a lot of dream interpretation literature, one can find somewhat hackneyed interpretations of commonly found symbols – the worst of these are so-called "dream diction-aries" which take individual symbols completely devoid of context and ascribe meanings to them. A forest, for example, might be equated with "the unconscious". But interpreters as early as Jung warned against this sort of thing, as we have seen from many of his quotes cited in this volume already, for example, when he advises that "we should not pare down the meaning of the dream to fit some narrow doctrine" (Jung 1954, para. 318), which includes his own doctrine.

First and foremost, it's an *unknown forest.* What does that suggest? Sticking to the imagery given to us, it is a forest he is "not sure which way to go" in. Forests are places where it is easy to get lost, and it's not an artificial environment either. It's a natural one. So it's just him and nature – a man living in the world, tracing a path on his own, trying to get to a place of safety and security. He's not scared, but he doesn't want to just plop down in the woods either; obviously he doesn't *belong* there but needs to get *to where I need to go.* But he is not traveling the "well worn paths" to get there. Why not? He tells us: because they won't tell him where he needs to go. They will just keep him lost.

Let's connect this to his quest for sobriety: the IS is telling us that his hard work in maintaining sobriety feels *as if* he has to blaze a new trail for himself because the "well worn" ones (i.e., those traveled while he was still drinking) will not take him where he is supposed to be. It's a new experience, somewhat daunting but also exciting. As we have seen many times before, the IS just shows us how things are without comment. The patient and therapist can assess from there if it is a picture of progress or of stagnation or even regression. In this case the IS is telling us the patient is working hard on his sobriety and that it's like blazing a trail through the wilderness. That gives us a good feel for how it must be for him, so it provides us with diagnostic information. He's not "backtracking", "going in circles", or "getting more lost" – all of which would be poor prognostic signs. He's not being attacked by monsters or evil people – which would suggest inner conflicts impeding the process. But he could use a bit more guidance, the dream seems to be saying, since he feels he is doing it on his own. The therapist and other supporting people are notable in their absence.

There is plenty more one can do with this dream; what was done in this case was to focus on the images themselves and connect them with the dreamer's situation – the dream was interpreted as above and presented to the patient, for whom the interpretation "clicked" and resonated. He felt he "got" the dream after that. And since the imagery of "finding a new trail" was a metaphor for the work of maintaining sobriety, this was utilized in therapy by suggesting the patient – who liked to go for nature walks – now go on such walks *mindful* of the symbolism found in the dream. The patient then thought of his continued positive efforts every time he went on a walk in the forests near his home, only now the experience was more meaningful and powerful, and in a non-verbal and very sensual way, as it was conveyed through the imagery of the dream.

This technique is but one example of integration because we are integrating dream life with waking life – naturally they should be connected, but of course many of us do not think about them in this manner. Plenty of evidence I have reviewed in this volume shows that they are, but still the persistent idea that dreams are just zany, meaningless brain malfunctions that have nothing to do with "reality" can be difficult to shake.

Other ways to use this are when a person has a recurrent character that is constantly fighting the dreamer; these characters are usually alter egos (like Mr. E's un-killable enemies) or strong emotional impulses. During waking life, when such feelings come on, the dream has provided for us a way to visualize the conflict that the patient can use to conceptualize what is going on in the moment. In the right patient (i.e., one who has at least a modest amount of psychological mindedness), this can be a helpful way to de-escalate overwhelming affects. The patient overwhelmed with anger feelings can, with enough practice, see that the recurrent dream conflict is showing itself in waking life, and the same integrative efforts can be used (facing the fear, reconciling with the anger, etc.), only because of the dream imagery we have an additional tool that allows us to visualize it clearly.

Viewing the dream from multiple points of view

The next dream will demonstrate the technique of recounting the dream from the point of view of a character not the ego; at the same time we will be seeing Jung's concept of "compensation" in action, as well as an example of confirming one's dream interpretations with clinical data to ensure your interpretation is accurate. Recall that compensation as Jung defined it was simply "the rest of the story" – the experiences in life not picked up on by the conscious ego, but in the dream material nonetheless. Here is the dream, from a 33-year-old female:

> *I'm in a dark alley, lost. I see a building where there is a convenience store and I go in. There's a bunch of side passages and tunnels leading out of the store with signs – some of them neon – but they don't help. I can't figure out where I'm supposed to go. I grab a "hot pocket", but I drop it and it gets dirty. I go up to the desk manager, and ask him which way I should go but he dismisses me. He finds me annoying.*

The waking context of this dream was that the patient had been plagued with indecision for many years. She was unable to decide on a place to live, her job, and her current romantic relationship. She often commented on how when she was younger she felt much more confident than now, but for various reasons now she felt incompetent to make decisions and so she was paralyzed. By now, hopefully, the reader can see how this context produced such a dream. Why? Notice how the theme in the dream – indecision – is so vividly depicted in imagery. In Dream Hack terms, her life was going *as if* she was stuck in a dark alley and everywhere she went was just more confusing passages and "signs" that didn't really tell her anything.

That much is fairly obvious and reflects what we already know. But what else does the dream depict that she doesn't know? What is the "compensation", or the "rest of the story"? Turns out there is quite a lot. There is an important when-then here: she is plagued with indecision, she "reaches for a hot pocket". Knowing that the IS put this odd detail in here for a reason, I interpreted this to mean that she had a tendency to reach for "comfort food" (i.e. quick and easy, heavily processed microwave food), especially when stressed about decisions. It was not something we had discussed in therapy up to this point, so this was a prediction based on the dream. I decided to get confirmation by asking the question – "does getting stressed about decisions sometimes have you reaching for 'comfort food'?" She said yes, and that she used to be much lighter and had gained weight from it over the years. Confirmation was therefore obtained – the IS told us both what was going on, and working on the dream with her led to greater insight for both of us.

The IS also tells us how helpful this behavior is: it isn't! It doesn't give her what she really needs because she "drops it" and it "gets dirty" – meaning it is tainted and unpalatable. Remember this is not literal food, it's metaphorical food: i.e., sustenance, "nourishment", etc. It's an image of "what I need". And notice the IS shows us the kind of "food" she reaches for is the largely artificial kind – a "hot pocket". Compare this to the "fruit" from the lucid dreamer in the last chapter. Nothing against hot pockets per se, but in dreams fruit has more connotations with non-artificiality, originating from "nature", etc. I'm interested in the symbolic connotations for the use of this imagery here; considering the theme of this dream, it appears that what she really needs is a feeling of self-assuredness and a sense of knowing where she is and where she is supposed to go. Lacking this, she reaches for food, which does not end well. The IS is simply showing the ego what she does and how it turns out.

Then she encounters the "desk manager". In therapy as we worked on this dream, I asked her to describe this character for me so I could have a better idea of what he was about, and because already I was suspecting that we needed to foster integration having these characters get to know one another better. She said he looked about the dreamer's age and had dark hair "like mine is", she added, referring to herself. He was also somewhat in shadow and he wore a "visor" – a curious detail that we will understand in a moment. In any case, he was an unknown figure and so therefore a symbolic character that was in somewhat of a conflict with the dreamer in that he was irritated with her and withholding information from her. Was this an animus character? Or perhaps some other kind of alter ego? Or maybe he was some other kind of character? So to get more information, and to foster integration in a fairly direct manner, I asked her to recount this dream from the point of view of the desk clerk. This exercise can often be a bit jarring for patients, and it may require a bit of explanation so as not to sound hokey or odd. In any case, here was the result:

> I'm working in my store when this ditzy girl comes in, fumbling around and dropping food. She's irritating because she is so flaky and doesn't know anything. She asks me where things are and I just tell her to go figure it out for herself.

Already we can see that this character has quite a bit of "alter ego" in him. From the imagery, which the dreamer compared to herself in hair color and age, and the fact that he forms a clear mirror-image contrast with the dreamer in terms of the general theme: being "lost" and not knowing where things are. And given that the patient's upbringing and value system viewed assertiveness and self-confidence as stereotypically "masculine", and this character embodies these virtues when the dreamer does not feel that she does, I might also label this an "animus" character, or a figure who embodies characteristics that the dreamer feels are associated with the opposite gender. Knowing this leads us to the conclusion that the best way to foster integration is to help these characters interact better and function in harmony with one another.

The above interchange helps to highlight one of the key problems in her indecision. At some point there came a split in her, and the ego identified itself with a "ditzy, flaky girl" type ego, while the decisive and knowledgeable resources became relegated to "other" – to a masculine alter ego. The desk clerk knew what things were, and might even have been a good "advisor"; the last detail I intuited from the "visor" he was wearing. Dreams often pun like this; many dream researchers and therapists have noted this tendency, and now we can perhaps see why: a pun is a conceptual blending of two concepts. In conversation we can use accidents of language to say one thing while meaning another for comedic (and often groan-inducing) effect. But the IS is using it not necessarily to be funny (though it can be "funny and serious" as Jung puts it), but because of the conceptual blending. In the work of memory consolidation and symbolic storytelling, concepts become condensed symbols that embody many ideas visually. So the desk clerk looks to be a part of her psyche that "advises" and provides guiding intuitions and assurance in the rightness of them, and the dream is telling us that she is cut off from that part.

So following this exercise we focused on reintroducing her to this side of her psyche; integrating her with the desk clerk meant drawing upon some creative anger – "hey, I'm important and I need you to tell me something!" to help counter the self-image as "ditzy and flaky". In this case, the patient was indeed able to do this successfully, armed with vivid images of the concepts and conflicts that the IS so eloquently weaved together for us, and she was able to find her voice and strength again, making important relationship and career decisions and even losing over 50lbs by giving up the compulsive eating, which she was only able to do after recognizing the emotional needs this behavior was trying to actually fill.

Commenting on dreamer behavior

Another technique we can use in therapy while we are exploring dreams with a patient is to take advantage of the fact that the IS "tells it like it is" when it comes to the dreamer's behavior. With this technique we use two essential principles about dreams. First, recall that not only did Jung observe that the process responsible for dreaming seemed to have access to information unavailable to consciousness, but dream researchers have been able to observe this phenomenon in laboratory study. So the dream is a picture of the patient's life from a more objective, less filtered point of view. Second, having given up on Freud's idea that dreams are distortions and concealments, but rather recognizing that dreams *reveal* what is going on, we can be confident of one simple fact: dreams never lie. The IS calls it exactly as it sees it.

These two principles tell us that stories created by the IS where the dreamer as the protagonist will give us a lot of insight into things that the dreamer does in commonly encountered (i.e. "memory consolidated") situations. This is one of the reasons I warn people against telling me their dreams; it tells me about their bad habits! Though, to be fair, they also tell me the good habits, too (dreams also tell me when someone is ego-inflated, which is not necessarily something they would want me to know). But as Jung put it, Nature is not diplomatic. You get what you get.

In any case, when we see a recurrent pattern of behavior in the ego we can use it in therapy as a way to remove the blinders on those habits. Here is an example, from a 46-year-old female, with comments from the dreamer added:

> *I keep having a recurrent dream of an old boyfriend whom I have NO interest in whatsoever. Yet I keep dreaming about him. He lived out West in the mountains in a rural setting. I really liked that place even though the relationship didn't work out. Anyway, I keep dreaming that I'm in town waiting for him to show up so I can go up into the mountains, but he never shows up and I'm very frustrated and disappointed. What is so disturbing about the dream is that I seem to be obsessing about this guy and I don't have any feelings for him anymore.*

So does she? I don't think so. Here's why: if that were a part of the picture, the IS would have just said so. Romantic interest in the boyfriend is notable in its absence. The fact that the patient is worried that she is dreaming about him because "maybe it means I really still have feelings for him" despite the fact that she has been happily married to someone else for many years is actually a legacy of the Freudian "wish-fulfilment" idea that has filtered its way into the public consciousness. Remarkably, even though the wish-fulfilment hypothesis has drifted out of favor, the idea continues to linger.

In any case, I was able to allay her fear about that by sticking to the image: if you were really wishing for him, why did you not have romantic feelings for him in the dream? She didn't, which led to an "oh, right." And that was that. Moreover, we know that this character is someone who has not interacted with the dreamer for years and so is much more likely to be a symbol rather than a statement about the boyfriend.

But a symbol of what? Skipping the play-by-play, I will just say that we came to the conclusion that he was a symbol of "the mountains" – the natural setting which evoked strong feelings in her; she has a powerful love of natural settings, and the context of this dream also was one of spiritual searching and questioning also. The boyfriend was a personification of all the memories she had there. And it was striking, once we realized this, that it was not *him* that she longed for, but the *mountains*. This fact led me to recognize the universal spiritual associations that get tacked on to mountains – Mt. Olympus, Mt. Fuji, etc., the examples of the "places of the gods" that are high mountains in world mythology and folktale are nearly endless. In my earlier work I point to some neurobiological reasons why this probably is (Goodwyn 2011).

So how can we use this therapeutically? Look at the dreamer's behavior in these recurrent dreams. She is longing to "go to the mountains" – i.e., connect with the divine through its expression in beautiful wilderness settings. But she doesn't go. Why? Because she is "waiting for an old boyfriend". That is, she is stymied by the memories and they are of no help to her, says the IS, because they never show up. So in effect, she doesn't get to go where she wants because she is waiting around for him. When I posed this observation to her, the patient laughed and said "you're right! Why don't I just go out there myself? To heck with that guy!" Mission accomplished. Since then this patient has made a point of taking trips to such places and reports it as very healing and balancing for her.

But it would not have been possible – or at least arriving at this insight would have taken quite a bit longer – had we not been able to take advantage of the dream material and the keen insights of the IS. Moreover, such insights can sometimes be used in a manner which circumvents patients who are especially resistant because they aren't coming from me. She is the one who dreamed this, after all. I didn't make this stuff up. That said, some patients will still avoid and/or resist such insights – expect that possibility and recognize that it is likely a sign of more severe pathology.

This technique is helpful all throughout the dream interpretation process, and we have seen several examples of it in action already. For example, we noted that Mr. E had a habit of always attacking and fighting whenever any conflict arose, and the IS showed us how that usually wound up – with just more fighting and bombs and destruction. Our bunny rabbit dreamer was locked into a habit of always running away from the rabbit, instead of the thousand other things she might do. We saw how the technique of lucid dreaming could change this behavior *while dreaming* and how it could dramatically change dream content and stop recurrent nightmares. Using it in therapy is just the next step. But as in everything in therapy, be mindful of the timing. There is a right time to bring these considerations into the consulting room; be sure to have a firm therapeutic, trusting bond.

Finishing the dream

Another tool we can use in therapy once a patient has reported a dream is to ask them to return to it and "finish it". This requires a certain level of psychological mindedness that not all patients have, so you have to use this technique only on those patients who are able to relax and enter a state of passive receptiveness to the autonomous images that will eventually emerge. It requires a reduction of the conscious will to control mental imagery and so you obviously want to be sure your patient has such a capacity. If they do, this maneuver can help you figure out a tough dream, or if nothing else it can provide you with more clinical data to work with, to be "filed away" in your mind to be used later.

One example, from a man in his early 30s:

I am walking down the street with my girlfriend and this disheveled guy comes along and starts making rude sexual advances toward her. I get in his face and we start having a shouting match, but I woke up before I found out what happened next.

From therapy you discern that this unknown rude guy embodies a number of impulses that the dreamer has perhaps too harshly disavowed himself of. The dream tells us why: he perceives the idea of making sexual advances as rude and boorish and *not* him, however other clinical material suggests that the dreamer was only well defended against such impulses and he was very conflicted about them. The dream, of course, shows us this scenario in pictures. While his girlfriend is minding her own business – notice her total inactivity in this dream, even when he and the rude guy are arguing – he is engaging in this fierce conflict. But unfortunately we were cut off from how it ends; that piece of information might tell us a lot. Do they reconcile somehow, or come to an understanding at least? Does one kill the other? Does the dreamer chase off the guy, or vice versa? We don't know, and all of these possibilities would lead to a different clinical picture, and suggest a different line of questioning and exploration with him.

To figure it out, we can ask the patient to finish the dream in the consulting room, remembering that undirected fantasy, according to dream researchers, is heavily overlapping with dream content; clinical experience shows this to be the case as well, provided the subject is not "cheating" by directing the images too much in the manner of a daydream/fantasy sequence. Only allowing the imagery to emerge into consciousness organically will make this technique useful. Fantasies directed by the ego, however, will be too heavily filtered through the defenses of the ego and can wind up being overly-inflated stories that only highlight the defenses rather than the larger picture.

In this case, when asked to do this, the dreamer's conflict only escalated, until it became physical and the dreamer actually killed the other man. Now we know how deep the conflict goes. We know we will have our work cut out for us helping the dreamer come to better terms with this other side of his experience – sexuality – such that he can become more comfortable with them without feeling like a rude and boorish interloper.

Dreams about the therapist, dreams about each other

We have discussed a number of ways you can use dreams creatively to further the goal of integration. And one of the primary ways in which we do that is by taking advantage of the fact that the IS has a separate, wider perspective on the patient's life situation. But don't forget that *you* are also part of the dreamer's "situation". The IS will occasionally have things to say about you, too. So what about the case where *you* wind up in your patient's dream? In short: we use the same approach and look closely at the images and how they are behaving. In dealing with such dreams, Kaufmann (2009: 38) observes that the unconscious of the patient is able to provide a helpful perspective to the therapist, and he feels this particular point is not emphasized enough. This is for good reason, as we often think of *ourselves* as being the instrument of healing and integration for our patients. I don't think we are, however. Rather, the patient's natural healing mechanisms heal them, and we as therapists merely help the patient best utilize them. Not unlike most medicine, in fact. And we do this by helping them to stop self-(re)injuring, provide a safe environment that gives them time and energy to heal, teaching them to pay closer attention to their own healing impulses and instincts, and encourage healthy habits. In other words, psychotherapy heals in precisely the same manner that pretty much all other forms of healing do.

The IS will comment on how you appear to your patient by depicting you in the dream as part of its narrative. If you (meaning, that is, the dream image of you in your patient) are behaving in an inappropriate manner, it's time to step back and try to figure out what is going on; why does your patient feel *as if* you are doing X? As we have seen so far, the IS says exactly what it means, expressing the current situation without comment or judgment – it is up to us to decide what is needed from that point.

Therapist August J. Cwik (2011) suggests one can use dreams to detect transference and countertransference issues by looking at how you are behaving in your patient's dreams. He also reminds us that "transference is always a countercountertransference" (17). In this manner Cwik points out that trans-ference (unconsciously motivated behaviors and attitudes directed at the therapist) and counter-transference (unconsciously motivated behaviors and attitudes of the therapist directed at the patient) are not isolated phenomena, but interact with each other immediately and continually. Cwik thus suggests treating such dreams as of a more collective/collaborative nature, *as if* dreamt not solely by the patient or therapist, but by a combination of both, as "all material arising in the analytic encounter is more or less co-created" (17), that is, not treating the dream material as emerging solely from the patient alone, but recognizing the interactive nature of the dream-making process.

Jung's advice was, when he appeared in one of his patients' dreams, to treat the dream character in the exact same manner he would anyone else: since the therapist is well known to the patient, the dream is typically about the therapist – but importantly the dream is also about *how the therapist appears to the patient.* He did not dismiss such dreams or treat them lightly, as he felt they contained useful and more objective information about the therapy: "When a patient dreams 'I tell Dr. Jung that,' or 'he calls my attention, etc.,' that is information for me personally, for the doctor. The patient's unconscious addresses me and says, 'now listen Dr. Jung.' Then I have to say something to that man. I have to take an active part" (McGuire 1984: 267). Cwik (2011) adds to this approach by observing that the unconscious of the therapist plays a part as well in dream construction; through the dyad of patient and therapist, dreams and images self-organize and emerge within the awareness of both and close attention to these can further facilitate the healing process.

Thus, clinical experience shows that dreams, in any sort of intense, closely interacting relationship, such as patient-therapist, siblings in daily contact, spouses, parents and children, etc., can be thought of as emerging from a kind of shared space, where the IS is utilizing information from both to create its narratives about each other. I refer to this phenomenon as "having each other's dreams", because it has that kind of feeling to it. But this is not some mysterious occult phenomena; it happens naturally as a consequence of the fact that the IS treats the ego as simply yet another player in the dramas it creates. The ego only has a special place in the sense that the dream imagery is colored by the ego's perspective to a degree, but the IS will still make observations about its behavior as it would anyone else it is "familiar with", such as someone whom the dreamer interacts with on a regular basis. So, naturally when I dream about these significant others, it can actually be relevant to them. Recall in the alchemy dream, the IS made a point of including the dreamer's sister in the grueling and terrifying exercise of tumbling through the hot machine. There was no need to include the sister in that dream – the same meaning would have been present. Only she *was* there. Why? I predicted that, based on this dream, the dreamer's sister was going through as life changing a process right there with her. As it turns out, she was at the end of her marriage and during therapy the sister got divorced. So, in that sense, the patient was having her sister's dream as well as her own. As mentioned earlier, clinically this is not an unusual happening, and it represents another tool we can use to understand dreams.

Chapter 8

The king of Annwn

Absolute truth ... cannot be established anywhere, and least of all in psychology.
(Jung and Meyer-Grass 2008: 73)

I can't help but wonder if Jung felt the above (likely intentionally flip) statement represented an absolute truth about our ability to discern absolute truth or not. In any case, in this chapter we will be talking about the spiritual aspect of dreams and how you can use them to help patients become more integrated in terms of their own belief system, whatever it may be. For the title of this chapter I used the Welsh word "Annwn": the Otherworld of Welsh mythology where many wonders take place, where time is nonlinear, and where the gods and fairy folk dwell. In this realm – perhaps equivalent to the "realm" of dreams, the IS is the creator and ruler.

We have already seen that, given the phenomenon of psychological resonance, strongly recurrent motifs can show up in the dreams of anyone. So, too, can highly idealized characters such as gods and demons, dragons and so forth show up. As such, the dreamworld may be partially what such places in mythology refer to – an incredibly vivid and sensually rich environment where one can meet fantastical creatures and the impossible is possible, all of which is created by the IS. It is easy to see why dreams have been attributed to divine sources across the world. But beyond that, there are some dreams which seem to stretch the boundaries of time and space we are normally comfortable with. In particular, I have noticed that patients who have experienced recent loss often not only dream of the deceased, they also report strange occurrences, uncanny coincidences, precognitive and/or telepathic dreams, and so forth. This also seems to happen with some trauma survivors and may coincide with dissociability as a general trait.

In any case, dreams have been recognized as connected to the mysterious, the spirit world, and the paranormal since the dawn of humankind, but it is interesting that even such staunch materialists as Freud (along with those less committed to materialism such as Jung, Stekel, Boss, and many others) have insisted on the reality of paranormal dreams, including dreams with precognitive, telepathic, and clairvoyant features, and a perhaps surprisingly large number of studies have been done on these sorts of dreams (Van de Castle 1994: 405–438), the results of which are interesting to say the least. My comment here is that though we often speak of "the scientific community" as if it were a monolithic entity with a single ruling dogma concerning such things, there is no consensus on paranormal and parapsychological phenomena regarding dreams (and quite a bit else besides). Rather there is intense controversy. For my part, though I have plenty to say about this subject, it would take us far afield of our primary goal here to go too deeply into this subject; I only add that whether such phenomena are valid or not, our patients (for the most part) believe in them when pressed. Thus, what most concerns us here is not the admittedly fascinating subject of what these dreams mean in terms of "absolute truth", but more *what do I do with* such dreams if my patient reports them?

Note that the plausibility of such stranger things depends greatly on our metaphysical position on the mind-body problem. If, for example, one ascribes to a strict materialism/physicalism with respect to the mind (i.e., the mind is nothing but the brain and entirely derived from/equivalent to physical interactions), then paranormal events such as precognition and telepathy are simply impossible. Other metaphysical positions, however, such as dualism, idealism, or various kinds of dual-aspect or neutral monisms – the latter of which would have likely appealed to Jung (Atmanspacher and Fuchs 2014), and are ascribed to by contemporary psychoanalytic dream researchers like Solms and Turnbull (2002) – allow that such things are likely rare but not impossible and in any case completely natural and deserving continued serious investigation.

But enough of that – whatever one thinks about such things, it would be a mistake to apply one's personal bias or metaphysical preference (for or against) prematurely when a patient reports such things to you. Moreover, if you present yourself as highly skeptical (whether you are or not), patients will hesitate to report such dreams to you, which may cause you to miss important clinical material – whatever one may think of it. By the same token, if you present yourself as overeager to hear such things, patients may feel pressure to report them to you in order to feel "special" or to avoid rejection. Neither of these situations is preferable. Whatever the case, a neutral stance which honors the patient's experience of the world, and takes it at face value – but also with a grain of salt – is probably the most cautious course.

The mystery of the dream character

When it comes to dream characters, there is a tendency to think of them as if they were the dreamer but in a different guise. Perhaps this tendency is another legacy of the "substitution" idea forwarded by Freud. In this volume, I have not ruled out the possibility that some characters can be "alter egos", such as the dream from Mr. E where he was told to beat up his "best friend".

But I do not advocate for assuming *all* characters are alter egos at the outset. Rather, I believe we can only arrive at that conclusion if the imagery dictates it; in other words, I think we need to stick to the image before we can make that designation. Characters that resemble the ego, whether strongly such as in the child-killer dream, or vaguely such as in dreams that are about the "best friend" (especially if they are unknown best friends, or friends that have been out of contact with the dreamer for a long time), can be considered alter egos. Characters that are more "distant" from the ego will appear and behave differently to varying degrees.

Which points out something rather mysterious about dream characters in general. And that is, even in the case of the alter ego character, that character behaves like another human being (or humanlike creature, or anthropomorphic creature, etc.). That is, they have their own interests, intentions, motivations, and personalities. All of these – because we are dealing with a dream – are *not* the dream ego's interests, motivations, intentions, etc. Thus, these characters appear to represent separate personalities that we encounter while dreaming, all of whom have their own agenda, and whose behavior is sometimes so different from the ego's that they come into conflict. What is so strange about this is that it is all happening "under the same roof" – meaning in the head of a single person, the one who is having the dream. Shouldn't they all be pretty much the same person? How is it we have all these people running around in our heads? Are we all crazy? It would be different if we could account for these characters as "mere figments of the imagination", as if they were characters like in a fiction writing exercise, but in the case of consciously imagining another character, we find *ourselves* to be arbiter of the character's motives, dialogue, etc. In the case of the dream characters, the dreamer does not know what these are necessarily, since they simply emerge in the dreamer's experience unbidden, with each character having their own unknown and self-derived goals, intentions, and so forth.

Perhaps the problem is with the terminology of "in the head/in our heads". This terminology, I think, is a holdover from Cartesian dualism, where the universe is divided rigidly into what is in my head and what is not, and never the twain shall meet. This sort of metaphysics certainly does make dream characters and the riotous variation of their motives, personalities, and desires, that are sometimes exactly the opposite of the dreamer's, mysterious indeed. The terminology also assumes that everything going on in my conscious experience must be entirely bounded by my brain – hence the emphasis on "in the head"; but again, nobody is a brain in a vat (except perhaps some philosophers). Rather, everyone's brain is continually interacting all day and night with the surrounding physiological and physical environment. This means that the physical correlates of the mental experience we all have are *not* entirely associated with the brain alone, but the irreducible interactive matrix of your brain with all the other brains, environments, history, body, etc. (see Chalmers 2002, and Kelley et al. 2007 for discussions) up to this point. This simple fact makes the term "in the head" quite vague – I think we can dispense with it. It is too imprecise.

Rather let us stick with more phenomenological descriptions of experience, recognizing that the brain is fantastically relevant and important, but that there is even more going on than the brain alone, acting in concert in a holistic manner to correlate with the experiences we have. And many of these experiences are of characters that have motives and intentions all their own and opaque to the dreamer.

But do dream characters have thoughts? Do they have consciousness? Obviously, proving that a dream character is conscious runs into some of the same difficulties we might have if we were to try to prove anyone is conscious. At a certain philosophical level, we really can't *prove* it (research into artificial intelligence runs into the same problem). But we might get some clues to this question if we test whether or not dream characters were capable of a number of behaviors commonly associated with conscious beings. Surprisingly, this question has been investigated. Tholey (1989) used experienced lucid dreamers to try to find out by having them ask questions of dream characters they met in their dreams. They found that dream characters not only could perform the tasks put to them (if they felt like it!), they could express things without the dreamer understanding the meaning of them even after awakening that could become understood only after help understanding them. Dream characters could lie, they could compose rhyming verse and sing, they could do math problems, and they were "especially ingenious when it is a question of outwitting the dream ego" – something I find quite humorous.

Interestingly, recurrent characters remember their previous interactions with the dreamers in subsequent dreams, sometimes becoming lucid before the dream ego does. Dream characters can also help the dreamer remember things from their (waking) past which they had forgotten about. Moreover, when asked directly if they have consciousness, they often answer "yes" (wouldn't you?). All this led Tholey to conclude:

> From the phenomenological findings, nothing contradicts the assumption that dream characters have consciousness in a specific sense. Herefrom the conclusion was drawn, that in lucid dream therapy communication with dream characters should be handled as if they were rational beings ... we have concluded, on the basis of our findings, that for practical purposes, dream characters are to be taken as seriously as if they had a consciousness of their own.
>
> (Tholey 1989: 567)

Tholey also noted that conflicts with dream characters, when resolved peaceably, often resulted in a reduction of anxiety symptoms and subsequent nightmares, which suggests that such characters seem to represent or embody intrapsychic conflicts – providing more support for this interpretive principle yet again. This evidence seems to suggest that there can be more than one consciousness associated with a single brain and body (in a particular context), and that the dreamer's is but one of many active during a dream, and possibly at other times, given that the dream characters have memory of previous interactions.

But a little reflection reveals that "dream characters" sometimes means gods, angels, demons, and everything in between, as well as the dead. That they can be considered conscious, too, gives us plenty of reason to, as Tholey suggests, take them seriously, regardless of one's metaphysical leanings. With this data in mind it is easy to understand why ideas of possession, spirits, ghosts, and so forth can be so convincing – if such ideas emerge from dream characters or other mental states in which a consciousness not your own is communicating with you, it is difficult to see how that differs functionally from the idea of conversing with a ghost, spirit, or what have you. Thus, even though thus far we have been arguing that a number of characters in dreams are "symbolic" – there is clearly more to them than this. In other words, many of them are likely not only symbolic of a particular situation, feeling, instinct, intuition, or what have you, but they *also* have been self-organized out of the IS's *prima materia* with possibly conscious intentionality, feeling, and so forth.

The possibilities for philosophical exploration of this concept are obviously great, but again I will have to leave that to the experts (for now). Many questions arise from this fascinating stuff, but for our purposes here I have only to recommend that dream characters be taken seriously, not reduced to such-and-such neural mechanism or "brain malfunction" (any more than our everyday consciousness can be so reduced), and not *merely* a symbol or narrative device or trope. Until proven otherwise, it is best to treat them as an obviously very special sort of "person", and to recognize that many more than only one consciousness may be roving about "in our heads".

Guardian angels

There are times when a dream character can serve the function of a "guardian angel" – that is, a character who appears with helpful advice and encourage-ment for the ego. This seems especially true, clinically, in the case of trauma. That is, patients who have suffered from severe trauma may dream recurrently of an angel, a god or goddess, or a grandparent (usually deceased) to appear in the patient's dream and offer helpful advice. Kalsched (1996) discusses several examples of these types of characters.

Mr. E was no exception – though we did not review them in the chapter on trauma dreams, Mr. E had a number of dreams involving his deceased grandfather, whom he described as having a very loving relationship while he was alive. During the course of therapy, his grandfather appeared several times (or he would dream about "being at grandpa's house"). Needless to say, when he spoke, we both listened, particularly given the above considerations about dream characters.

It is important to recognize where our method of staying very faithful to the imagery of the dream takes us. It means taking seriously the idea that the patient's grandfather is speaking to him from beyond the grave – perhaps self-organized ego of the IS that behaves as the grandfather would have (remember the creative capacity of the IS is very high) if one cannot stomach the more mysterious alternative. This is, of course, assuming the grandfather is *dead in the dream*, meaning the ego is aware that his grandfather is deceased, even though he is speaking with him. This is an important distinction, because – as ever – we will assume the IS means what it says, and if the dead grandfather appears in a dream, but the ego thinks he is still alive in the dream, it means something different than if he appears in a dream but the ego knows he is dead. In Dream Hack terms, dreaming of a deceased loved one that you are not aware is deceased is "treating them *as if* they were still alive". In that case, I would be concerned about unresolved or complicated grief, a subject we will get to later.

For now, let's take a look at such "guardian angel" characters in general terms, followed by a few examples. There are two types of these – ancestor figures and outright spirits. Both are signified by the IS as "helpful spirits" by similar mechanisms: helpful behavior, their tendency to be older than the dreamer, either in age or in being "eternal" in appearance. If they are family members, they are signified by the fact that they are dead *but the dreamer knows it* and interacts with them anyway. If they are unknown they are normally clothed in some sort of numinous trappings – light, ethereal beauty, magical abilities, thunder and lightning, etc. Their behavior cues us into their nature as "guiding spirits" in that they appear typically to aid the ego make difficult choices, but ones which tend to foster integration.

In the case of Mr. E, for example, whenever his grandfather appeared, he offered advice to face fears, work through difficult trauma material, but also he offered support, encouragement, and inspiration. In another dreamer's dream series, a mysterious old man with a staff appeared from time to time to offer helpful (and sometimes stern) advice on how to work through various difficulties. As a therapist, you have to judge whether such characters are fostering integration or not, because not all supernatural or ghostly characters will be so benevolent, particularly if they are embodying or personifying things like primitive rage or self-destructive impulses. The proof is in the imagery itself, as always, and a discerning eye can tell the difference in terms of what the behavior of the character appears to be suggesting to the ego.

Note that these sorts of characters have been identified as "inner guides" by a number of Jungian therapists such as Kalsched (1996, see also Jung 1954, 1990; Stein 1998; Edinger 1992), using the word "inner" to perhaps relegate such characters to the individual – keeping them safely inside someone else's head, in other words. But imagine a situation where more than one person dreams of the same sort of guiding character – remember we saw how people in close interpersonal contact can "have each other's dreams" so to speak, as a result of their daily interaction. Such a character, then, if capable of fully conscious-seeming behavior, can quickly acquire a transpersonal sort of existence among a group (especially if such a character and the stories associated with her or him are *resonant*). Carry this concept out to its logical conclusion and we can see that dreams may play a significant part in many if not all developing religious systems from the very beginning. Obviously I am not the first person to suggest a dream origin/contribution to religious and spiritual ideas; the idea has been around for a while, I only hope that the present volume adds a little something to this conversation that might pull it away from arguments that seek to reduce religion excessively to dream-related neural mechanisms and "malfunctions" (for example, as in McNamara and Bulkeley 2015).

Here is an example from a 36-year-old female:

> *I have been dreaming of my dead grandmother lately. I've had a lot of family drama going on [in waking life] and it has been really stressing me out. So I was in my house and she was there and I asked her what I should do. Suddenly I was transported to the tomb of my great-grandmother. I was at a loss of what to do next.*

The context was that this patient was of South American descent and, within her family and culture, belief in spirits and waking communication with them was not unusual. What is interesting about this dream is the when-then: when I ask my grandmother for help, I am transported to the tomb of my great-grandmother.

Since the subject of this chapter is focusing on dreams and spiritual beliefs, we need not go through the full exploration of this dream. Instead I bring it up here to illustrate how you can take a dream like this and use it to spur further questions. I want to know why the IS chose to depict the tomb of her great-grandmother – who was she? In this case, the patient went on to explain her relationship to her great-grandmother was very positive, and her memories of her were very loving and admiring. The interesting thing is the IS chose to depict the *tomb* and not the great-grandmother herself. Why? Sticking to the image, it seems the tomb is the answer to the question "what do I do?" that was asked of the grandmother.

So then, what should we make of the tomb as an image? Tombs and gravestones in particular are locations imbued with great significance. It is (as are all ritualistic expressions) a way to conceptually blend concrete physical things such as places and objects like stones and the spirit of a loved one. After all, if a person is dead but their spirit lives, isn't their spirit free of the trappings of time and space? Can't they be spoken to *anywhere*? But if that is the case, and indeed the beliefs typically go this way, then why do we need a special set-aside (i.e. sacred) place where such activity is somehow "more" or "preferred"? I think, for reasons developed in my previous book (Goodwyn 2016), that this is because a grave site is a specific place that is bounded and conceptually tied to the person. It is a way to make the all-too-ethereal realm of spirit and bring it into tangible reality. A grave site does this nicely, evoking the proper psychological state of mind wherein one can perhaps more effectively commune with the deceased.

So why stones? Stones are used for grave sites all over the world and their use as such stretches into prehistory. Again, it is a way to blend the abstract and the spiritual with the concrete and physical. While any object might do, a stone is particularly apt for this job because it is nearly permanent – as the soul is thought to be. It has weight and physicality, yet it is not malleable or ever-changing. It endures as the soul endures. These are resonant ideas, easy to imagine and hard to forget. They are recurrent and so find their way in all sorts of places, continually reinvented or carried on.

But what about a tomb? Tombs are, again, made of stone usually, or metal which is also permanent. But a tomb perhaps signifies something larger than a mere person. Just consider the tombs of Egypt, for example. Those did not simply signify a single person insofar as they signified or embodied an entire nation. In the case of this dream, since the details were so sparse, the spiritual exercise was simply about getting the patient to think of these ideas and help her develop her own answer to the problems they seemed to address. The essential message of the dream itself seemed to be: "when faced with excessive family drama that is stressing you out, return to the essence of the family." In this case, the "essence" or "soul" of the family seems to be what the "tomb of the great-grandmother" is about. I also recommended she go *visit* that tomb with this dream in mind, in hopes that perhaps more wisdom may come to her; my goal is to foster and encourage the natural integrative efforts of the IS. I'm trying to "get on its side". Subsequent clinical material helped to discern that this was a helpful exercise for her.

Finding spirituality

Another theme that one may come across is the theme of finding spirituality in general, which I equate (more or less) with finding a larger meaning and context in which to place oneself. Many times what patients can suffer from is *alienation* (see Edinger 1992 for discussion): a sense of feeling disconnected from life and others. This comes, I think, often enough from having a poor sense of belonging and identity – a subject I could write an entire book about, and touched on quite a bit in Goodwyn (2016). But ultimately alienation is about feeling like you are not a part of anything larger than yourself. In the hyperindividualistic culture of Western first world nations, it is a very common thing to see clinically. During the course of therapy in these cases, integration means not only integrating the separating parts of the self, but *also* helping them integrate themselves within some kind of larger context, whether it be family, society, or what have you. The pervasiveness of consumer culture is a powerful force that strongly encourages everyone to think of themselves as part of an atomized world where each person is chasing their own private destiny in total disconnect from everyone else. It makes for a good market society but doesn't help the human heart very much. The remedy for alienation is integration. And finding a spirituality of some kind (provided we avoid extremisms, which are tempting to the alienated for this very reason) can be a common theme in the dreams of patients on this particular journey. Here is an example:

> *I'm in a desert, alone and wandering across the dunes. I come across several abandoned concrete buildings that are empty. Then I cross a large sand dune and see a mighty ocean, brilliant blue, full of people playing and laughing on the tall waves. Looking at the water I see it is alive: it's God. It is so beautiful I wake up in tears.*

In this case, the context was one of the early part of therapy dealing with serious problems concerning alienation. We can see it depicted vividly in the imagery: alone in a desert, where nothing grows. There is no water anywhere, and the only landscape features are dunes and artificial, abandoned buildings of "concrete" – a hint that part of this dreamer's problem is an inability to think less concretely and more flexibly. Concrete is rigid and permanent, so these environments of rigidity and permanent inflexibility are shown for what they are – abandoned of life and meaning. The IS is showing us that the dreamer has been wandering this environment for an unspecified period of time, *then* he discovers the "mighty ocean" that is brilliantly vivid, deep blue (a color cross-culturally associated with ideas of spirituality in itself, probably because of the association with the sky), and not only is it full of life, it *is* alive and it is "God". The fact that he is having this dream means the awareness is already there that this quest for Deity is a major concern in his life. In Dream Hack terms, it's *as if* he's been wandering the desert for a long time, and only now has he found God in the world and not in some rarefied ivory tower in the sky.

The universal symbolism of the ocean as associated with Creation is certainly present here. Oceans or the "primordial waters" are depicted in creation myths worldwide as the source, the beginning, and the primordium. Many alchemists speaking about the *aqua vitae* were not talking about water, ethanol distillates, or even the common ocean but *this* kind of ocean: that which is equivalent to God. It is a strongly pantheistic dream as well, where the spirit of god not only "hovers over the waters" but *is* the water itself.

The dreamer's emotional response to this dream is interesting as well: tears (need I mention that tears share a great similarity with sea water?); why is this dreamer crying? When asked, he responded that he wasn't really sure. It was something very hard to describe. Such answers are common when dealing with imagery of this nature – recall the IS speaks in the language of images and symbols, and such expressions are notoriously difficult to verbalize entirely. When pressed, the dreamer could only describe "great relief ... like coming up for air after thinking you're going to drown". In other words, these are tears of joy, of great meaning, and of tremendous longing and seeking finally fulfilled, perhaps.

In therapy, finishing this dream might be a useful exercise to further this patient along; the very ineffability of the symbols could then be engaged directly in the patient's imagination, allowing them to continue the process of reconnecting and "getting one's feet wet" by walking into the water. In such an exercise, the point of which is to use the symbolism directly without trying to translate it and abstractify it, would be to direct the patient's attention to the feelings that emerge in the exercise. As we have seen from several lines of evidence, dream narratives are driven by emotional needs and issues. This helps us to get at them in a direct manner.

Waking life and the dead

So far I have given several examples of how to incorporate dream imagery into the patient's life, whether it be to have them mindfully hike through the forest of recovery from alcoholism, returning to the tomb of the great-grandmother, or seeing the Divine spark in the mundane and the commonplace – all of which can be particularly powerful since they utilize highly resonant dream images. This practice is basically "dreaming the dream onward", whether it be in undirected fantasy in the consulting room or going out and blending dream elements with waking life in a mindful and reflective manner.

A final way in which this technique can be useful revolves around grief work. As I explore in some earlier work regarding grief (Goodwyn 2015), complicated grief sometimes results after the death of a loved one, wherein a person is plagued with poor functioning and extreme symptoms related to the death and the lost attachment long after the person in question has passed away. In the referenced work, I go through several ways in which cultures around the world help to facilitate grieving to the end goal of (not coincidentally) *integrated* grief, where the loss is still felt but it does not cause severe loss of functioning or symptoms.

One of the key aspects of achieving integrated grief is getting the patient to a place in which conflicted feelings about the loss and "unresolved issues" with the deceased can be dealt with. I will give an example from a 50-year-old female who lost her mother when she overdosed on prescription pain killers:

> *I had another dream about my mom. This time she is standing at the doorway of my bedroom. She seems to be offering me something but I turn away.*

The context of this recurrent dream was one of numerous uncanny experiences in her home: often she felt her mother's presence intensely. Other times she noticed that things had been moved around in her house. One in particular disturbed her: a stack of papers that had been placed in a cabinet found its way onto her desk.

I did not worry myself with questions of whether or not my patient was "making things up" or hallucinating. I'm also not interested in investigating the paranormal. Instead I took her story at face value and tried to make sense of it in light of the narrative principles we have been discussing so far. Such stories of uncanny experiences surrounding deaths – particularly those fraught with conflict or which are unexpected – are very common, though I suspect too few therapists ask about them. The dream helped provide a few clues: the mother is trying to give the patient something but she turns away from her in the dream.

This aroused suspicion in me that we hadn't quite gotten to the heart of the conflict over her mother's death. From the dream imagery I formulated a hypothesis that she was angry with her mother and that's what prompted the fractionation behind the complicated grief she was having. Asking her directly if she was experiencing anger toward her mother opened up a whole conversation about the circumstances of her death; her mother had been "doctor shopping" in search of opiate pain medications, and it was the abuse of such medications which killed her. This caused a great deal of pain and anger in the patient, understandably, but it appeared not only through the dreams but in the narrative surrounding the uncanny experiences that the conversation was not over, despite the fact that her mother was dead.

It became apparent that one way to frame the experiences was one in which her mother was still attempting to contact her. Whatever one thinks of the veracity of such occurrences, we known that this type of narrative is highly resonant because of its recurrence: cultures around the world subscribe to beliefs that the dead can sometimes need the help of the living (usually close family members) in order to ease their passing onto the next world, however envisioned, and pain, anger, and conflict can hinder the process and cause the dead to make mischief or even levy curses upon the community (Goodwyn 2015), therefore most cultures have various practices in place to prevent this sort of misadventure by continually contacting the deceased and enacting various rituals in order to facilitate their "moving on" from the liminal space they are in immediately after death to their final resting place in the Otherworld.

In these cases, you need to lay the groundwork by asking what their beliefs are about life after death and the survival of the personality. Most people feel the soul survives bodily death, and that moreover we can still communicate with them. Even in the case of a hardcore atheist or highly skeptical agnostic, it is usually possible to treat these characters in an "as if" manner. Emotionally when dealing with grief, it can be helpful to continue to treat such people as if they are still alive because such practice affects our personal emotional reactivity and behavior.

With that out of the way you can move on to the dealing with such characters as Tholey suggested, like they have full blown consciousness. And if this is so, the next logical questions for this patient are: "what do you think your mother wants?" "Do you think she knows how you feel?" "Would you like to tell her right now how you feel about her death?", and – with an eye toward integration – "is there any way you can forgive her?" The last question will be difficult to pose without seeming like you are dismissing her anger. Of course dismissing anger is not our goal. Integrating it, giving voice to it, allowing it to be felt and contextualized – these are our goals. This narrative seems to be "behind" the uncanny experiences and the dreams both; the experiences she was having at home fit the pattern that her mother was trying to "give her something" (like in the dream), but the dreamer wouldn't have it. Since one common way to make amends is to give someone something, I suggested that might be what was happening here. This caused a change in the patient's overall approach to the experiences, from one of worrying about "going crazy" or "is this really real?", which is a dead end when it comes to the work of integration, to "what does this mean? what might she want?", which is more forward looking. All of this work led to a discussion mainly about the patient's anger at the deceased and how to best manage it. The dream prompted the work to begin with, and recognizing the theme of the dream and its commonality to the uncanny experiences she had helped to connect the two into a single solid narrative.

Chapter 9

Conclusion

> Everything that is resisting us in our psychology is a god or demon because it
> does not conform to our wishes.
>
> (Jung speaking in McGuire 1984: 182).

This book grew from a lifelong interest in dreams, but the story does not end
here. As we have seen, the interpretation of dreams as an aid to health and
wellbeing is probably as old as humanity, with the modern psychodynamic
version of it starting with Freud, to be expanded and revised extensively by
those who came after him, perhaps foremost among the earliest expansions
coming from Jung. Since then decades of psychodynamic therapists and
theorists have added to the ongoing discussion, and joining in have been the
dream laboratory researchers such as Calvin Hall, Robert Van de Castle, and
G. W. Domhoff. Still more players have joined the game with the advent of
neuroscientific study aided by neuroimaging, with the input of Allan Hobson,
Robert Stickgold, and many others.

What I have tried to do with this volume is distill all the above insights into
something useable for the everyday clinician, with plenty of room for comment and additional insights or even debates. Interested lay readers can of
course use the techniques described herein as well to help them understand
themselves and their lives better, gaining from the insights put together every
night from the Invisible Storyteller.

Asking about dreams

Of course, not everyone is interested in dreams or even remembers them.
Dream research shows that we probably dream several times every night, but
most of these dreams are lost. Dream recall, however, is, like many things, a
skill that can be refined with practice. If your patient is interested in discussing
dreams, there are three basic practices you can suggest to help facilitate this
process.

First, have them journal their dreams. The act of writing down the dream
continues the storytelling work that the raw dream material gives you, so

journaling it is not actually a passive exercise in "recall", but an active process of storytelling and creative activity. It also, obviously, protects from forgetting later since it's written down. But another thing this does is prime one's mind to recall better because you train yourself to do so with repeat practice of this technique.

Second, have them time awakening to be at a multiple of 90 minutes after they fall asleep. This will give them the best chance to wake up in the midst of a REM period, during which time dream recall is maximal. The longer one goes from a REM period, the more difficult dream recall is (Domhoff 2003, *passim*), so if you have them time wakening to be, say 6 hours or 7.5 hours after going to sleep, they will be in the midst of a REM period and so have a better chance to remember the dream.

Third, if after all that they wake up and they still can't recall any dreams, have them sit quietly in the dark room and concentrate for at least a few minutes on trying to remember any dreams. Minimize distractions and have them gently try to put themselves into a receptive state of recollection. Many times this works, and it becomes more effective with practice. Often it is the bustle of morning activity which edges the dream out of working memory. Calming that down and quietening it can help bring the dream into awareness.

Discussing dreams

When you listen to a dream, since our method here suggests staying faithful to the imagery as given, the most important thing is to gather as many details as you can about each part. What did that house look like? What did the character look like? What were they doing? Note the dreamer's behavior in each instance. Find out how each scene *felt* – a detail that is very important, as it may help us to understand some of the subtler aspects of the dream image.

In this book we worked on nine basic principles of understanding dream imagery. If you develop a method of asking about dreams and thinking about these as you discuss them, going through all of them becomes second nature and you will find you can quickly zero in on the most interesting and relevant parts. In the order we discussed them, the principles were:

1   Resonance: This principle tells us just how resonant this particular dream is, and how deeply it goes into universal themes. It tells us how "big" this dream is.
2   Context: recognizing that dreams do not happen in isolation, but in the context of the dreamer's current life situation. This principle examines how the dream relates to the dreamer's current life as a whole.
3   Characters: recognizing what characters in dreams represent, either as aspects of the dreamer's own mind/life experience, or as symbols for

relationships, and more importantly, why the IS uses particular people to symbolize them.

4   Setting: from abstract to familiar, the setting tells us much about the dreamer's current life situation and overall emotional quality. The details of the setting tell us more precisely *what* these things are.

5   Scope: the overall narrowness of vision vs. expansive, comprehensive view, the scope tells us a lot about the state of the dreaming ego and just how well connected s/he is with his/her life situation.

6   Storytelling: recognizing the narrative aspects of a dream adds context and meaning by putting together events in a particular order. Asking "why *this* order?" opens the door to better understanding of the dream.

7   Conflict: the overall level of conflict tells us a great deal about how the dreaming ego is relating to the rest of the mind and to the waking world. High levels of conflict, and looking at the specific imagery used in the dream often show us aspects of internal conflicts previously unnoticed.

8   Intensity: besides conflict there is overall intensity, turmoil, and general "storminess" or emotional force. This can tell us the overall level of creative/destructive energy going on at the time of the dream.

9   Integration: This final factor involves the over-arching connection between dreams that occurred over a long period of time and how the dreamer is or is not changing to meet new challenges. This principle guides us toward psychological healing, development, and expansion as we grow older.

When you come up with an interpretation, make sure you confirm it with subsequent clinical material, either by further observations or by follow up questions. For example, if I had been listening to the bunny rabbit dream, and formulated a hypothesis that the rabbit embodied playful, creative, and per-haps childlike feelings and behaviors that the dreamer was "running from" metaphorically, I would ask her directly about her creative and playful impulses, assuming these subjects have not come up already. Questions like "are you a playful kind of person? Do you get a chance to let loose and just be silly sometimes? Do you have any creative outlets?" In a more advanced therapy, where much of this will have already been discussed or revealed, you can be more direct about your observations: "might this dream be talking about how you feel terribly uncomfortable outside of very rigid boundaries of behavior?" or something like that.

If your interpretation is correct, then you can set to work on helping the integration effort. Help her to engage in a dialogue with that bunny rabbit with questions like "what does this character want, do you think?" Or you can have them recount the dream from the rabbit's point of view. Point out the dreamer's behavior and ask why they did *that* rather than something else. Why run from the rabbit? Why not just go into the mountains yourself, rather than wait for an old boyfriend – a relationship which went nowhere? Why immediately attack the supposed "child killer" in the garden as opposed to talking to him?

Dream images and characters can and should be referred to in sessions when you are sure you have a good handle on their meaning, as they not only emerged from the pre-verbal utterances of the IS, they will speak to them when used in creative ways. Mr. E, for example, had the "authority figure" who told him to hurt his friend, whom he later rebelled against. But we discerned from the therapy that this authority figure represented rigid, unyielding ideas of "what I'm supposed to do" that he clearly had second thoughts about, but nevertheless were frequently turned inwardly against himself and his own feelings of vulnerability. In therapy we can use this interpretation to point out when that character seems to be "present" – i.e., when the patient begins the pattern that prompted the dream in the first place; that is, being in a conflicted state of pain and anxiety, while at the same time feeling rage against himself for feeling that way. In therapy, we can ask "it seems like you're stuck in that barbwire cage right now", or "I wonder if I'm hearing that authority figure wanting to beat up on the man in the wheelchair right now". Because the IS put together things that reflect recurrent emotional patterns, they *will* be in evidence in therapy with you, so long as you are able to see the symbolism and how it depicts their situations. Once you do, of course, you can use the imagery just as the IS uses it – in this way you foster integration, aiding the efforts of the Invisible Storyteller, taking part of and utilizing the tools Nature provides to promote emotional healing and mental wellbeing, complementing the other techniques, medications, or therapies that you normally use.

References

Antrobus, J. 2000. *Theories of dreaming*. In Kryger, M., Roth, T. and Dement, W. (Eds.). *Principles and Practices of Sleep Medicine, 3rd ed.* Philadelphia: W. B. Saunders, pp. 472–481.

ARAS. 2010. *The Book of Symbols*. New York: Taschen.

Atmanspacher, H. and Fuchs C.A. 2014. *The Pauli-Jung Conjecture and its Impact Today*. Exeter: Impact Academic.

Beauchemin, K. and Hays, P. 1995. Prevailing mood, mood changes and dreams in bipolar disorder. *Journal of Affective Disorders* 35: 41–49.

Bierlein, J.F. 1994. *Parallel Myths*. New York: Ballantine.

Braude, S.E. 1995. *First Person Plural*. New York: Rowman and Littlefield.

Brown, D. 1991. *Human Universals*. New York: McGraw-Hill.

Brugger, P. 2008. The phantom limb in dreams. *Consciousness and Cognition* 17: 1272–1278.

Bryant, R.A., Wyzenbeek, M. and Weinstein, J. 2011. Dream rebound of suppressed emotional thoughts: the influence of cognitive load. *Consciousness and Cognition* 20: 55–522.

Bulkeley, K. and Domhoff, G.W. 2010. Detecting meaning in dream reports: an extension of a word search approach. *Dreaming* 20: 77–95.

Chalmers, DJ. (Ed.). 2002. *Philosophy of Mind*. Oxford: Oxford University Press.

Cicogna, PC., Occhionero, M., Natale, V. and Esposito, MJ. 2007. Bizarreness of size and shape in dream images. *Consciousness and Cognition* 16: 381–390.

Cipolli, C., Bolzani, R. and Tuozzi, G. 1998. Story-like organization of dream experience in different periods of REM sleep. *Journal of Sleep Research* 7(1): 13–19.

Clarke, J., DeCicco, TL. and Navara, G. 2010. An investigation among dreams with sexual imagery, romantic jealously, and relationship satisfaction. *International Journal of Dream Research* 3(1): 45–50.

Coleman, W. 2016. *Act and Image*. New Orleans: Spring Journal, Inc.

Crick, F. and Mitchison, G. 1983. The function of dream sleep. *Nature* 304: 111–114.

Cwik, A.J. 2011. Associative dreaming: reverie and active imagination. *Journal of Analytical Psychology* 56: 14–36.

Da Silva, S.G. and Tehrani, J.J. 2015. Comparative phylogenetic analyses uncover the ancient roots of Indo-European folktales. *Royal Society Open Science* 3: 150645.

DeCicco, T., Donati, D. and Pini, M. 2012. Examining dream content and meaning of dreams with English and Italian versions of the storytelling method of dream interpretation. *International Journal of Dream Research* 5(1).

Domhoff, G.W. 1993. The repetition of dreams and dream elements: a possible clue to a function of dreams. In Moffitt, A., Kramer, M., and Hoffmann, R. (Eds.). *The Functions of Dreaming*. New York: SUNY Press, pp. 293–320.

Domhoff, G.W. 2003. *The Scientific Study of Dreams*. Washington:American Psychological Association.

Domhoff, G.W. and Schneider, A. 2008. Similarities and differences in dream content at the cross-cultural, gender, and individual levels. *Consciousness and Cognition* 17: 1257–1265.

Doricchi, F., Iaria, G., Silvetti, M., Figliozzi, F. and Siegler, I.. 2007. The "ways" we look at dreams: evidence from unilateral spatial neglect (with an evolutionary account of dream bizarreness). *Experimental Brain Research* 178: 450–461.

Edinger, E.F. 1992. *Ego and Archetype*. Chicago: Open Court.

Edinger, E.F. 1994. *Anatomy of the Psyche*. Chicago: Open Court.

Eiser, AS. 2005. Physiology and psychology of dreams. *Seminars in Neurology* 25(1): 97–105.

Eliade, M. 1974. *The Forge and the Crucible*, 2nd Ed. Chicago: University of Chicago Press.

Fiss, H. 1993. The "royal road" to the unconscious revisited: a signal detection model of dream function. In Moffitt, A., Kramer, M., and Hoffmann, R. (Eds.). 1993. *The Functions of Dreaming*. New York: SUNY Press, pp. 381–418.

Foulkes, D. 1993. Introduction to the Functions of Dreaming. In Moffitt, A., Kramer, M., and Hoffmann, R. (Eds.). 1993. *The Functions of Dreaming*. New York: SUNY Press, pp. 1–9.

Foulkes, D. 1999. *Children's Dreams and the Development of Consciousness*. Cambridge: Harvard University Press.

Freud, S. [1900] 1998. *The Interpretation of Dreams*. New York: Avon.

Globus, G. 1987. *Dream Life, Wake Life*. New York: State University of New York Press.

Goodwyn, E. 2011. *The Neurobiology of the Gods*. New York: Routledge.

Goodwyn, E. 2013. Recurrent motifs as resonant attractor states in the narrative field: a testable model of archetype. *Journal of Analytical Psychology* 58: 387–408.

Goodwyn, E. 2015. The end of all tears: a dynamic interdisciplinary analysis of mourning and complicated grief with suggested applications for clinicians. *Journal of Spirituality in Mental Health* 17(4): 239–266.

Goodwyn, E. 2016. *Healing Symbols in Psychotherapy*. New York: Routledge.

Greenberg, R. 1987. Self-psychology and dreams: the merging of different perspectives. *Psychiatric Journal of the University of Ottawa* 12(2): 98–102.

Hall, C. and Nordby, V. 1972. *The Individual and His Dreams*. New York: New American Library.

Hartmann, E. 2001. *Dreams and Nightmares*. Cambridge: Perseus Publishing.

Henderson, R.S. 2011. What do dream animals want of us? *Jung Journal: Culture and Psyche* 5: 133–142.

Hobson, JA. 1988. *The Dreaming Brain*. New York: Basic Books.

Hobson, J.A., Pace-Schott, E.F. and Stickgold, R. 2000. Dreaming and the brain: toward a cognitive neuroscience of conscious states. *Behavioral and Brain Sciences* 23: 793–1121.

Holmyard, E.J. 1990. *Alchemy*. New York: Dover.

Jung, C.G. 1953. *Two Essays in Analytical Psychology*. Collected Works, volume 7. Princeton: Bollingen.

Jung, C.G. 1954. *The Practice of Psychotherapy. Collected Works*, volume 16. New York: Bollingen.

Jung, C.G. 1967. *Alchemical Studies. Collected Works*, volume 13. New York: Bollingen.

Jung, C.G. 1989. *Mysterium Coniunctionis. Collected Works*, volume 14. New York: Bollingen.

Jung, C.G. 1990. *Dreams.* Princeton: Princeton University Press.

Jung, C.G. 1993. *Psychology and Alchemy. Collected Works*, volume 12. New York: Bollingen.

Jung, L. and Meyer-Grass, M. (Eds.). 2008. *Children's Dreams: Notes from the seminar given in 1936–1940.* Princeton: Princeton University Press.

Kahan, T.L., LaBerge, S., Levitan, L. and Zimbardo, P. 1997. Similarities and differences between dreaming and waking cognition: an exploratory study. *Consciousness and Cognition* 6: 132–147.

Kahn, D. 2013. Brain basis of self: self-organization and lessons from dreaming. *Frontiers in Psychology* doi:10.3389/fpsyg.2013.00408.

Kalsched, D. 1996. *The Inner World of Trauma.* New York: Routledge.

Kaufmann, Y. 2009. *The Way of the Image.* New York: Zahav Books.

Kelley, E.F., Kelly, E.W., Crabtree, A., Gauld, A., Grosso, M., and Greyson, B. 2007. *Irreducible Mind.* New York: Rowman and Littlefield.

Koukkou, M. and Lehmann, D. 1993. A model of dreaming and its functional significance: the state-shift hypothesis. In Moffitt, A., Kramer, M., and Hoffmann, R. (Eds.). *The Functions of Dreaming.* New York: SUNY Press, pp. 51–118.

Koulack, D. 1993. Dreams and adaptation to contemporary stress. In Moffitt, A., Kramer, M., and Hoffmann, R. (Eds.). *The Functions of Dreaming.* New York: SUNY Press, pp. 321–340.

Kracke, W.H. 1993. Reasons for oneiromancy: some psychological functions of conventional dream interpretation. In Moffitt, A., Kramer, M., and Hoffmann, R. (Eds.). *The Functions of Dreaming.* New York: SUNY Press, pp. 477–487.

Kramer, M. 2007. *The Dream Experience.* New York: Routledge.

Kramer, M. and Glucksman, M.L. 2006. Changes in manifest dream affect during psychoanalytic treatment. *Journal of the American Academy of Psychoanalysis and Dynamic Psychiatry* 34(2): 249–260.

Laberge, S. and DeGracia, D.J. 2000. Varieties of lucid dreaming experience. In Kunzendorf R.G and Wallace B (Eds.). *Individual Differences in Conscious Experience.* Amsterdam: John Benjamins, pp. 269–307.

LaBerge, S. and Rheingold, H. 1990. *Exploring the World of Lucid Dreaming.* New York: Ballantine Books.

Limosani, I., DÁgostino, A., Manzone, M.L. and Scarone, S. 2011. Bizarreness in dream reports and waking fantasies of psychotic schizophrenic and manic patients: empirical evidences and theoretical consequences. *Psychiatry Research* 189: 195–199.

McGuire, W. (Ed.). 1984. *Dream Analysis: notes of the seminar given in 1928–1930.* Princeton: Princeton University Press.

McManus, J., Laughlin, C.D., and Shearer, J. 1993. The function of dreaming in the cycles of cognition: a biogenetic structural account. In Moffitt, A., Kramer, M., and Hoffmann, R. (Eds.). *The Functions of Dreaming.* New York: SUNY Press, pp. 21–50.

McNamara, P. 2014. *The Neuroscience of Religious Experience.* Cambridge: Cambridge University Press.

McNamara, P., Andresen, J., Clark, J., Zborowski, M., and Duffy, CA. 2001. Impact of attachment styles on dream recall and dream content: a test of the attachment hypothesis of REM sleep. *Journal of Sleep Research* 10: 117–127.

McNamara, P. and Bulkeley, K. 2015. Dreams as a source of supernatural agent concepts. *Frontiers of Psychology* 6(283): doi:10.3389/fpsyg.2015.00283.

Mikulincer, M., Shaver, P.R. and Avihou-Kanza, N. 2011. Individual differences in adult attachment are systematically related to dream narratives. *Attachment and Human Development* 13(2): 105–123.

Moffitt, A., Kramer, M., and Hoffmann, R. (Eds.). 1993. *The Functions of Dreaming*. New York: SUNY Press.

Nielson, T. and Levin, R. 2007. Nightmares: a new neurocognitive model. *Sleep Medicine Reviews* 11: 295–310.

Nielson, T.A. and Stenstrom, P.. 2005. What are the memory sources of dreaming? *Nature* 437 (27): doi:10.1038/nature04288.

Payne, JD. and Nadel, L. 2004. Sleep, dreams, and memory consolidation: the role of the stress hormone cortisol. *Learning and Memory* 11: 671–678.

Pesant, N. and Zadra, A. 2004. Working with dreams in therapy: what do we know and what should we do? *Clinical Psychology Review* 24: 489–512.

Purcell, S., Moffitt, A., and Hoffmann, R. 1993. Waking, dreaming, and self-regulation. In Moffitt, A., Kramer, M., and Hoffmann, R. (Eds.). *The Functions of Dreaming*. New York: SUNY Press, pp. 197–260.

Schredl, M. and Sartorius, H. 2010. Dream recall and dream content in children with attention deficit/hyperactivity disorder. *Child Psychiatry and Human Development* 41: 230–238.

Shamdesani, S. 2012. *C. G. Jung: a Biography in Books*. New York: W. W. Norton.

Siegel, J. 2001. The REM sleep-memory consolidation hypothesis. *Science* 294: 1058–1063.

Smith, C. 1993. REM sleep and learning: some recent findings. In Moffitt, A., Kramer, M., and Hoffmann, R. (Eds.). *The Functions of Dreaming*. New York: SUNY Press, pp. 341–362.

Soffer-Dudek, N., Wertheim, R. and Shahar, G. 2011. Lucid dreaming and resilience in the face of exposure to terrorism. *Journal of Traumatic Stress* 24(1): 125–128.

Solms, M. and Turnbull, O. 2002. *The Brain and the Inner World*. New York: the Other Press.

Sproul, B. 1991. *Primal Myths*. New York: Harper-Collins.

Stein, M. 1998. *Jung's Map of the Soul*. Chicago: Open Court.

Stevens, A. 1996. *Private Myths: Dreams and Dreaming*. Cambridge: Harvard University Press.

Stickgold, R., Hobson, J.A., Fosse, R. and Fosse, M. 2001. Sleep, learning, and dreams: off-line memory reprocessing. *Science* 294: 1052–1057.

Strauch, I. 2005. REM dreaming in the transition from late childhood to adolescence: a longitudinal study. *Dreaming* 15(3): 155–169.

Strauch, I. and Meier, B. 1996. *In Search of Dreams*. New York: SUNY Press.

Tholey, P. 1988. A model of lucidity training as a means of self-healing and psychological growth. In Gackenbach, J. and Laberge, S. (Eds.). *Conscious Mind, Sleeping Brain*. New York: Plenum, pp. 263–287.

Tholey, P. 1989. Consciousness and abilities of dream characters observed during lucid dreaming. *Perceptual and Motor Skills* 68: 567–578.

Ullman, M. 1969. Dreaming as metaphor in motion. *Archives of General Psychiatry* 21(6): 696–703.

Uther, H.-J. 2011. *The Types of International Folktales*. 3 vols. Helsinki: Finnish Academy of Science and Letters.

Van de Castle, R. 1994. *Our Dreaming Mind*. New York: Ballantine.

Van der Hart, O., Nijenhuis, ERS., and Steele, K. 2006. *The Haunted Self*. New York: W. W. Norton.

Vertes, R.P. and Eastman, K.E. 2000. The case against memory consolidation in REM sleep. *Behavioral and Brain Sciences* 23: 793–1121.

Von Franz, M.-L. 1980. *Alchemy*. Toronto: Inner City Books.

Walker, M.P., Liston, C., Hobson, J.A., Stickgold, R. 2002. Cognitive flexibility across the sleep-wake cycle: REM-sleep enhancement of anagram problem solving. *Cognitive Brain Research* 14: 317–324.

Wilkinson, M. 2006. The dreaming mind-brain: a Jungian perspective. *Journal of Analytical Psychology* 51: 43–59.

Wyatt, R., Goodwyn, E. and Ignatowski, M. 2011. A Jungian approach to dreams reported by soldiers in a modern combat zone. *Journal of Analytical Psychology* 56: 217–231.

Zadra, A.I. and Pihl, R.O. 1997. Lucid dreaming as a treatment for recurrent nightmares. *Psychotherapy and Psychosomatics* 66: 50–55.

Index

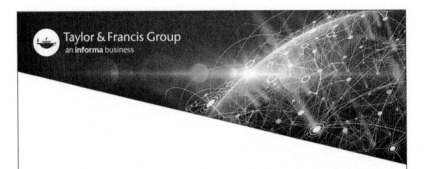

Printed in Great Britain
by Amazon

81932118R00106